Heretical Fictions

# eretical Fictions

Religion in the Literature of Mark Twain

Lawrence I. Berkove and Joseph Csicsila

UNIVERSITY OF IOWA PRESS, IOWA CITY

University of Iowa Press, Iowa City 52242

Copyright © 2010 by the University of Iowa Press

www.uiowapress.org

Printed in the United States of America

Design by Omega Clay

The University of Iowa Press is a member of Green Press Initiative and is committed to preserving natural resources.

Printed on acid-free paper

Library of Congress Cataloging-in-Publication Data

Berkove, Lawrence I.

  Heretical fictions: religion in the literature of Mark Twain / by Lawrence I. Berkove and Joseph Csicsila.

    p.   cm.

  Includes bibliographical references and index.

  ISBN-13: 978-1-58729-903-2 (pbk.)

  ISBN-10: 1-58729-903-8 (pbk.)

  1. Twain, Mark, 1835–1910—Religion. 2. Religion in literature. I. Csicsila, Joseph, 1968– II. Title.

  PS1342.R4B47 2010

  818'.409—dc22   2010002373

To our families,
for the support and encouragement
they have given us over the years

CONTENTS

Scholarship is always a collaborative enterprise. Academic critics are assisted by the work of others, usually by the advice and cooperation of others, and certainly by the instruction of their teachers. So vast and varied is the state of Twain scholarship that it is not feasible, or even possible, to document all our indebtednesses, but it is true in our case that engagement with that scholarship has contributed to our education and our sense of a standard to which we aspired. At the general level, our bibliography is a record of the most important readings we have consulted. Some of these sources, whether or not we cited them directly, opened a way for us. Others, especially if we took similar ideas in different directions, were sufficiently well thought out to induce us to examine our positions more carefully. One of the major benefits of teaching is the opportunity to try out ideas with our students. Our footnotes single out a few of them whose insights on assignments were especially valuable, but we recall many rewarding moments in our courses when the excitement of discovery rose to the point where all of us, teachers and students alike, transcended our formal roles and became equal colleagues.

At the individual level, the priority of influence both in time and impact goes to Leo Marx, who introduced one of us to Mark Twain and inspiringly taught him enduring lessons of how to read and think about literature. Although we differ herein with one of Marx's interpretations, any disagreement is specific and respectful, and does not extend to his general analytical technique. More recent colleagues have encouraged us in our path and in this particular enterprise. Of these, Alan Gribben heads the list for freely sharing information and his expertise with us, and painstakingly critiquing and proofreading our manuscript. Others who have been outstandingly helpful are Forrest Robinson, Victor Doyno, Thomas A.

Tenney, Joseph McCullough, Jeanne C. Reesman, Tom Quirk, Robert H. Hirst, and the late Sherwood Cummings, James D. Wilson, Stanley Brodwin, and Henry Nash Smith. R. Kent Rasmussen has been an unfailing source of information, and we are grateful to Barbara Snedecor, of Elmira College, for collaborating with us on a National Endowment for the Humanities (NEH) grant in July 2007 that enabled us to try out our ideas with talented students from all parts of the country in a summer session on Mark Twain. Our listing of these colleagues herein does not imply their total agreement with our views, but their conception of scholarship was sufficiently generous for them to encourage us even though honest differences of opinion might have existed.

We are grateful beneficiaries of the facilities and staffs of libraries, especially those of the University of Michigan–Dearborn; Eastern Michigan University; University of Nevada, Reno; California State Library at Sacramento; Nevada Historical Society, Reno; University of California Bancroft Library at Berkeley; and the Mark Twain Project. We also thank the University of Michigan–Dearborn, especially Drew Buchanan of the Office of Sponsored Research, for important funding in the form of grants over the years for necessary research and travel. A special note of thanks to Pat Healy and Cindy Young of Eastern Michigan University for their assistance in the preparation of the manuscript. We would like to express our gratitude as well to the Provost's Office at Eastern Michigan University for a Faculty Research Fellowship, without which this project could not have been completed in such timely fashion.

Last in the order of listing but first in our hearts are our families, especially our lovely and loving wives Gail Berkove and Vail Csicsila. In more than one way, their constant encouragement, practical support, and inspiriting devotion made our work a labor of love.

. . . . .

Parts of this book are revised and expanded versions of material previously published in scholarly journals. For permission to reproduce from the following essays we thank the journals in which the originals appeared: From *The Mark Twain Annual*, passages from "'No Mere Accidental Incidents': *Roughing It* as a Novel," vol. 1 (2007): 7–17; from *Thalia*, passages from "The Trickster God in *Roughing It*," vol. 18.1&2 (1998): 21–30; from *Essays in Arts and Sciences*, passages from "*A Connecticut Yankee:* A Serious

Hoax," vol. 19 (May 1990): 28–44; passages from "The Gospel According to Hank Morgan's Newspaper," vol. 20 (October 1991): 32–42, copyright owned by the University of New Haven; from the *Mark Twain Journal*, passages from "'The Reality of the Dream': Structural and Thematic Unity in *A Connecticut Yankee*," vol. 22.1 (Spring 1984): 8–14; (revised) passages from "'The Poor Players' of *Huckleberry Finn*," vol. 41.2 (Fall 2003): 16–26.

For the past three generations, factual information about Mark Twain has increased very rapidly. Previously unpublished or lost manuscripts have been discovered and made available, existing texts have been edited and made more accurate, new letters and writings have been found, and a great deal of fresh biographical information has been uncovered. Even a single piece of new information has the potential to alter the whole picture a little bit, but the virtual flood of it has radically affected the general scholarly understanding of Twain. As recently as the mid-twentieth century he was regarded mainly as a brilliant and genial humorist with the gift of nostalgically evoking a more innocent and near idyllic era of our national history. But now that picture is changed to that of a social critic of an era that was neither as innocent nor as idyllic as we had thought. Because this new conception is founded solidly on a vastly broadened base of new information and new interpretations, it is unlikely that it will prove to be only an evanescent phase of comprehending the author and the man. However, the process of reinterpretation continues in response to the problems and questions that this modern image of Twain has not settled. The issues addressed in this book are not minor matters: a rational defense for Twain's ranking as a literary artist and the establishment of a consistent set of values from his early work to his last.

In recent years interpreters of individual works of Twain have begun to pay more attention to these issues. Previously, but continuing to the present day, they typically proposed a reading of some work, marshaled evidence to support their claim, and ended with a conclusion about that work and perhaps implied an unpursued suggestion that the conclusion could be extended more widely. If all parts of a text were not congruent with their conclusions, they evoked biography to account for the discrepancies: for example, Twain spread the composition of the work over too long a period and lost the intense focus that was needed to unify it; he needed to bulk up a book to reach a certain number of pages and so introduced filler material; he was freshly persuaded by some source material he was reading and applied it to his text even though it did not fully comport with his original conception; some aspect of his personal life changed his mood and colored his writing; he changed his mind about his original idea when he was part way into the text and went off in a new direction; or he lost his nerve at some point and abandoned his original bold plan for some less controversial and safer ending. All these reasons, and more, have been cited to explain away interpretive difficulties. Most interpretations have been supported by plausible explanations drawn from Twain's personal life or career, but very few considered the possibility that Twain's artistry was somehow more sophisticated and integrated than the constantly changing state of biography suggested.

The total effect of this laissez-faire situation has been to multiply interpretations not only to the point where they cannot all be true but to where any coherent sense of Twain cannot be evoked. This has direct implications for his artistic reputation. If he stands for this, at one time, and that, at another time, and arbitrarily fluctuates widely and wildly between extremes of good humor and bleak pessimism, sometimes in the same work, and between contradictory attitudes toward what are normally settled convictions in thoughtful individuals toward major values—God, humankind, and ethics—and if his major works are flawed by indecision and contradiction, how does this confusion about purpose and execution justify the high reputation he has? After all, like unsystematic philosophers, he might be granted moments of sublime inspiration and performance and yet be denied the praise that is reserved for those whose lifetime of endeavor results in some integrated vision of life. Addressing this problem, this book supplies a rationale and reasons that justify Twain as one of literature's most accomplished writers.

We now know that the world he contemplated was far more complicated than we had earlier thought. But Twain's was a remarkable mind, and however he acquired his undoubted genius, he had the ability to conceptualize a world picture. The task that preoccupied him toward this end was what to make of the contradiction between the grand ideals of his country and culture—freedom, justice, equality, and a humanitarian reverence for life and individuality—and the obvious inability of his country and culture to enact those ideals into practical and lasting elements of a humane society. Human nature, as always, was complex and intractable, but when Twain pondered the reasons why, over the span of recorded history, universal human aspirations should fail so signally of realization, he was led inadvertently by his religious upbringing to an unexpected answer. Tentatively and circumspectly at first, but eventually explicitly and boldly, Twain became a critic of God. He lived in an age which read Tom Paine and listened to Robert Ingersoll, which saw the spread of atheism and generated agnosticism, and which thrilled to the audacity of Zola's ringing charge against a corrupt system: "J'accuse!" The resolve to seek the truth wherever it led induced Twain to raise his sights above society, organized religion, and human nature, to God. Still believing in God, Twain accused him. Our study attempts to demonstrate the centrality of that decision to Twain's literature.

To that end, *Heretical Fictions: Religion in the Literature of Mark Twain* knowingly advocates several ideas that are controversial in that they diverge from conventional views and are intended to provoke reconsiderations that will lead to deeper as well as fresher insights. This book was not undertaken on a whim or some desire for novelty; it originated simply in the search to determine if there might be unity of purpose and consistency in Twain's literature. We have tried hard not to project our own preferences into our arguments. We carefully followed the leads of evidence and pragmatically adopted the conclusions which worked until we finally realized that the conclusions fell into a pattern. The leads and the evidence, as well as the conclusions, are presented here openly, for all to check. Most of the component interpretations herein have been extensively "field tested" many times over several decades in the authors' graduate and undergraduate literature courses, in presentations at academic conferences, in publications, and in classes taught by former students and colleagues who have implemented our ideas. The test of utility, therefore, has been thoroughly demonstrated. The test of fact is more complicated, but we are satisfied that we are in conformity with the majority of facts and at least have accounted for most of the others. It is now time for our results to be drawn together and presented as a complement and extension to the work of the fine scholars who have preceded us and inspired us with their dedication, even though it involved revealing harsh truths, to a more accurate understanding of the literature of one of America's greatest authors.

．．．．

The texts of Twain's works prepared by the Mark Twain Project (MTP) are regarded by most Twain scholars as definitive. Editions of Twain's works that do not follow the MTP texts are, except for certain limited purposes, generally regarded as unsuitable for literary analysis. Hence, even the Oxford University Press edition, although of a more recent date of publication than some of the MTP texts, is valuable chiefly for its making available first edition versions of many of Twain's works, but not for literary analysis. We have therefore used MTP editions, wherever available, as our basic texts, and have identified them in our chapter notes. We have deviated from this practice only where they did not exist, and in those cases have identified the texts we used. Because many readers may be unaware of the importance of the MTP texts and because the use of other versions is still widespread, we have included chapter numbers as well as page numbers in our source references so that readers can find quotes in whatever versions they have access to. We have kept abbreviations to a minimum, and those very few that do appear, e.g. MTP or SLC (Samuel Langhorne Clemens) are standard and commonplace in Twain scholarship.

Twain's Countertheology

I form the light, and create darkness: I make peace, and create evil:
I the Lord do all these things. —Isaiah 45:7

Perfect consistency can hardly be expected in human affairs, but Mark
Twain poses more than the usual number of problems for readers searching for any key to his writings. He is one of the most brilliant and accomplished ironists in the history of literature. Hence, in addition to the
complexity of his thought, a large part of the difficulty in arriving at a satisfactory understanding of his mind and art is due to the elusiveness of his
irony. Attempting to summarize his beliefs, then, can be confusing. It can
be proven, for instance, that Twain at times criticized wealth but at other
times made strenuous efforts to acquire it; praised the United States and
also denounced it; was both pro- and antidemocratic; was critical of quack
medicine and nostrums yet experimented with faith healers and endorsed
health products of doubtful results; extravagantly complimented friends or
associates and shortly thereafter extravagantly denounced or denied them;
was both realistic and sentimental; was alternately anti-Catholic and ap-
preciative of Catholicism; was both antireligion and devoted to Christianity; and so on. In short, there is hardly an area of his existence where he
did not eventually contradict himself. Supportive evidence for all of these
contradictory positions, and more, can be readily found in his fiction, letters, speeches, notebooks, and autobiography.

Nevertheless, although Twain modified or changed his mind frequently
on many issues of the day, in the area of private religious beliefs he was
surprisingly consistent. This is especially true of his literature, which offers numerous insights into his mind and his art. Few would dispute the
fact that religion was a main concern of Twain's during his entire life. From

1

often shockingly heretical perspectives, Twain preached all his life in his literature a distinct departure from a conventional Christian message: that *because of God's malice* life is deceitful and humans are not meant to achieve in it their dearest goals of freedom, happiness, and fulfillment. This vision is at the center of his most important works and forms the organizing principle of his literary oeuvre. His major works are each artistically constructed around this idea, and it constitutes a recognizable common fingerprint which each shares with all others.

Religion, the conviction that God exists and dominates existence, was the sun around which Twain orbited, like Halley's comet, elliptically—now closer, now farther away—but always recurrently. While there are levels of social and political morality in his books, at the deepest level is the common theme of all his literature: a sense of the *ultimate* relationship of humanity and God to each other.

A tradition stretching over thousands of years has granted humans— prophets, saints, theologians, philosophers, and authors—the right to criticize humanity in order to "justify the ways of God to man." But it is an exceptional author who "presumes God to scan" and will call him to account. Inevitably, we ask such an author, "Who are you, and what are your qualifications to judge 'the Judge of all the earth'"? Individuals wounded and embittered by tragedies in their lives and brash youths and arrogant intellectuals have sometimes passed judgment on God for his sins and shortcomings, but seldom has so much of an extraordinarily gifted and balanced major author's extensive oeuvre, spanning more than forty years, been devoted to the process of painstakingly examining and reexamining God and his creation, recording the virtues and flaws of both parties and arriving at original conclusions on the basis of equity.

Religion itself was a central and controversial topic in the English-speaking world in the mid-nineteenth century, and in small communities—such as Hannibal, Missouri—where the opportunities for exposure to intellectual discussions were largely restricted to Sunday sermons and church doctrine, its prominence was intensified. Religion saturated American culture. On the national level, the belief in "manifest destiny" helped power the expansion of the nation across the continent and beyond. "The Battle Hymn of the Republic" imbued the Union cause with religious fervor; biblical literalism on the issue of slavery contributed to the decision of many to support the Confederacy. Capitalism received a boost from religious teachings that associated wealth with virtue; religion was a main factor in the rise and spread of social relief and improvement organizations such as the Red Cross, the Young Men's Christian Association (YMCA), and labor unions. Even Darwinism, usually regarded as inimical to religion, was given a supernatural cachet with the endorsement of the teleological phrase "survival of the fittest" by the wing of it led by Herbert Spencer and the spiritualist Alfred Russel Wallace. It would have been peculiar if Twain, of all American authors so deeply representative of his time and place, had not engaged this topic. He did wrestle with it, and with surprising frequency. In fact, it is a major feature of his literature.

The topic of religion, although often mentioned in Twain studies, has until recently been relatively neglected as a subject of extended scholarly examination in its own right. Given its vastness and the many facets from which it may be viewed, scholars have been understandably hesitant about undertaking any detailed discussion of it, but it is much too important to be left on the shelf. However, in the past few decades some noteworthy books and articles have started to address the topic. The penetrating essays of Stanley Brodwin and James D. Wilson, two perceptive authorities on Twain's religious views, largely concentrate on biographical materials.[1] Howard G. Baetzhold and Joseph B. McCullough's *The Bible According to Mark Twain* (1995), though insightful on Twain's relationship to the Bible, particularly the Old Testament, and most particularly Genesis, is an edition of Twain's frequently irreverent variations on biblical passages. More recently, William Phipps (2003) and, especially, Harold K. Bush Jr. (2006) have produced publications calling more attention to the importance of Twain's theology, inferring from biographical information for literary interpretation.[2] Joe Fulton, too, has written usefully about the theological aspects of Twain's works, with emphases on Bakhtin, genre form, and religion in general.[3] Tom Quirk's *Mark Twain on Human Nature* (2007) and this present book share considerable common ground, though our emphasis on Twain's Calvinistic heritage ultimately leads us in different directions.

There are significant differences between what Samuel Clemens allowed the world to know about his deepest thoughts and what was hidden but can be revealed in Mark Twain's writings. Fortunately, he left behind a considerable number of compelling manuscripts and letters about his personal beliefs which simultaneously assist an understanding and yet also make things perversely difficult. One of the most explicit of these follows, but within itself provides us with a rationale for *not* regarding it as a definitive pronouncement. It is a creedal statement, which Paul Baender tentatively dates to the years 1880–1885.

I believe in God the Almighty.

I do not believe He has ever sent a message to man by anybody, or delivered one to him by word of mouth, or made Himself visible to mortal eyes at any time or in any place.

I think the goodness, the justice, and the mercy of God is manifested in His works; I perceive that they are manifested toward me in this life; the logical conclusion is that they will be manifested toward me in the life to come, if there should be one.

I do not believe in special providences. I believe that the universe is governed by strict and immutable laws. If one man's family is swept away by a pestilence and another man's spared, it is only His law working; God is not interfering in that small matter, either against the one man or in favor of the other.

I cannot see how eternal punishment hereafter could accomplish any good end, therefore I am not able to believe in it. To chasten a man in order to perfect him might be reasonable enough; to annihilate him when he shall have proved himself incapable of reaching perfection might be reasonable enough: but to roast him forever for the mere satisfaction of seeing him roast would not be reasonable—even the atrocious God imagined by the Jews would tire of the spectacle eventually.

There may be a hereafter, and there may not be. I am wholly indifferent about it. If I am appointed to live again, I feel sure it will be for some more sane and useful purpose than to flounder about for ages in a lake of fire and brimstone for having violated a confusion of ill-defined and contradictory rules said (but not evidenced,) to be of divine institution. If annihilation is to follow death, I shall not be *aware* of the annihilation, and therefore shall not care a straw about it.

I believe that the world's moral laws are the outcome of the world's experience. It needed no God to come down out of heaven to tell men that murder and theft and the other immoralities were bad, both for the individual who commits them and for society which suffers from them.

If I break all these moral laws, I cannot see how I injure God by it, for He is beyond the reach of injury from me—I could as easily injure a planet by throwing mud at it. It seems to me that my mis-conduct could only injure me and other men. I cannot *benefit* God by obeying these moral laws—I could as reasonably benefit the planet by withholding my mud. [Let these sentences be read in the light of the fact that I believe I have received moral laws *only* from man—none whatever from God.] Consequently I do not see why I should either be punished or rewarded hereafter for the deeds I do here.[4]

This profession of faith seems straightforward enough, but it is, in fact, problematic. For one thing, its similarity to Tom Paine's statement of creed and other of his theological arguments in *The Age of Reason* is evident to anyone who has read both writings. We know that Twain was sufficiently influenced by his reading of Paine to consider himself a deist in his young manhood. But we also know that Twain later attempted to become a believing Christian while he was courting Olivia Langdon and subsequently in their early married life. While it is plausible—mainly on the basis of the stationery and ink used in the undated manuscript—that the document was *written* in the early 1880s, even Paul Baender, the editor of the 1973 publication that first included the creed, admits that the date of *composition* is "conjectural" (Twain, *What Is Man?* 585). It is at least possible, therefore, that the untitled manuscript was composed while he was still a deist. But even if the editor's dating is correct and its date of composition corresponds to that of its writing, it is doubtful that Twain retained these beliefs later in life. The beliefs expressed therein are incompatible with those contained in *What Is Man?* (1906), which Twain claimed were begun "twenty-five or twenty-seven years" earlier (124), or with other short works of theological import written in the last decade or so of his life. It would seem, then, that the validity of this statement is limited to a period of Twain's intellectual life, and does not apply to his entire career. Another possible significance is that it is the product of his rational mind—that is, he thought that was what he believed at the time he wrote it—but does not reflect deeper beliefs he tried to suppress.

One shortcoming is that it omits crucial beliefs that we know he inherited from Calvinism. Even its first sentence is open to question. What does he mean by "God"? During the course of his career he sometimes and inconsistently distinguished between the God of the Bible (or of Calvinistic Presbyterianism) and the "true" God, which he partly defines here in a deistic way. In general, when he referred to the notion of God that he preferred, it was to the deistic God of impartial and immutable laws but who remains unresponsive to prayer. Though Twain regarded this conception of God as ultimately benevolent, even he recognized that this conception and those laws made no provision for what he valued as "sentimental justice," divine expressions of individualized compassion and approximations to human standards of fairness (*Notebook* 363, composed between May 30 and June 11, 1898). Most of Twain's thought and animus in his literature, on the other hand, is devoted to the revealed God of the Bible, whom he typically treats as a whimsical, angry, malevolent, and manipulating trickster deity. This view derived from the enduring Calvinistic legacy of his youthful years, which he could never throw off. Similarly, Twain was inconsistent in his references to hell. Usually it was to the specific place of punishment designated in the New Testament, but sometimes it was to the world he believed all humans experience between the cradle and the grave, made deliberately dysfunctional, illusory, and frustrating by the creator. As is the case with his use of "God," Twain sometimes slips from one meaning of hell to the other, or straddles the line between them, in the selfsame context. Hell, however, never has a mild meaning, and even his most favorable conception of God falls considerably short of the view of an infinitely loving and merciful personal God taught by all Bible-based religions.

Finally, it is necessary to consider how *useful* this abstract statement is to understanding Twain's literature. Does it help us to penetrate particular works of his literature? Does it help us to relate, say, an early book of his to a later book and thus give us some sense of continuity in Twain's values? It is not our intention to dismiss this creedal statement; we acknowledge its importance and usefulness, but question its import as a stand-alone definitive statement of belief that applies to all stages of his career and leaves no questions unanswered. It simply does not fairly represent Twain's positions in the great majority of his literature, and is inadequate even as autobiographical evidence. We will recur to it and make use of it, however, as well as similar statements, but always in conjunction with other evidence from Twain's literary texts that affect its applicability.

Five of Mark Twain's books, along with several shorter works, seem most germane to a systematic study of his beliefs: *Roughing It* (1872), *The Adventures of Tom Sawyer* (1876), *Adventures of Huckleberry Finn* (1885), *A Connecticut Yankee in King Arthur's Court* (1889), and *No. 44, The Mysterious Stranger*[5] (composed between 1902 and 1908). These writings supply evidence for interpretations that fall into definite patterns. Twain's other books hardly contradict our thesis but are nevertheless omitted. Some, like

Tom Sawyer Abroad (1894) and *Tom Sawyer, Detective* (1896), are universally regarded as minor works. *The Prince and the Pauper* (1881), valuable for its examination of social issues and the influence of environment and circumstance on the individual, is nevertheless, as John D. Stahl maintains, "a significant step in the evolution of Mark Twain's thought and literary art" but "surely not a masterpiece" (592). *The Innocents Abroad* (1869), while permanently popular and not without religious content, is preeminently a travel book, and our focus is on fiction. For the same reason we have excluded *Life on the Mississippi* (1883) and *Following the Equator* (1897). Although we do not entirely pass over *The Tragedy of Pudd'nhead Wilson* (1894), Hershel Parker's exposition of its textual problems, and the consequent editorial controversy that would force us into a digression, persuaded us not to engage in an analysis of that otherwise very interesting novel.

Though complex, Twain's writings are not chaotic, and his fictional works contain characteristic thematic consistency and integrative principles. William James prefigured this realization with an acute observation:

> Place yourself . . . at the centre of a man's philosophic vision and you understand at once all the different things it makes him write or say. But keep outside, use your post-mortem method, try to build the philosophy up out of the single phrases, taking first one and then another and seeking to make them fit "logically," and of course you fail. You crawl over the thing like a myopic ant over a building, tumbling into every microscopic crack or fissure, finding nothing but inconsistencies, and never suspecting that a centre exists. (*Pluralistic Universe* 117)

In Twain's case, the way to this "centre," his core of consistent beliefs, is through his fiction. His mind is organized as his literature is—in layers. His surfaces and topical levels include currents and crosscurrents, usually entertaining and interesting, but often moving in different directions and sometimes at odds with each other. What remain the same, however, are the deep tidal swells of his mind that drive his creativity. They move steadily and always in the same direction, and they order his fiction, although at first glance they may seem to have little or no connection with what happens closer to the surface.

Twain's capacity to keep his depths separate from his more worldly interests is early attested to in an exasperated preface to his readers in his final contribution to the *Galaxy* magazine in April 1871:

VALEDICTORY.—I have now written for *The Galaxy* for a year. For the last eight months, with hardly an interval, I have had for my fellows and comrades, night and day, doctors and watchers of the sick! During these eight months death has taken two members of my home circle and malignantly threatened two others. All this I have experienced, yet all the time have been under contract to furnish "humorous" matter once a month for this magazine. . . . I think that some of the "humor" I have written during this period could have been injected into a funeral sermon without disturbing the solemnity of the occasion.

Despite his low opinion of his output, his monthly contributions did not betray his inner turmoil. On the contrary, they included some choice items of humor. Of course, many other writers besides Twain have managed to compartmentalize their minds and keep their personal lives and professional work separate. But the *Galaxy* work represents early Twain. He soon learned how to continue to preserve this compartmentalization and restrain the private sphere from intruding prominently into his public and professional appearance, and yet in his fiction integrate both spheres of his life. The public one, in which he gave play to his gifts of narrative and humor, was obvious on the surface and was the one that established and maintained his reputation. The private sphere, in which he explored controversial religious ideas and pondered their implications, he concealed by various artifices, but these private meditations are not only detectable in most of his fiction, they give depth and unity to it and the entire corpus of his works. His techniques will be discussed in the analyses of individual literary works, but for now we will address the subject of the source and nature of his distinctive and recurrent themes.

The most significant by far of the many exposures Twain had to religion was to the Calvinism of his youth. It defined him, and his prolonged response to it is essential to understanding his literature and finding in his fiction a ground of consistency. He was reared in an environment of frontier Calvinist Presbyterianism—a hard and fundamentalist form of Protestant orthodoxy.[6] Mabel Donnelly has given us some idea of its severity by calling attention to excerpts from the official Calvinist *A Short Catechism for Children* (1864), which were published in the *Hartford (Conn.) Daily Times* in 1869. It took the form of question-and-answer exchanges that were to be studied by both adults and children as a way to memorize doctrine. Three examples from it follow:

Q. Does your wicked heart make all your thoughts, words, and actions sinful?

A. Yes; I do nothing but sin.

Q. Is your life very short, frail, and uncertain?

A. Yes; perhaps I may die the next moment.

Q. What would become of you if you die in your sins?

A. I must go to hell with the wicked.

Q. Cannot your good thoughts, words or actions recover you, by the covenant of works?

A. No; everything I do is sinful.

Q. What are you then by nature?

A. I am an enemy to God, a child of Satan, and an heir of hell. (3)

His indoctrination in this religious outlook took root in his mind, and not only was it never replaced, but it continued to grow his entire life. It may be too strong to say that it flourished in his mind, because the evidence is irrefutable that he fought it from the days of his young manhood until his death and sought to extirpate it by successively embracing deism, evangelical Protestantism, determinism, and the new science of psychology.[7] It nevertheless persisted despite this lifetime of opposition. Twain recognized this tendency in himself in 1884 when he wrote to William Dean Howells about "a but-little considered fact in human nature: that the religious folly you are born in you will *die* in, no matter what apparently reasonabler religious folly may seem to have taken its place meanwhile, & abolished & obliterated it."[8] The term "folly," however, understates the real crux of the matter, which is that Twain saw Bible religion as worse than foolish, but as the worship of a real but cruel and evil deity.

It is no secret that Twain, especially in his later years, was critical of God. In a very real sense, Twain's literature arises out of his attempt to discredit theodicy, the justification of divine tolerance of evil. Unlike the pious apologists for God in every religion, Twain *blamed* God for evil. He did not mind the God of deism, such as appears in "Captain Stormfield's Visit to Heaven" (1909/1995).[9] God, in that work, is sublime, remote, liberal to a fault, and somewhat vapidly ineffectual. Twain's quarrels were with the God he learned about from Calvinism, and all the quarrels had at their root Calvinism's take on the problem of evil: where it came from, how it comported with belief in a kind and loving God, why it existed.

Although Twain largely focused on God as depicted in the Old Testament, the Calvinism of Twain's youth was trinitarian, and it remained his default position.[10] He seems not to have followed Tom Paine in his incredulity that there could be two testaments from one God—"I now go on to the book called the New Testament. The *New* Testament! that is, the *new* will, as if there could be two wills of the Creator" (477)—although that created difficulties for Twain whenever he attempted to infer God's nature from God's actions. For example, in the relatively little Twain had to say about Christ, he seemed to respect Christ—with several major exceptions. Twain's typically respectful attitude is displayed throughout the Holy Land portions of *The Innocents Abroad*, and also in chapter 3 of "Captain Stormfield's Visit to Heaven," when Stormfield arrives at an inappropriate gate of heaven and is frustrated by his inability to explain to the head clerk which world he comes from until he at last hits upon what he considers his planet's definitive feature:

> "I don't seem to make out which world it is I'm from. But you may know it from this—it's the one the Savior saved."
> He [the clerk] bent his head at the Name. Then he says, gently—
> "The worlds He has saved are like to the gates of Heaven in number—none can count them." (Baetzhold and McCullough 152)

Generally, insofar as Christ represents mercy and salvation offered to all, as in this example, Twain withholds criticism and even appears to be complimentary.

The major exceptions occur later in his career, and unmistakably reveal his trinitarian perspective. One of them appears in an item written between April 11 and 15, 1896, in his notebook: "~~God as Christ~~ If Christ was God he is in the attitude of one whose ~~indignation~~ anger agst Adam has grown so uncontrollable . . . that nothing but a sacrifice of life can appease it; & so, without noticing how illogical the act is going to be, God condemns *Himself* to death—commits suicide on the cross, & in this ingenious way wipes off that old score" (*Notebook* 290).[11] Another exception occurs in Letter 10 of "Letters from the Earth" (1909/1962), when Satan writes:

> The first time the Deity came down to earth, he brought life and death; when he came the second time, he brought hell. . . .
> Now here is a curious thing. It is believed by everybody that while he was in heaven he was stern, hard, resentful, jealous, and cruel; but that when he

came down to earth and assumed the name of Jesus Christ, he became the opposite of what he was before: that is to say, he became sweet, and gentle, merciful, and all harshness disappeared from his nature and a deep and yearning love for his poor human children took its place. Whereas it was as Jesus Christ that he devised hell and proclaimed it!

Which is to say, that as the meek and gentle Savior he was a thousand billion times crueler than ever he was in the Old Testament—oh, incomparably more atrocious than ever he was when he was at the very worst in those old days (45).

Twain was never in doubt that only a horribly malign God would have created hell as a way to nullify death's blessing of an escape to the refuge of the grave from all further persecution. Hell was "contrived to pursue the dead beyond the tomb" (45). Calvinism's zealous justification of hell only exacerbated Twain's basic hostility toward it.

All Bible-based religions share three common beliefs about God: he is omniscient; he is omnipotent; and he is benevolent. Of these three fundamental attitudes toward God, Twain agreed with only the first two. On the matter of God's benevolence, Twain dissented heretically. Progressing from Tom Paine's criticism of the Bible to a censure of the God of the Bible, Twain apprehended God as an ingenious, deceptive, and malevolent monster who, while promising love, mercy, and salvation, visited an awful and perpetual wrath on all creation because of Adam and Eve's original infraction of his law, an infraction that they were in fact predestined to commit.[12] Twain's heresy can therefore be seen to be aimed at God as conceived by the stern version of Calvinism that he encountered in his early years.

Twain blamed God for a situation which his contemporary Ambrose Bierce, who also came from a Calvinist background, described with angry eloquence: "This is a world of fools and rogues, blind with superstition, tormented with envy, consumed with vanity, selfish, false, cruel, cursed with illusions—frothing mad!" (*Collected Works* 10:77). Going to the root of the theological proposition, Twain was outraged at the duplicity he found in God according to Calvinism. For example, although humans were adjured to act morally, the world into which they were born was so thickly laid with temptations, obstacles, and deceptions that not only was it in effect impossible to live a blameless life but whoever even tried to act morally was put at a disadvantage. Salvation in a blissful life to come was dangled before humanity, but Calvinism taught—and Twain believed—that only a tiny fraction of the race had been predestined to heaven; the rest were from eternity predestined to hell. Without realizing it, therefore, most humans were in a Sisyphean situation: no matter how hard and earnestly they attempted to merit salvation, they were doomed to failure and damnation. Twain correspondingly pondered the idea that the human race was not only damned but that this life was already hell. In counterpoint to his occasional reflections that humans were hapless victims of their evil destiny was his frequent conviction, based on observation, that humans were also hopelessly foolish and wicked and doing their damnedest to make their life a hell. With only occasional exceptional lapses, Twain thus believed that *both* God and humanity were evil: God for first introducing evil into the world and then condemning his creation, and humanity for behaving so damnably bad.

This representation of Twain's beliefs is not new to Twain scholarship and is especially obvious and even explicit in Twain's late writings. But it remains to demonstrate how complexly and interestingly it operates in Twain's entire oeuvre. The most controversial aspect of this entire conception is that which assumes that Twain truly believed in God. If we take Twain either autobiographically or biographically, especially in his extended philosophical treatise *What Is Man?*, in his later years he replaced a belief in God with a belief in secular determinism. But the record of his other literature written before, during, and even after that dialogue shows a God-haunted mind recurring to scenarios involving God, angels, devils, and mysterious divine strangers. Although he tried not to, throughout his whole life he believed in the existence of God. As his comment to Howells recognized, regardless of which church he attended or which philosophy he seemed to embrace, in his core he was a Calvinist.

Twain absorbed his youthful religious training in Calvinist Presbyterianism. It must have been intense to have left such a lasting impression on him. As Dixon Wecter observed in his biography of young Sam Clemens: "Presbyterianism and the Moral Sense it fostered—with its morbid preoccupations about sin, the last judgment, and eternal punishment—entered early into the boy's soul, leaving their traces of fascination and repulsion, their afterglow of hell-fire and terror, through all the years of his adult 'emancipation.' He did not believe in Hell, but he was afraid of it" (88). Whether or not Clemens was himself afraid of hell is a biographical topic worth pursuing, but Twain certainly was aware that a large part of his readers believed in hell and were afraid of it, and in his literature he therefore gave a great deal of attention to hell and Satan and proposed wittily unconventional speculations about both.[13]

Twain renewed contacts with Calvinism during his lifetime through his extensive associations with clergymen and religious people, but the record of his writings shows that he must also have devoted a good deal of thought to it during personal reflections. Calvinism, it should be said at the outset, is one of the older and more scholarly offshoots of Protestantism, with deep roots in Christian theology and biblical exegesis. In America in the nineteenth century it was one of the largest and most popular Protestant movements, though it had several divisions within it. A number of previous commentators over the years have observed that Twain revolted against the severe doctrine he absorbed as a child and encountered as a familiar religious position in the United States. Twain's mother appears to have set her son on the course to strict orthodoxy. She decided on his religious upbringing and, as Terrell Dempsey shows, she and Twain's sister adhered to the conservative "old school" wing of Presbyterianism which supported a stringent observance of traditional teachings (55–61).[14]

Traditional doctrine remained so characteristic a feature of his thought that even as late as 1899 his good friend William Dean Howells described him as a "creature of the Presbyterian deity who did make you,"[15] and one of Stanley Brodwin's articles supports Howells by quoting Clemens's description of himself as a "Brevet Presbyterian."[16] As is well known, Twain spent his life struggling with Christian—especially Presbyterian—doctrine, not infrequently making fun of it, denying it, and seeking to break definitively from its hold on him. Yet despite his overt and emphatic rejection of it, that theology, or rather his heretical take on it, appears in all periods of his literature—early, middle, and late—is a key to his main themes, and constitutes a defining signature, or rather a unique fingerprint, that enables us to reliably identify and better understand his work at all stages of his career.

He held internally opposing views about religion, but these contradictions are largely resolvable in his fiction. There it can be recognized how he came to terms with Calvinism and how it reciprocally affected his thought and modes of expression. Indeed, one of the deepest, if not *the* deepest, influences on Twain's artistry and his outlook on the world was his lifelong encounter with Calvinism, a fact Twain himself seems not to have fully recognized. It is therefore necessary to explain how his troublous Calvinistic orientation toward God and humanity inspired as well as antagonized him and became a prime source and driving force of his creative insights.

Although Twain undoubtedly was exposed to multiple religious and philosophical influences, his critical attitude toward humanity and its institutions had to have derived—whether consciously or not—from an orientation that human nature is fixed to be vain, corrupt, and predisposed from before creation to do evil, that all is predestined, and that "reality" is obscured and distorted by illusion. Only Calvinism fits this description, and it fits it closely. What we are doing, therefore, by identifying Calvinism as the probable source for what everybody agrees are Twain's radical disparagements of the ways that individuals behave and society operates, is making clear the connection between Twain's expressed values and their wellspring. Inasmuch as Twain resented and resisted his beliefs to the point of heresy, he cannot be regarded as a conventional Calvinist. On the other hand, because his beliefs were so shaped by what he opposed, neither can he be adequately described apart from Calvinism.

Because Twain was heretical in his view of God, he was, of course, heretical in his Calvinism. Stanley Brodwin's essay "Mark Twain's Theology" draws on many scholars to confirm Twain's lifelong association with Presbyterianism and to formulate an apt and luminous term, "countertheology," essentially a personal creed—what some scholars have called his gospel—that opposed the theology Twain had been taught.[17] Although there is much overlap between Twain's creed and that of traditional Calvinism, the "spin" that Twain puts on his gospel renders it daringly heretical from the perspective of Calvinism. Heretofore, Calvinist Presbyterianism has been referred to generically, but now it is time to lay out the specifics of Twain's religious creed, this "countertheology" that manifests itself at the core of his literature. Centrally planted in his most important works, this gospel drives his fiction and is a distinguishing feature of it. While some of its component parts have been mentioned in previous scholarship, the core of this countertheology has not hitherto been presented as such. Accordingly, and because its influence will be demonstrated in subsequent chapters, we summarize its main positions as derived heretically by Twain from Calvinism.[18] Twain's countertheology maintained:

1. There is a God. He is omnipotent, omniscient, but not benevolent. When he is not indifferent to creation, which he brought into existence solely for his own pleasure, he is capable of good and sometimes bestows it on his creatures, but more typically he is arbitrary, petty, malicious, cruel, and vindictive, and he is angry at the human race.[19]

2. Existence is an evanescent and transient phenomenon, just a thought of the omnipotent deity and a dream in the minds of all sentient creatures. The dream of life may furthermore be compounded by lesser, subordinate dreams—dreams within dreams. This world is therefore essentially unreal. It is not true substance but only hollow and empty appearance, an illusion, a vain and transient bubble of gaudy but fleeting colors. Its immateriality results from its having been spoken into existence and being sustained only by God's breath and thought. Those of its creatures that take it and life itself at face value are therefore deluded.

3. A consequence of humanity's original sin of disobeying God is what Twain calls God's "Primal Curse" of the "Moral Sense." (Twain himself in 1896 characterized Moral Sense as "the secret of [humanity's] degradation. It is the quality *which enables him to do wrong*. It has no other office. It is incapable of performing any other function" [Budd, "Man's Place in the Animal World," *Collected Tales* 2:207–216].) It renders the great majority oblivious to their own faults. It justifies injuries done to others and leads malefactors to be infuriated by acts of retaliation, which are seen as unwarranted. It enables humans to be content with the practice of small virtues in one aspect of their lives while they perpetrate large vices in other aspects; to cherish ineffective and cheaply pious wishes of brotherhood, justice, and peace while indulging in hatred, revenge, and war; to ignore or downplay the Old Testament's denunciation of the perversion of morality by covetousness, bribery, ethical insensitivity or cowardice, passion, lies, and the following of false doctrines and leaders, and the New Testament's condemnation of the hypocrisy of criticizing others for the motes in their eyes while the critics ignore the beam in their own. All of these examples, Twain believed, are common effects of the curse of the Moral Sense, whose twisted reasoning is made worse by the proud conviction of humanity that in the Moral Sense it possesses some unique and precious endowment that

elevates humans above the beasts, whereas in reality the Moral Sense is the means by which humanity earns damnation.

4. The human race is therefore not merely flawed by original sin but is *corrupted* by it. It has entirely lost the ability to use free will virtuously, and is so wholly inclined to evil that even what seem to be good deeds are tainted. As a consequence, so depraved is human nature that every single human being, even a newborn baby, is fundamentally evil and merits damnation.[20] God is angry at the human race and intends no good to the great majority of it. (In fact, as Warburton puts it, the reprobate majority is "dead to God" [128; see also 78, 102, 136, 146–147].) Nevertheless a few, the "elect," have been predestined to be born again and saved to eternal bliss in heaven, but this is due to no merit of their own but only to God's undeserved gift of grace that passes human understanding.

5. No humans can be saved by their virtuous deeds because no truly virtuous deeds are possible in the absence of God's grace, and because there can never be enough of them to outweigh the sinfulness of humans' nature and deeds. Those who are saved must have faith in God, but he alone decides whom he will save and for what reason.[21]

6. As a consequence of God's omniscience, everything is predestined from before creation. In other words, every incident however slight, every act, every gesture, every word, even every thought—"virtuous" or sinful—is predestined. Nothing happens "accidentally" or by chance.[22] Freedom is therefore impossible, at best only a delusion.

7. Most humans are reprobates, that is, they have been predestined from before creation to eternal punishment in hell: after the advent of Christianity, all non-Christians are; after the advent of Calvinism, all non-Calvinists and even most Calvinists are. Humans are predestined: first by God's plan and edict, and additionally by temperament, "the *law of God* written in the heart of every creature by God's own hand, and [which] must be obeyed, and will be obeyed, in spite of all restricting or forbidding statutes, let them emanate whence they may" ("Letters from the Earth" 38). Nevertheless, although humans can only be agents of God's will and must do as they are predestined, they are held responsible for the sins they commit.[23]

So depraved is human nature that if reprobated humans were not already predestined to hell by edict, the sinfulness of even those who appear to be the most virtuous would surely damn them. (This is sometimes known as "double damnation.")

8. God's predestination is immutable both in scheme and in detail. Being perfect, there is no possibility that God will ever change his mind and reverse his original decree. Those reprobated to hell will infallibly go there; those elected to heaven will never completely fall away from or lose grace, but will ultimately be eternally saved. What are called "special providences" (apparent exceptions to the course of nature or the law of averages—for example, miracles) are actually the workings of the immutable plan God predestined from before creation, and in the larger picture, because there may be collateral victims as well as beneficiaries from them, it may not be possible to definitely ascertain if they do more good than harm.[24]

9. Conscience is an inner voice instilled in us by God, affected by religious instruction but still independent of it, that monitors our moral condition and warns us that we are going astray. Inasmuch as humans are fundamentally evil, and even their virtuously intended motives are therefore corrupt, conscience functions primarily as an irritant to keep us uncomfortable, and is undependable as a guide to action. It moreover subserves our predestination and always cooperates with God's plan for us.

What is significant about this countertheology is that although Twain believed in this canted derivative of Calvinism (which in turn affected his view of God and all Bible religions), he resented and objected to all items in it on the grounds that they were either arbitrary, unfair, or deceptive, and that all were cruel. He did not take pleasure in them or congratulate himself on his own perspicacity; he held to them because he continuously found them to be accurate and efficacious in describing the world and the human race he knew and the God he believed in. In other words, he believed that those positions were true, but he hated those same tragic truths.

Who can know what these beliefs cost him? His literary judgments about life were reinforced by personal experience. Hamlin Hill observed that "Mark Twain was immensely interested in his destination after death. The truth is inescapable that, wherever he went after he died, much of the last decade of his life he lived in hell" (*God's Fool* xvii). Laura Skandera Trombley has documented the series of horrible and painful events during 1908–1909 that constituted what should have been—but clearly was not—the triumphant capstone of his life.[25] As a consequence of thinking blasphemous thoughts about the God he believed in, at times he must have suspected that the fatal tragedies that visited his beloved family—first his son, and later his wife and all but one of his daughters—were perhaps retributions. He must have ached at having converted his wife to his bitter way of thinking, she who entered into marriage with the expectation that he would join her and her family in their loving faith and that they would all reassemble in a blessed heaven. We have evidence that out of love he sometimes dissembled to Livy—what Howells called "heroic lies" (32)—about his disbelief in an afterlife. He must often have been nostalgic, at the very least, for the comfort religion offered about the love of God and the assurance of heaven. To the end of his days, he enjoyed hearing and singing African American spirituals, he knew many hymns by heart, and he was clearly familiar with the Bible, not just the parts that he considered immoral or lies, but the beautiful and tender parts as well, and the Bible's lofty conceptions and stately King James language evoked his admiration.

Twain's attitude, therefore, toward his own countertheology was profoundly ambivalent, and it will be seen how this ambivalence became a source of creative tension in his thinking. It contributed greatly to his deeply ironic vision, his ability to combine and to slip nimbly back and forth between humor and tragedy, and to his ultimate seriousness. As an American, Twain was sincerely devoted to freedom. He considered it a great good, and at the political level he supported its extension to all. But insofar as Twain was a Calvinist, and therefore a predestinarian, he believed at the same time that freedom was a chimera, and that the only thing worse than being denied it would be having it granted, for then nothing would remain to restrain humans from becoming as evil as their depraved natures incessantly urged.

Other American authors of Twain's time also began with childhood Calvinism, but whether they broke entirely away from it in adulthood or only modified it, none of the others seems to have so thoroughly internalized its doctrines and embodied them in his or her literature.[26] Calvinism in Twain's time differed from most other branches of Christianity in the emphasis it gave to the implications of God's omniscience. As Calvinism interpreted this quality, God not only knows everything that has happened and is happening, but he also knows with absolute certainty what will happen in both the immediate and distant futures. It follows then that as God *knows* what will happen, all future events that he knows about *must* happen. Therefore all events are predestined by virtue of the fact that God knows about them in advance. Calvinism was buttressed in this position by an abundance of passages throughout the Bible in which God predicts or ordains what will come to pass, but especially by the explicit New Testament references to predestination in Romans 8:29–30 and Ephesians 1:5, 11.

The weighty subject of predestination is an unusually vexed one in theology, and Calvinism, as a staunch advocate of it, hosts an extensive variety of discussions of it. The questions for us, however, are how much did Twain know about predestination, and what did he believe? In chapter 18 of *Adventures of Huckleberry Finn*, Huck—but not Twain—confusedly conflates a number of associated subtle variations of predestination in an unintentionally flip recollection of the "good" sermon he heard with the Grangerfords: "It had such a powerful lot to say about faith, and good works, and free grace, and *preforeordestination*, and I don't know what all" (147, emphasis added). The conflation is the tip of an iceberg of Twain's awareness of technically distinct theological differentiations from predestination.[27] He would certainly have had exposure to arguments on these topics in church sermons and access to more detailed explanations of them in the religious tracts that abounded in the nineteenth century. It appears that he did not retain an appreciation of the distinctions—what to Huck, though not to the Grangerfords' preacher, seemed hair-splitting subtleties—but the central fact of predestination was another matter. *That* Twain kept, and kept it separate in his own mind from superficially similar doctrines.[28]

Some Christian religions, uncomfortable with biblical assertions of predestination, have homiletically advanced the notion of foreknowledge as a way of interpreting these passages. As foreknowledge is usually understood, although God knows all in advance, his knowing does not cause humans to act in certain ways; having free will, they choose their actions—but in the way God foreknows. Foreknowledge has been analogized by a familiar situation: a parent puts some candy within the reach of a child who is very fond of it, warns the child not to touch it, and then leaves the room. Of course the parent knows that the child will soon succumb to the temptation of the candy, but the parent's knowledge does not cause the child to take the candy. The flaw in this analogy is that the knowledge of the parent is different in kind from the knowledge of God. The parent may be highly certain about what the child will do, but though unlikely it is always possible that for some reason the child will leave the candy alone. When an omniscient God knows, however, his knowledge is absolute certainty; the child will always act as God foreknew. Indeed, the fact that God foreknows ensures the child's action. Whatever value foreknowledge has as a homiletic tactic to mitigate the severe implications of God's omniscience and to make humans responsible through free will, it does not hold up to logical scrutiny. If God has omniscience, then all is predestined.

"Predestination" is often used interchangeably with other terms such as "fatalism," "destiny," "fortune," and "determinism," and sometimes with "necessity," probably because all these terms share the common consequence of abrogating, abridging, or circumventing freedom. Nevertheless, in their literal senses they reflect different etiologies that are important to distinguish them from each other. Fatalism is at root a belief in fate, a mysterious nonbiblical entity. As conceived by Greek, Roman, Norse, and other cultures, the Fates were shadowy personifications of vague, controlling forces beyond the gods and, in some cases, forces to which even the gods were subordinate. Fate seems to be intermittently active but purposeless insofar as some general scheme can be discerned directing it.[29] "Destiny" and "fortune" are sometimes used interchangeably with "predestination" as synonyms, although those vague terms also may sometimes serve as substitutes for it. One who claims, however, to be master of his or her own fate or in charge of his or her own destiny is either confused about the controlling character of fate, destiny, or fortune, or is grandiosely but confusedly affirming free will. Predestination is a specifically biblical idea, the effects caused by one all-knowing, all-powerful, and purposeful God who controls *everything* that happens in his universe, from the movements of heavenly bodies to the fall of a sparrow, and includes thoughts and feelings as well as words and actions. Predestination is general, total, and continuously in action; it operates, as they say today, 24/7. It excludes the possibilities of chance, accident, or luck. Implicit in the Old Testament, it is explicit in the New Testament.

"Determinism" in the modern sense is a nonreligious, scientific, or philosophical term that affirms that all effects are inevitably caused by operant antecedent conditions. Genetics, for example, determines what our physical makeup, and influences what our mental and behavioral characteristics, will be. Programming determines how computers will operate automatically, and animals and humans, at least to some extent, can also be conditioned or programmed to be predictable. Determinism is usually understood to be a mechanical function of the operation of immutable laws and as such can be applicable to particular cases, but not as the expression of a general and purposeful plan or ultimate cause that sets all into motion. "Necessity" refers to the compelling influence upon us of the condition of our environment or situation, or to invariable physical laws. These existing laws or conditions are only knowable restrictions, however, and not denials of freedom. A child born, therefore, to poor and uneducated parents is at a disadvantage compared to one born to well-off and educated parents; nevertheless, the former may succeed and the latter fail. But if someone jumps off a tall building to prove trust in God, it will not be God's disapproval that brings that person crashing down, but gravity. Miracles, if they really occur, could contravene necessity, but the laws of physics, chemistry, and biology are the knowable norms and conditions of existence, and it is prudent not to challenge or test them. Twain appears to have understood and generally observed the differences between these terms, and although he sometimes identified himself as a determinist in his later years, it remains to be seen if his fiction really reflects that position or if he was rather cloaking predestination under another name.

But what of free will? Many Bible-based religions affirm it, and cite scriptural texts that give assurances of the human capacity to choose. Here is one of those instances where the Bible appears to contradict itself, and where each religion that affirms free will attempts to explain its stand by the way it interprets the issue. If the issue is faced directly, however, and free will is defined as the ability to surprise God, then it is obvious that if God is really omniscient, he cannot be surprised. "Free will" does not therefore come close to meaning that humans are, or can be, totally free, but is only a manner of saying that we may not be strictly controlled, that our leash has some play to it. Ultimately, as Calvinism recognized, given an omniscient and omnipotent deity, predestination follows logically, as well as having a scriptural basis. Scripture nevertheless often affirms the idea of choice, but how free will might be compatible with divine omniscience is beyond the power of logic to ascertain. If free will exists, then believers have to accept it as a mystery, or on the basis that if not a matter contrary to reason, it is a quality above human reason. The frontier Calvinism which Samuel Clemens absorbed as a boy did not try to limit God's power. Nor, in his writings, and though he was often critical of God's power, did Mark Twain.

From its inception, America has been a country profoundly devoted to freedom, and in the nineteenth century there was an exhilarating feeling that freedom was on the rise, that its day had come, and that increasing numbers of humans both in the United States and in other lands were becoming beneficiaries of it. It is strange to reflect that while all this was happening, many Americans were Calvinists and supposedly committed to a belief that all was predestined. Exactly how this could be is a question yet to be adequately answered, but a working presumption based on analogy with members of other faiths might be that then, as now, despite a sincere belief in particular doctrines of their religion, relatively few Calvinists were scrupulous about affirming those doctrines rigorously outside of church, or assiduous in applying them to their practical, mundane, day-to-day lives. In chapter 5 of *Tom Sawyer*, while describing a church service Tom attended, Twain understatedly supplies an example of how little impact a doctrinal sermon might have on a congregation.

> The minister gave out his text and droned along monotonously through an argument that was so prosy that many a head by and by began to nod—and yet it was an argument that dealt in limitless fire and brimstone and thinned the predestined elect down to a company so small as to be hardly worth the saving. (50)

As this passage suggests, however, although Tom and his fellow congregants did not show much interest in the sermon, and even the minister did not treat it as exciting information of great intrinsic importance, Twain was aware of its significance and regarded as ironic the contrast between its fearful doctrines and the congregation's passivity about their import. But if most other Calvinists did not show much concern about the church's doctrines, Twain did. He took the Bible and Calvinistic doctrines seriously enough to brood over them, and to be one of that small minority of American Calvinists who internalized Calvinist indoctrination to the degree that he denied that humans were, or even could be, free.

It is not that he was scornful of freedom or did not value it—on the contrary, in both his personal and public lives he considered it precious, longed for it, advocated it, and actively promoted it—but in his private thoughts and especially in his fiction he constantly confronted its impossibility. The reason for this is easy to understand, its impossibility being a direct consequence of the fact of God's omniscience. If all humans are predestined, what is the meaning of having political or economic freedom? When predestined humans go into a voting booth, what kind of choices can they make? Puppets might believe that they are making choices, while all the time they are being controlled by strings invisible to them. Freedom, like God's benevolence, was therefore for Twain an elaborate hoax. It promised much, but failed to deliver. On the contrary, although freedom is one of the great themes of his fiction, his position on it is a denial of its possibility. In all of his major works and many of his minor ones, he consistently demonstrates that freedom is a delusion and that none of his protagonists achieve it; if anything, their struggles for it result in making clearer the fact of their predestined bondage.

Dream, impersonation, and hoax are three interrelated subthemes—aspects of his grand theme of the deceitfulness of life and the impossibility of humans achieving freedom, happiness, or fulfillment—that run through Twain's fiction as he sought to explain why freedom, happiness, and fulfillment remain forever beyond the human ability to secure them. As he saw life, governed by the predestination of a hostile God, they work separately and together to restrict or divert humanity's aspirations to freedom, happiness, and fulfillment and lead life instead into a state of perpetual illusion that degrades all its hopes into agents of frustration or punishment. Although this is Twain's view, at least at his creative level, only two of his protagonists in our samples—the older narrator of *Roughing It* and August Feldner of *No. 44, The Mysterious Stranger*—even sense the enormity of the deception they are living. Repeatedly his protagonists are insidiously victimized by waking dreams, either ones they believe their own or ones they are "charmed" or "enchanted" into, which blind them to truth so successfully that they do not even recognize retrospectively what has been done to them. As described, the dream process in effect hoaxes them, because the border between dream and hoax is not clear-cut, and the leitmotifs overlap. Dream leads to hoax, and hoax works through dream; the manner of operation may differ, but the purpose and result conspire to the same ends. But in Twain's main fictions a major hoax lurks at the center of each and organizes and controls the entire work. He characteristically aims his hoaxes at readers, and a large part of the hoaxes' effectiveness is the readers' delayed and chagrined realizations—or maybe shock—at having so misread the signs. Although it can be difficult for readers to detect the hoaxes, once they do a clarification results, and many things fall into place.

Impersonation participates in both dream and hoax but works more subtly than either. There are two kinds of impersonation: that which the individual enters into "knowingly" and voluntarily, and that which is imposed upon the individual from outside. Impersonation is transformative; it changes the individual from one personality into another. It differs from imitation, which is a light and conscious form of play acting that is obvious and can be started or dropped at will without consequence. Impersonation is a deeper and riskier empathetic experience which must be "lived" but can get out of the individual's control and take over. It makes no difference if an individual believes that he or she is knowingly fitting into a desired social or professional role, or if an individual is maneuvered by predestined circumstances into a role; once the role takes over and the individual's values are changed from achieving independence to achieving the values of the role, a personality change has taken place, and the individual thenceforth serves the malign purpose or pleasure of the governing force.[30]

Although Calvinism was the locus of concentration for Twain's religious orientation, not all of the important ideas that he assimilated from his youthful indoctrination were uniquely Calvinist; some would have been found in the teachings of most Christian denominations. The insubstantiality of this world and its transience, for example, are standard Christian teachings. Practically every biblically derived religion regularly reminds its adherents that the striving after riches, power, status, fame, and worldly enjoyment are exercises of vanity because they are hollow achievements, the insubstantialities of dream. All students of Bible religions know this, yet few internalized this lesson as deeply as Twain did, who brooded on it for most of his life. Increasingly in his fiction, life is depicted as an illusion or a dream,[31] and so is identity. To him, even time participates in this monstrous hoax, and all that occurs in "real time" is in truth dreamlike, pleasantly delusive if romantic, nightmarish if "realistic," but in any case susceptible to being switched arbitrarily to other scenarios, like incidents in a dream.

We do not maintain that Twain was fully aware in the earlier part of his career of the power and range of these inclinations in his thought. Like other young people, while he knew what his religious indoctrination had been, he did not at the beginning realize how deep and strong its grip on him was or would be. Over the course of his life, he would discover that he kept recurring to the same positions, that they accorded with his experience, and that they accounted more accurately for what he encountered in life and thought than any alternatives. At some point, however, certainly by the early 1880s, he knew where he stood. He would occasionally explicitly try out elements of his gospel on friends, as he did in one of his addresses to the Monday Evening Club in Hartford, Connecticut, in which he denied free will: "I observed that the human machine gets all its inspirations from the outside and is not capable of originating an idea of any kind in its own head and . . . that no man ever does a duty for duty's sake but only for the sake of avoiding the personal discomfort he would have to endure if he shirked the duty; also I indicated that there is no such thing as free will and no such thing as self-sacrifice" (Blair 337).[32] Still, it is possible that even then he did not fully acknowledge the nature of his gospel or recognize the extent to which it had a way of insinuating itself into his fiction.

But if Twain had been fully aware of his inclinations, and had openly preached his countertheology, who would have bought his books? His was not a cheery message and, if promulgated, would have soured his reputation as a popular author before it got fairly started. Twain wanted to sell books and establish his reputation as a writer, and for most of his career, therefore, he was very circumspect about advancing his beliefs openly. This circumspection, in fact, has a great deal to do with his development as a writer. He turned the liabilities of potentially objectionable beliefs into assets by skillfully devising attractive ways of masking them. His core values are expressed in all his main works, but they are usually so sugarcoated or indirect and concealed by attractive and entertaining surface features of his fiction that these vehicles for his ideas have long been mistaken for the whole. Without a doubt, Twain had a genius for humor and was a brilliant author, so it is not surprising that readers should enjoy him for richly abundant qualities which are also easily accessible and have not searched closely for features of his thought considerably more difficult to recognize and not very "enjoyable" once found. Only in recent decades, after Twain achieved the status of a major literary figure and letters and hitherto unpublished materials became more fully available, has the interest in deeper and concealed aspects of his art and his life encouraged more attention to his use of irony and more careful research into his informal writings.

We know, for example, that Twain not only was raised as a Presbyterian but that he wanted to be a minister and preach the gospel. In a letter written on October 19 and 20, 1865, Twain revealed to his brother and sister-in-law something immensely telling:

> Now let me preach *you* a sermon. I never had but two **powerful** ambitions in my life. One was to be a pilot, & the other a preacher of the gospel. I accomplished the one & failed in the other, **because** I could not supply myself with the necessary stock in trade—*i.e.* religion. I have given it up forever. I never had a "call" in that direction, anyhow, & my aspirations were the very ecstasy of presumption. An But I *have* had a "call" to literarture, of a low order—*i.e.* humorous. It is nothing to be proud of, but it is my strongest suit, & if I were to listen to that maxim of stern *duty* which says it is m that to do right you **must** multiply the one or the two or the three talents which the Almighty entrusts to your keeping, I would long ago have ceased to meddle with things for which I was by nature unfitted & turned my attention to seriously scribbling to excite the **laughter** of God's creatures. (*Mark Twain's Letters* 1:322–323)

This most interesting admission might be dismissed as the exaggeration of a young idealist were it not reiterated thirty years later, in 1906, by another autobiographical revelation:

> Humorists of the "mere" sort cannot survive. Humor is only a fragrance, a decoration. Often it is merely an odd trick of speech and of spelling. . . . Humor must not professedly teach, and it must not professedly preach, but it must do both if it would live forever. By forever, I mean thirty years. . . . I have always preached. That is the reason I have lasted thirty years. (Twain, as qtd. in DeVoto, *Mark Twain in Eruption* 202)

The greatest part by far of Twain's writing career lies between these two statements, which have two major points in common: that he "preached" in his fiction, and that his brilliant use of humor was paradoxically serious in motive and subordinate and ancillary to the messages he was preaching. There is also one major difference: before he was fairly under way in his career he had initially wanted to preach *the* gospel; afterward he covertly preached *his* gospel in the form of a resentful countertheology.

Roughing It

How much better is it to get wisdom than gold! And to get understanding
rather to be chosen than silver! —Proverbs 16:16

Roughing It (1872) is underestimated both as a work of literature and as the
main product of a crucial era and phase of Mark Twain's development. Not
that the book has not been complimented. On the contrary, from the beginning it has been justly celebrated and enjoyed as a comic masterpiece by
critics as well as amateur readers, and until World War II it and *Life on the
Mississippi* (1883) were generally considered to be Twain's main contributions to American literature. But hardly any of the praises it has received
adequately describe what an even more extraordinary achievement it is:
a work of mature but daring artistry, subtly organized, full of the sparks
of genius, and an outstanding example of the dictum that the greatest art
is that which conceals itself. Examined closely, the book reveals a serious
dimension that must be reckoned with in any satisfactory understanding
of its totality and its place in Twain's canon. More than merely a loose
collection of youthful high-spirited sketches about adventures in the new
territories of the West and Hawaii, *Roughing It* is that *and* an artistically
sophisticated exposé of the divine hoax of the human search for the good
life, freedom, wealth, and happiness.

Several notable studies of Twain's early years as an artist have appeared
in recent decades, among them Jeffrey Steinbrink's *Getting to Be Mark
Twain* (1991), Jeffrey Melton's *Mark Twain, Travel Books, and Tourism*
(2002), Joseph Coulombe's *Mark Twain and the American West* (2003),
and James Caron's *Mark Twain: Unsanctified Newspaper Reporter* (2008).
These four books, as well as others, have identified many of the conditions
and inspirations that contributed to Twain's formation as an artist dur-

ing the period leading up to his writing of *Roughing It*. Arguably the most profound influence on Twain during his time out West in the early 1860s, however, came from the writers of Nevada's Sagebrush School. These writers advanced Twain in numerous ways as a serious artist, but particularly in the art of the literary hoax. He had, of course, previously encountered literary hoaxes in the writings of American humorists, such as Poe and the writers of the Old Southwest, whom he read before the Sagebrush authors, but in Nevada hoaxes and swindles were practically everyday occurrences in the mining business, and the Sagebrushers not only reflected this situation in their literature but also developed such skillful ways of incorporating hoaxes in their writings as to have raised literary hoaxes to a new level of artistry. So great was the effect of the Sagebrush School on Twain during his almost three-year stay in Nevada that it is impossible to separate his mastery of the art of hoax from the literature he wrote for the rest of his life. It was during this period that Twain came to see a grand pattern of hoaxing throughout all creation. The hoaxes he noticed taking place on the Comstock, the ubiquity of hoaxes in nature, and the fatal affinity for hoaxes he detected in human nature merged with his belief in a vindictive deity who tricked humanity, and thereafter became an ideological unit in his thinking.[1] As a consequence, in the great majority of novels, short stories, and humorous pieces he wrote, central but subtle hoaxes are so deeply embedded in most of them as to constitute essential elements of both their style and content. *Roughing It* is the first of his major works in which Twain makes use of this approach.

Artemus Ward (the pseudonym of Charles Farrar Browne) also made a deep and lasting impression on Twain during this period. Ward was already a nationally famous humorist when he visited Virginia City, Nevada, for three weeks in December 1863 to give some lectures and to socialize with the journalists of Twain's newspaper, the *Territorial Enterprise*. Twain was immediately captivated by Ward's lecture style, and became in effect a convert to Ward's manner of seeming to ramble loosely over a number of topics while actually advancing a covert theme almost subliminally. Before Ward left Nevada, Twain had not only assimilated Ward's platform style but had learned how to adapt it to his own writings. In 1875 Twain wrote a letter to his Nevada friend Dan De Quille in which he shows awareness of this technique and its importance.

Dan, there is more than one way of writing a book; & your way is *not* the right one. You see, the winning card is to nail a man's interest with *Chapter 1*, and not let up on him till you get him to the word "finis." That can't be done with detached sketches; but I'll show you how to make a man read every one of those sketches, under the stupid impression that they are mere accidental incidents that have dropped in on you unawares in the course of your *narrative*.[2]

De Quille was about to write his book *The Big Bonanza*, and it is highly probable that *Roughing It* was the model Twain was going to use to teach De Quille the technique he had adapted from Ward. This statement in his letter explains the seemingly loose style of *Roughing It*, with its abundance of "detached sketches," and also goes far toward accounting for the "evasion" chapters of *Adventures of Huckleberry Finn* (1885) and the whole of *A Connecticut Yankee in King Arthur's Court* (1889), for Twain continued to practice and refine the technique he learned from Ward of employing disguised modes of organization.

Roughing It contrapuntally overlays an extended contrast of conspicuous youthful and comic enthusiasm upon a very subdued level of somber realization that the hilarity of those experiences was either superficial or illusory. The book's comic view has always been overwhelmingly evident to commentators, but whatever seriousness they recognized in the book has often tended to be seen as anomalous, the author's transient and aesthetically dissonant indulgence of ephemeral personal moodiness.[3] This seemingly anomalous or recessive element, as purposeful as it is persistent, leads to the book's structure of values that organize it and provide its thematic relation to his other major works. However appealing are its surface features, the book's intellectual power stems from the perspectives of age and reflection that show how the variety and charm of those sunnier impressions are unreliable and dissipate, and leave behind disillusioning but enduring lessons that life is predestined and that happiness is not an achievable end in itself, especially the happiness brought about by material possessions or change of scenery or experience. The book's humor derives almost entirely from the sugarcoating of Twain's artistry as an entertainer; but Twain's heretical Calvinism supplies the book's core values. Once the book is understood as a balanced contest between two radically different views of life—indeed it bears comparison to some artists' use of "negative space" to create a "figure/ground" effect, alternate and initially overlooked pictures on the same canvas—it greatly deepens and grows in stature as a tour de force of literary artistry.

Besides being one of Twain's most enjoyable books—a virtual and virtuoso compendium of choice American humor from the nineteenth century—*Roughing It* is also one of his most puzzling books. It is generally read as a travel book with a strong autobiographical component consisting mainly of chapters of humorous incidents (often supplemented by fictional embellishment) of which he was presumably a participant or witness, and of reflections that are loosely connected by chronological sequence. While this view describes the book's surface, it misses the serious countertheological themes which underlie the book and tie it together tightly and powerfully into a work which bleakly surveys life as rigged by predestination and, most especially, by the vain dream of evading God's doom of earning one's bread by the sweat of one's brow. The Bible's teachings about human nature and God's control of all that happens are generally acknowledged in *Roughing It* in a theoretical way but ignored or downplayed in practice by the many individuals in the book in search of an earthly Eden or infected with silver fever. This deliberate internal contradiction underscores the book's themes of human folly and the tragic vanity of existence. Far from being a book of youthful talent but limited artistic merit, *Roughing It* is instead therefore an early but dazzling manifestation of Twain's maturity, the first full-scale demonstration of the artistic brilliance activated by the marriage of his countertheology with the literary techniques he assimilated from the writers of Nevada's Sagebrush School and the humorist Artemus Ward.

If there is one thing almost everyone agrees about in regard to *Roughing It*, it is that it is not a novel. But there is less agreement on what it is. The book used to be thought of as sort of an autobiography until scholarship demonstrated its unreliability for that purpose.[4] It is often considered to be a travel book, but it can be argued that its humor, imagination, and fictional content overshadow its value as an account of places visited. Many view the work as simply a book of humorous episodes and reflections loosely connected by its travel or autobiographical frame, but below that humorous surface the book does have thematic coherence, and those themes are quite serious: Calvinistic emphases on predestination, the corruption of human nature, and the imminence of hell.[5] It may therefore be worthwhile to reconsider the book as novelistic if not a novel, because carefully considered, the novel category describes the book no less satisfactorily than the other categories, and mostly better.

Roughing It exhibits so many characteristics of fiction that it is surprising that most readers have resisted considering it a novelistic work of fiction. It has a protagonist whose name by default in a work supposedly autobiographical is Mark Twain, but the persona is basically fictitious, as are most of his incredible adventures. The book's first chapter, which introduces and describes the protagonist, is almost entirely fiction. He characterizes himself as very naïve, and begins to depict a self-deprecating, gullible, modest, and humorless stance that is maintained throughout the book until the last chapter.[6] Biography establishes that this characterization was not true of the real Mark Twain, but the fiction contributes a great deal to the success of the book and to some degree was extended to the public persona of Mark Twain. In fictionalizing himself, Twain followed the lead of humorists of Nevada's Comstock Lode and the Old Southwest, and of those before who did the same thing in travel letters and fiction cast as autobiography, and carried the technique to its logical extension in a work of novelistic length.[7] Why, then, not call this book about a fictitious narrator a novel as we normally do with other similar works?

The fact that the protagonist of *Roughing It* undergoes character development from frivolous to grave is often overlooked. The description he gives of himself in the first chapter, apart from being fictitious, is humorously naïve and contributes greatly to the pleasure of reading the book, but that picture alters by degrees throughout the book until it is reversed by the end. A main technique by which Twain accomplishes this, and accomplishes it brilliantly, is a hoax device which might be called the "misleading past tense." By its means, most episodes in the book are told absorbingly by the narrator in the simple past tense in such a way as to lead readers to think that the young narrator's first conclusions about these episodes are also final evaluations. But they are not; the narrator knew when he wrote them that he was recording only the mistaken conclusions of his younger self *up to that moment* in his life, and that in the light of subsequent events he will expose the errors of those premature conclusions, usually as cases of self-deception. The purpose of this device is to take readers in, to hoax them, and it is done sometimes blatantly and sometimes subtly.

Perhaps the most delightfully notorious example of the blatant form of this device is the episode in chapters 31–33 in which the protagonist and several of his companions become lost in a blizzard on their way to Carson City. Twain sneaks up on readers by enticing them into a romantic frame of mind—and for Twain, romanticism was typically tantamount to falsehood. First, the protagonist mentions the plight of a young Swede who walked into a blizzard and "disappeared into the white oblivion. He was never heard of again. He no doubt got bewildered and lost, and Fatigue delivered him over to Sleep and Sleep betrayed him to Death" (31:209).[8] The story appears, by itself, pathetic, and the capitalized personifications (a romantic device) intensify the tragedy by making the Swede appear to be a victim of conspiring supernatural forces. Next, the protagonist and his companions likewise get lost in the blizzard, travel in a circle, and lose their horses when they dismount. Deceived by the romantic lies they read in books, they are unsuccessful at building a fire. As they feel the cold they assume that death is upon them. They each make a final confession and discard a prominent vice to which they had been attached (more romantic conventions). The protagonist weeps as he contemplates what he might have done if more years of life had been granted him (yet another romantic convention) and then,

> We put our arms around each other's necks and awaited the warning drowsiness that precedes death by freezing.
> It came stealing over us presently, and then we bade each other a last farewell. A delicious dreaminess wrought its web about my yielding senses, while the snow-flakes wove a winding sheet about my conquered body. Oblivion came. The battle of life was done. (216)

This passage, with its dramatic situation, resignation to the inevitable, and lofty language, is pure romanticism. If true, it should have ended the book. Instead, it only concludes the chapter.

Twain continues the hoax through the first paragraph of chapter 33, then ends it swiftly with two sentences that transition abruptly from the ethereal to vulgar reality.

> I do not know how long I was in a state of forgetfulness, but it seemed an age. A vague consciousness grew upon me by degrees, and then came a gathering anguish of pain in my limbs and through all my body. I shuddered. The thought flitted through my brain, "this is death—this is the hereafter."
> Then came a white upheaval at my side, and a voice said, with bitterness:
> "Will some gentleman be so good as to kick me behind!" (217)

It is a companion's voice. The travelers are not dead. Not only that, but they are only fifteen steps away from a stage station where their horses stand under a shed. Readers are undeceived, seemingly simultaneously with the narrator. But what had deceived the readers? Their own romantic expectations. The misleading past tense had been the means by which they, through their gullibility, had been enticed to a setup (with malice aforethought) by the protagonist narrator. Of course, by implication, the older narrator is wryly aware of his youthful folly.

Four additional examples among many in the book will illustrate how readers are hoaxed more subtly by the device of the misleading past tense. In chapter 1, when the naïve protagonist learns that he has been offered the position of secretary to his brother, he declares, "I had nothing more to desire. My contentment was complete" (2). In chapter 3 he sums up with enthusiastic praise the experience of being carried across the continent in a stagecoach away from a "tiresome city life" to new adventures: "we felt that there was only one complete and satisfying happiness in the world, and we had found it" (11–12). Chapter 23 begins with an even stronger statement of satisfaction, but is directed toward a different experience at Lake Tahoe: "If there is any life happier than the life we led on our timber ranch for the next two or three weeks, it must be a sort of life which I have not read of in books or experienced in person" (152). A similar glorification in chapter 28, which we may now suspect is hyperbole, describes yet a fourth experience, the greenhorn narrator's account of how he slipped out of camp one day and began hunting for ore under the assumption that any shiny rocks would be precious mineral: "Of all the experiences of my life, this secret search among the hidden treasures of silver-land was the nearest to unmarred ecstasy" (185).

Apart from the fact that these four experiences contradict each other in their superlative claims to be the happiest of the narrator's life, each of these extravagant claims about happiness is also soon contradicted by subsequent experiences. The stagecoach ride turns into a series of embarrassments, disappointments, and unpleasant, even frightening, incidents. By the time the stagecoach reaches the alkali flats of Utah, "truly and seriously the romance all faded away and disappeared, and left the desert trip nothing but a harsh reality—a thirsty, sweltering, longing, hateful reality!" (18:124). The timber ranch idyll with a friend ends with a forest fire that destroys their timber, turns the lakeside firmament above into a "reflected hell!" and reduces them to being "homeless wanderers again" (23:156). (The word "again" is subtly eloquent, for it implies that the narrator and his companion had been homeless wanderers before, a not inaccurate representation of the situation of Gold Rush emigrants—or of the whole human race after expulsion from Eden.) The protagonist is "smitten with the silver fever" after arriving in Nevada and is enticed by it into quitting his "sublime position" and instead following "the road to fortune" (26:174). And the "unmarred ecstasy" of the secret search is marred within hours by the narrator's humiliating lesson that what he had pounced upon as gold nuggets was only "granite rubbish and nasty glittering mica that isn't worth ten cents an acre!" (28:188).

Immediately following this latter revelation the narrator launches into an elegantly rhetorical and extravagantly romantic lament:

> So vanished my dream. So melted my wealth away. So toppled my airy castle to the earth and left me stricken and forlorn.
> Moralizing, I observed, then, that "all that glitters is not gold."

Ballou, the experienced miner who broke the news to him, follows up with antiromantic realism (including a pointed biblical allusion) when he says that "I could lay it up among my treasures of knowledge, that *nothing* that glitters is gold."[9] Chastised and humbled, the narrator concludes: "So I learned then, once for all, that gold in its native state is but dull, unornamental stuff, and that only low-born metals excite the admiration of the ignorant with an ostentatious glitter. However, like the rest of the world, I still go on underrating men of gold and glorifying men of mica. Commonplace human nature cannot rise above that" (28:188).

These last lines are very rich but also complex. Both the first and second lines contain romantic sentiments, including the admission that the narrator had been living a dream, but are in a state of internal contradiction, a truth revealed but paired with an admission that it is not followed. The last line, instead of resolving the contradictions, raises the unanswered question of why "cannot" is used instead of "does not." The sentence is also a bitter reflection at odds with the romantic perceptions throughout most of the book that stem from the naïve "innocence" of the narrator. In addition, the phrase "once for all" in the first line is another artful example of the misleading past tense, for if it were literally true, the narrator would have been permanently enlightened and most of his subsequent entertaining misadventures would not have occurred. Instead, the narrator exposes himself as having a learning defect: after grasping an important truth he promptly forgets it and immediately reverts to his normal naïveté. In fact, as chapter 29 bears out, not only the narrator but also the rest of the company, including Ballou, become "stark mad" with excitement over not real discoveries and the production of ore but just the undeveloped prospects of mere rocks (193–194). In short, the episode implies that even where some humans may know the truth well enough to teach it to others, their nature is incapable of assimilating it to the point where they govern their own actions by it. The narrator who wrote the entire book and ended it with a somber moral (79:542) of course knew in chapter 28 that the conclusion his younger self arrived at was a false dawn and would soon be forgotten, and that he would revert to his normal type of being prone to err. The pessimism of the book's penultimate paragraph goes even further than its admission that the knowing narrator continues to "usually" make gross errors; it extends to the implied recognition that he *cannot* escape his type.

The pattern of the technique of the misleading past tense, then, is to induce readers to uncritically accept the younger narrator's hyperbole and consequently suffer vicarious letdown and remorse when his romantic gullibility is inevitably exposed and the realistic consequences of his foolish exaggerations unfold later on.[10] In effect, readers are set up by the misleading past tense into reacting before all the cards are laid on the table. When the last card is played not by the youthful and naïve narrator but by his older and wiser self with information he withheld, it trumps the readers' hands. The fact that Twain uses the same technique repeatedly is in itself evidence that *Roughing It* is not an unpremeditated and merely amusing record of travels, but an artful work of fiction which largely aims at tricking the reader. The subtle tricking, furthermore, is not gratuitous; it is always done when the youthful narrator is carried away to happy ecstasy by romantic enthusiasms, and it always has the same consequence: the narrator and the readers are undeceived when they are returned with a jolt to sad reality.[11]

Twain varies the force of these tricks, spaces them just sufficiently far apart to make difficult the detection of their pattern, and usually cloaks them with humor so that readers are strung along and hindered from catching on before the book's end. While he does this, however, Twain also artfully drops risky clues about the character of the narrator, betting, as it were, that they will not be picked up and connected. If readers could easily recognize the clues in the course of reading, they might see where his portrayal of the narrator is heading. By forcing readers to wait until the end to learn his purposes, Twain secures the benefits of surprise, and additionally drives home the point that readers are no more likely than his youthful narrator to gather the evidence that was there all along, and reach the correct conclusion. The pattern of character development is the same in all incidents: the narrator is deceived, either by himself or some other agency, and increasingly loses some of the fresh and romantic naïveté projected in the first chapter. Conversely, the pattern of disappointments increasingly and inevitably propels the narrator toward the glum personality he acquires at the end.

A few selections from the book reveal the pattern of how Twain forecasts the fully matured character of the narrator with hints. In chapter 1, for instance, not just a definite distancing from the youthful narrator's romantic extremes is implied in line three by the prefacing of the whole enthusiastic outburst with the words "I was young and ignorant," but also the objective use of the past tense is used. Those words suggest an older and wiser narrator who admits to having once been so ebullient but is now no longer so and, in fact, is disapproving of the happy excessiveness of his earlier self. This is the first instance in the book of its recurring motif of a contradictory contest between the earlier and later selves of the narrator, a contest which at times is overt but is more often covert and always implants an ambiguity that tinges the younger narrator's optimism with ominousness. Additional instances occur throughout the book.

In chapter 2 one occurs in the conclusion of the sentence describing how the protagonist and his brother brought four pounds of statutes and six pounds of dictionary with them as baggage, "for we did not know—poor innocents—that such things could be bought in San Francisco on one day and received in Carson City the next" (4–5). The second half of the sentence, with the interjection "poor innocents," makes explicit a retrospective criticism from the mature protagonist of a naïve act of his younger self, which seemed at the time to be a prudential provision. In chapter 8, after the travelers register excitement at encountering alkali water for the first time, an older and disillusioned narrator interjects a surprisingly blunt criticism: "In a small way we were the same sort of simpletons as those who climb unnecessarily the perilous peaks of Mont Blanc and the Matterhorn, and derive no pleasure from it except the reflection that it isn't a common experience" (52).[12] Chapter 28 ends with the same sour note already quoted from the experienced narrator when the folly of the youthful narrator's secret search is revealed: "[L]ike the rest of the world, I still go on underrating men of gold and glorifying men of mica. Commonplace human nature cannot rise above that" (188). The pessimism of this remark is clearly out of keeping with the character of the youthful narrator. The remark must come, therefore, from a disillusioned narrator who has yet to make his full appearance. Indeed, the surface charm and humor of the book are mainly dependent upon the youthful narrator's being repeatedly deceived by his illusions. Chapter 44, for example, opens with its report of how every man on the Comstock entered into the gambling fever of believing that the wildcat mine claim into which he had poured his money "would infallibly be worth a thousand dollars a foot." Then comes this chilling statement: "Poor fellow, he was blessedly blind to the fact that he never would see that day" (285). Again the source of this comment could only be a disillusioned narrator who knew what was to come, a very different personality from that of the young and naïve narrator.

These critical interpositions occur with some frequency throughout the book and reach their peak in the last chapter. There, the older narrator reports how a practical joke permanently soured him on that sort of humor, how he sailed to New York via the Isthmus of Panama on a trip that was haunted by cholera that killed two or three people every day, and how he found home a dreary place where few of the grown people he had known remained prosperous and happy. More important, he characterized his "pleasure trip" to the West as "seven years of vicissitudes"—a strange judgment of a narrative that is widely hailed as a comic achievement. Most important is its explicit moral: "If you are of any account, stay at home and make your way by faithful diligence, but if you are 'no account,' go away from home and then you will have to work, whether you want to or not" (542).

The contrast of this depressing advice to the hopes of the naïve, happy, and optimistic narrator of the first chapter could hardly be greater. But the concluding moral also reveals the later narrator to have been characterized not so much by wanderlust as by a restlessness which drove him from one experience to another, from one place to another, vainly seeking everywhere for the ideal place, for the ideal job, and for a level of income, prestige, or sufficiency in which he could rest. There was no such place in the New World or even in the paradisiacal Hawaiian islands, and the probable reason for this restlessness has more to do with human nature than with place or climate, and recalls the original, biblical reason why humans were expelled from the Garden of Eden and turned into fugitives and vagabonds (Genesis 4:12). Twain's Calvinistic background had much to do with the shaping of the protagonist. The book recounts with delightful surface humor the protagonist's destined and futile attempts to escape God's doom for humankind until at the end he accepts that East or West, the results are, and always will be, the same. Vicissitude is the condition of life; "roughing it" will be man's lot as long as he draws breath.

Clearly, the protagonist becomes more mature and changes in a book that artfully invents and arranges incidents, continually hoaxes readers, and steadily attacks romantic illusions and replaces them with disenchantingly realistic insights. With fact all but swamped by fiction, *Roughing It* is neither serviceable autobiography nor travel writing, and its humor, though undoubtedly choice, is definitely only a surface feature. Insofar as the book demonstrates that realism is the necessary alternative to the deception of romantic illusion, and the book is therefore a portrait of character shaped by theme and illustrated by the incidents of plot, *Roughing It* works more satisfactorily as fiction than as travel literature, autobiography, romance, or even a loosely related collection of humorous episodes.[13]

The presence in *Roughing It* of a central theme is one more and perhaps its most important indication that it is novelistic in technique. A travel book or a mere collection of humorous anecdotes does not need a unifying thematic structure, but a novel does. *Roughing It*'s main theme is stated in chapter 36: "It is a pity that Adam could not have gone straight out of Eden into a quartz mill, in order to understand the full force of his doom to 'earn his bread by the sweat of his brow'" (233). The entire book leads up to, enlarges, and ends with the idea that it is futile to try to escape God's doom for humanity. From first to last, the protagonist of *Roughing It* is always looking for a way to strike it rich and escape work, to swindle those more gullible than he and thus escape work, or to go to someplace Edenic and rich or fertile, like Nevada, California, or Hawaii, where he can escape working for his food. Reviewing the book from this perspective, we are able to see how each plan, each scheme, is a dream; how each chapter is shaped novelistically to demonstrate the futility of this dream; and why *Roughing It* is even didactic in its concluding moral.

One last novelistic feature about *Roughing It* relates to its similarities to other, more famous works by Twain, the novels *Huckleberry Finn* and *A Connecticut Yankee*. It is worth noting that both of those novels have more than a few elements of travel books in them, both have humorous incidents, both are narrated by a first-person narrator; that *Huckleberry Finn* has more than a few connections to Mark Twain's life; and that *A Connecticut Yankee* is partially narrated by a character who identifies himself as "M.T." In other words, the line separating *Roughing It* from two works that are quite definitely novels is very thin. Add this to the above analyses and the line virtually disappears.

From the perspective of structure based on theme, within the text of *Roughing It* are layers, and these layers run counter to each other. The surface level is, as most literary critics observe, rambling, loose, unorganized, funny. But at its deepest level, the book is coherent and serious. On its entertaining but deceptive surface, *Roughing It* appears to be only a loosely anecdotal travel book that recounts Twain's travels to, and humorous adventures in, the Far West and Hawaii. Looked at more closely and deeply, however, the book may be seen to be surprisingly serious and its structure a repeated pattern of hoaxes and deceptions. The travels of *Roughing It* are ironic; distances are traversed, time passes, and variety is experienced, but the changes are illusions. With the possible exception of the protagonist, the characters in the book remain the same; they learn nothing, gain nothing, and in the long run they have gone nowhere and might as well have stayed at home. They start off as sinners, act as sinners, and wind up as sinners. It is not that there is no difference between home and the locations to which the characters travel but that they are similar in that they either resemble ruined Eden or are reminiscent of hell, which, as sinners, the characters are never far from. The pattern of repeated ironic undercutting of all hopes and enthusiasms supports the book's pessimistic themes that characterize progress, happiness, and freedom as divine hoaxes.

On its broadest and most literal level, the book opens with its callow narrator excitedly confessing that "that word 'travel' had a seductive charm" for him (1:1–2). The first paragraph continues with the young narrator confessing to having "envied" his brother and to having "coveted" his distinction and financial splendor. Toward the end of the paragraph, after his brother offers the narrator the "sublime" position of secretary under him, the narrator enthuses: "It appeared to me that the heavens and earth passed away, and the firmament was rolled together as a scroll." Many readers recognize that this language sounds biblical and infer an experience of lofty spirituality, but the allusions are in fact to Revelations 6:14 and 21:1, which refer to Judgment Day, when the final reckoning will be made. Having just confessed to the sins of envy and covetousness, expressed an eagerness to be seduced, and confused true sublimity, which belongs to divinity, with an administrative appointment that was lowly even by earthly standards, one would think that the narrator had little reason to be enthusiastic about his prospects on Judgment Day. Because the irony of the allusions would have been more detectible to the Bible-reading public of his time than to today's general readership, Twain was taking a daring chance of his audience balking at the inappropriateness of the allusions. This is the first time we encounter in this study what will be seen to be the Twainian characteristic of boldly risking detection of important and obvious ironies but shielding them by emplacing them in a complicating context such as humor, narrative interest, diversion, or ambiguity, which deliberately distracts from their implications. In this case, the prefacing of the young narrator's admissions by the clause "I was young and ignorant" affords Twain some protection against an audience backlash while he uses the protection of ambiguity to set some precedents of technique and theme that will be followed up in later chapters.

Although the book opens with the optimistic burblings of its immature narrator, it concludes with the undercutting pessimism of the now experienced narrator drawing the discouraging moral that "if you are of any account, stay at home and make your way by faithful diligence; but if you are 'no account,' go away from home, and then you will *have* to work, whether you want to or not." Upon his own return home, he reports, he found it "a dreary place," with few of his youthful acquaintances prosperous or happy: "some of them had wandered to other scenes, some were in jail, and the rest had been hanged." At the end of his travels and adventures he was therefore hardly farther ahead of his fellow townspeople, for what had started out as a three-month "pleasure trip" to Nevada turned out for him to be "seven years of vicissitudes" (79:542).[14]

What sort of vicissitudes? It is worth noting that although *Roughing It* abounds in episodes that are hilarious to read, the narrator never joins in the hilarity. For readers, the contrast of the humorless narrator with the rollicking stories he tells is in itself one of the humorous features of the book, but if we probe his humorlessness we uncover a truly serious and extensive dimension to him and the book. Like *Huckleberry Finn* and *A Connecticut Yankee*, *Roughing It* is rooted in Twain's deeply internalized Calvinism.[15] Early, middle, and late, Twain saw the human race as doubly damned both by its fatally flawed nature and by divine predestination. He saw postlapsarian life as designedly hellish, marked by humankind's Sisyphean efforts to escape God's curse of Adam. *Roughing It*'s underlying structure is largely a demonstration of the thematic operation of Twain's bitter belief not in the justice of this curse but in its empirical accuracy.

The theme appears explicitly in chapter 36, where the narrator, after having worked a week at a quartz mill, observes that Adam should have had that exhausting experience. To escape this doom by striking it rich was supposedly one of the reasons the narrator went to Nevada in the first place. An earlier and indirect statement of the theme occurs in chapter 30, when the narrator and his partners, having begun the labor of excavating the ledges of their silver mine claim, decide that there has to be an easier way of making money than actually working: "We never touched our tunnel or our shaft again. Why? Because we judged that we had learned the *real* secret of success in silver mining—which was, *not* to mine the silver ourselves by the sweat of our brows and the labor of our hands, but to *sell* the ledges to the dull slaves of toil and let them do the mining!" (197). The theme is here somewhat disguised by irony. Using again the technique of the misleading past tense, the narrator appears to have made a triumphant discovery. At this point he withholds from the reader the later discovery that the "*real* secret" did not amount to anything. But in the quoted passage, the slang meaning of "sell"—to hoax or to swindle—implies that the ledges were not worth anything and that the only way the narrator and his partners could profit by their claim was to deceive and take advantage of some later and more naïve "dull slaves of toil." The narrator's association of toil with slavery is a subtle recognition that human beings are not meant to be free as well as an implication that a person may escape slavery by conning someone else to do his or her share of the work. Here and elsewhere throughout the book, humans are shown to have no hesitation in cheating their fellow humans for easy profit.[16] This view of things conforms to the tricky double bind of the Calvinistic concept of double damnation: most human beings are damned to hell because of original sin, but even if they had not already been damned by predestination, their sinful natures would inevitably damn them.

In this book the hope of escaping the curse of work is always characterized as a delusion, a dream. "Silver fever," the lure of wealth which attracted everyone to Nevada in the first place, is literally characterized by the older narrator as a "disease" (26:175). Infected by it on a prospecting trip, his younger self "fled away as guiltily as a thief" from his comrades, "crawled about the ground," and collected glittering stones, believing in "a delirious revel" that the glitter was precious metals (28:185). When one of his partners subsequently identifies the stones as mere mica, the narrator falls from romantic "ecstasy" into romantic despair: "So vanished my dream. So melted my wealth away. So toppled my airy castle to the earth and left me stricken and forlorn" (28:188). Later, the partners travel to a mining camp where all claims are given "grandiloquent names" and are hyped with the "frenzied cant" of hyperbole. The miners are described as "stark mad with excitement—drunk with happiness," but retrospectively the narrator admits that it was all "a beggar's revel. There was nothing doing in the district—no mining—no milling—no productive effort—no income—and not enough money in the entire camp to buy a corner lot in an eastern village" (29:193). Not only are the narrator and his friends caught up in these dreams, but all prospectors are as well. Trying to escape work, they unwittingly condemn themselves to a life of illusion, solitary wandering, and hard labor. The pocket miner of chapter 60 is described as one decaying example among multitudes who were "dead to the common interests of men, isolated and outcast from brotherhood with their kind," and who lived in "the most touching and melancholy exile that fancy can imagine." The pocket miner in particular is "one whose dreams were all of the past, whose life was a failure; a tired man, burdened with the present, and indifferent to the future; a man without ties, hopes, interests, waiting for rest and the end" (412–413).[17] Here we are induced to see the hellish deception that began with the hope of escaping conventional labor by discovering wealth but ultimately brings him to abandon all hope. His life had been wasted on a dream, and now the only relief that was left him was more dreams that enabled him to evade confronting the bitter truth of reality.

Twain even goes so far as to affirm predestination by a repetition of nuanced instances of characters overtly acknowledging that there are no accidents. The first time occurs in chapter 38, and it sets the mood for the rest. The narrator is at Mono Lake in California and is observing with distaste the specialized life forms that exist around it:

> Providence leaves nothing to go by chance. All things have their uses and their part and proper place in Nature's economy: the ducks eat the flies—the flies eat the worms—the Indians eat all three—the wild-cats eat the Indians— the white folks eat the wild-cats—and thus all things are lovely. (247)

What starts off as an affirmation of divinely ordained ecological balance in nature ends as a sarcastic observation of the natural rapaciousness of life and is also a commentary on the perverse cruelty of Providence. Yes, everything is perfectly controlled by it, and the result is hellish. The stark and forbidding landscape of Mono Lake, like that of Darwin's Galapagos Islands, where everything is stripped down to essentials, is made to appear the site of Twain's revelation of nature's part in the brutal hoax of existence.

A humorous example of this otherwise grim theme occurs in the midst of chapter 53, Jim Blaine's story of his grandfather's old ram. Blaine has digressed to an explanation of the reason why savages ate some missionaries sent to convert them: "Prov'dence don't fire no blank ca'tridges, boys. That there missionary's substance, unbeknowns to himself, actu'ly converted every last one of them heathens that took a chance at the barbecue. . . . There ain't no such thing as an accident" (366). Blaine's Uncle Lem served a similar providential service when he was killed by an Irishman's falling on him with a hod full of bricks. "People said it was an accident. Much accident there was about that. He didn't know what he was there for, but he was there for a good object. If he hadn't been there the Irishman would have been killed." But why could the Irishman not have fallen on Uncle Lem's dog, which was nearby? Because "the dog wasn't appointed. A dog can't be depended on to carry out a special Providence" (366). Obviously, Twain is ridiculing someone who has reduced Calvinist theology to a ridiculous oversimplification. But besides humor for its own sake, this solitary example of a funny account of predestination serves another purpose for Twain; it diverts readers from picking up on the real functionality of the serious theme it mocks here.

A studied ambivalence attends the narrator's account in chapter 72 of how Christianity came to the Hawaiian islands through the agency of Providence. After describing how tabu-ridden and subdued by the hea-then priesthood the Hawaiians were, he then reports how King Liholiho, under the influence of imported whisky, challenged a major tabu by sitting down with women. "It was probably the first time whisky ever figured prominently as an aid to civilization," ironically notes the narrator, fully aware of how Protestant Christianity in America in the cause of temperance had turned against alcohol. But when no lightning struck Liholiho the people instantly understood the significance: "The superstitions of a hundred generations passed from before the people like a cloud, and a shout went up, 'The *tabu* is broken! The *tabu* is broken!'" The narrator's commentary is ironic on the literal level but is undercut by a double and deeper irony: "Thus did King Liholiho and his dreadful whisky preach the first sermon and prepare the way for the new gospel that was speeding southward over the waves of the Atlantic" (496–497).

A revolt ensues—the chiefs and pagan priests against the royal army—and the king wins, with the result that "idolatry and the *tabu* were dead in the land!" Then follows the narrator's sharpest irony, as he describes what was in effect a pyrrhic victory.

> The royalists marched gayly home to Kailua glorifying the new dispensation. "There is no power in the gods," said they, "they are a vanity and a lie. The army with idols was weak; the army without idols was strong and victorious!"
>
> The nation was without a religion.
>
> The missionary ship arrived in safety shortly afterward, *timed by providential exactness* to meet the emergency, and the gospel was planted as in a virgin soil. (498, emphasis added)

Given Twain's lifelong criticism of missionaries as being themselves doomed by the Calvinist contempt for all human motives and actions, this passage can only mean that the harsh and oppressive pagan religion was about to be replaced by one even harsher and more oppressive and whose success had ironically been prepared by whisky. As the narrator said earlier in a transparently ironic lament: "How sad it is to think of the multitudes who have gone to their graves in this beautiful island and never knew there was a hell!" (440). The missionaries were to fill that vacuum. For a moment, when they were without a religion, the Hawaiians were free. But Providence had predestined them not to remain so.[18] Where before they had observed the pagan tabus out of fear of death, now they will observe the Christian tabus out of fear of hell. The "truth" would again make them slaves.

The book's longest mention of predestination is done indirectly and intermittingly, over the course of the several narratives that relate to the Whiteman cement mine and the blind lead. They comprise several seemingly independent but actually linked episodes that begin in chapter 37. The narrator calls the mine "cursed" because despite its promise of great riches easily garnered, many are attracted to hunting for the mine but no one is able to find it. The discoverer of the "mine"—an outcropping of unclaimed soft, crumbly rock with many lumps of easily retrievable gold lumps throughout—found it while lost, but had such a harrowing experience returning to civilization that he has no wish to look for it again in the wilderness and gives the crude map he made to a prospector named Whiteman. Everyone knows this and watches Whiteman closely in order to trail him on his periodic expeditions to find the outcropping. The first episode, in chapter 37, relates how the narrator and his partners mistakenly thought that they were the only ones to notice Whiteman getting ready to leave town at night. But once it turns out that others had also noticed Whiteman, the narrator and his group call off their plan to follow him.

The next episode, apparently unrelated at first, occurs in chapter 41 when Higbie, the narrator's partner, explores an abandoned shaft near the rich Wide West mine, which had laid claim to all branches of the vein of gold and silver it had discovered. Higbie discovers that the ore at the bottom of the shaft is not from the Wide West vein. It was a "blind lead," an independent vein of ore that does not break the surface. Legally, it is free to be claimed and mined. Higbie and the narrator take another partner, and next morning the three men make the claim. By law, they now have ten days in which to do "a fair and reasonable amount of work on their new property" (262–263), which would seal their ownership of the claim. But if they do not, their right will be forfeited, and the property can be staked out by others.

Of course the first reaction of the partners is jubilation, and they naturally begin to imagine what they will do with their assured wealth. They dream plans of how to spend their prospective millions—money they do not yet have: move to San Francisco, buy a house and carriage, and take trips around the world. They do not even suspect that the blind lead has blinded them with the delusion of sudden and easy wealth. In short, they engage in the same kinds of happy ecstasy that earlier set up the narrator before he was undeceived when he was returned to sad reality.

This discovery, however, seems different from all the other enthusiasms because the blind lead has been established as an individual vein of ore safe from legal challenge, and without doubt the ore in it is rich. Because they have ten days in which to work on the mine, they plan to do it the next day. But that very afternoon the narrator learns that a friend is dangerously ill nine miles out of town. Acting on an impulse of friendship, the narrator decides to go help the sick man, first leaving a note for Higbie on the cabin table. Nine days later, fifteen minutes before midnight, the narrator returns to town and notices a huge crowd near the Wide West mine. As he passes a bakery a woman rushes out and begs the narrator to help her subdue her husband, who is having a fit. More than an hour later, after having fetched a doctor and waited until the man calmed down, the narrator leaves the family and returns to his cabin. There he finds Higbie "looking pale, old, and haggard"; none of the partners had done any work on the blind lead in ten days; the crowd the narrator saw was on their property waiting for midnight, and now "We're ruined—we didn't do the work—THE BLIND LEAD'S RELOCATED!" (266).

It turns out that Higbie and the other partner had never seen the note; Higbie had gone away for nine days after having thrown a note of his own through a broken window. And the third partner, rumored to have been called to California "on a matter of life and death," had not been seen on the streets since the night of discovery, and had also done no work. The situation smacks of coincidence, but the text is more pointed:

> It came out that Higbie had depended on me, as I had on him, and both of us on the foreman. The folly of it! It was the first time that ever staid and steadfast Higbie had left an important matter to *chance* or failed to be true to his full share of a responsibility.
>
> But he had never seen my note till this moment, and this moment was the first time he had been in the cabin since the day he had seen me last. He, also, had left a note for me, on that same *fatal* afternoon. . . . Here it was, on the floor, where it had remained undisturbed for nine days:
>
>> Don't fail to do the work before the ten days expire. W. has passed through and given me notice. I am to join him at Mono Lake, and we shall go on from there to-night. He says he will find it this time, sure.
>> CAL.
>
> "W." meant Whiteman, of course. That thrice accursed "cement!"
>
> That was the way of it. An old miner, like Higbie, could no more withstand the fascination of a mysterious mining excitement like this "cement"

foolishness, than he could refrain from eating when he was famishing. Higbie had been *dreaming* about the marvelous cement for months; and now, against his better judgment, he had gone off and "taken the *chances*" on my keeping secure a mine worth a million undiscovered cement veins. (266–267, emphases added)

As our emphases indicate, Twain loaded this passage with suggestions that what happened was predestined. The Calvinist principle that there are no accidents, that there is no such thing as "chance," lies behind the narrator's summary. The two good deeds that the narrator did were timed "accidentally" to derail him from doing the required work on the site and to keep him away from the site for exactly the number of days necessary to forfeit the claim. They not only extend the string of "coincidences" in the quoted passage but also hearken back ironically to the Calvinist position that good deeds count for nothing toward earning salvation. The ominous allusion to dreams continues to reinforce Twain's countertheological position about how the true nature of life is concealed by appealing deceptions that seduce humanity from confronting reality.

Higbie, also, was controlled by coincidences. Like Huck Finn on the Phelps farm, normally he left nothing to chance, but this one time he was faced with a temptation he could not resist and abandoned himself to chance. Of all times for Whiteman to appear, this was the worst, and Higbie compulsively joined him to search for an accursed mine not worth a fraction of what they had within their grasp, and was absent on that vain hunt for exactly nine days. (Twain's use of "veins," which suggests "vain," may additionally be a biblically inspired commentary on the frenzied hunt for wealth that can be effortlessly discovered instead of earned by sweat.) Recognizing the clues in this string of associated incidents enables us to see the operation in the book of an important deep theme and also helps us understand the changes in the narrator's personality from the first chapter to the last.

In chapter 55 the narrator recounts how his associate Dan on the *Enterprise* had been offered a chance to go to New York and, for one-third of the proceeds, sell an attractive mining property. Dan, however, did not want to go, so he told the principals to make the offer to Marshall, a reporter on another paper. The narrator is angered at having been overlooked, and Dan, admitting that it had not occurred to him that the narrator wanted to go, mollifies him by promising to recommend him if Marshall does not accept the offer. That night the narrator is oppressed by the thought that "it was the 'blind lead' come again" (379). Some time later, the shocked narrator reads in a newspaper that Marshall had accepted the offer, gone to New York, and sold the property for a million dollars. "Once more native imbecility had carried the day, and I had lost a million! It was the 'blind lead' over again" (403). Looked back on, the linked story of Whiteman's cement mine and the blind lead is an account of how every detail related to it falls into place to create a pattern which is a denial of "accident."

Although there was some autobiographical basis for the above events, we know that Twain modified certain details of his narrative for artistic reasons.[19] What the events add up to, as Twain lays them out, is the destiny that he was not meant to get wealthy. A cursed mine, a string of intricately manipulated "coincidences," a friend who should have known him better than to overlook him, all conspire to frustrate his hopes for wealth. Readers may be moved to reflect that if Sam Clemens had come into great wealth in Nevada, there might not have been the Mark Twain who went on to write great literature, but in 1872 Twain could hardly have known that. As he wrote it, *Roughing It* only demonstrates his belief that he was not meant to become wealthy in the West.[20] This belief was particular; it affected only one aspect of Twain's future. The fatalistic pessimism of the narrator at the end is the result of his having apprehended a larger pattern to his life that keeps him at every turn from easy wealth and happiness.

As the book describes the blasted hopes and blighted lives of the majority of prospectors who seek their fortune in the West and travelers who search for some lost Eden in remote islands, the narration suggests that they, too, are being controlled by a shadowy influence. Infected by "silver fever," the prospectors are driven by hellish delusions of hope. Not one recalls or sees the relevance to his situation of Dante's warning on the outermost circle of hell: "Abandon hope all ye who enter here." Twain does not quote Dante, but his vision is similar. In Twain's words, occasional uplifts consisting of temporary moments of misplaced ecstasies in which the prospectors savor anticipation of future riches that will never be realized are only "beggars' revels." Unrecognized by themselves, in search of great riches waiting to be discovered they have left behind families and friends back home and condemned themselves to solitary lives—rough, sometimes brutal, filled with small gains and large disappointments—at hard labor.

Wherever the narrator goes, there are reminders that his vision of glories is illusory and that all about him are hints of ruined Eden or of hell. Chapter 56 begins, for example, with the seemingly innocent remark that "all scenery in California requires *distance* to give it its highest charm" (385). Several sentences later, the narrator explains what he means by the illusion of charm. Up close he finds "a sad poverty of variety in species, the trees being chiefly of one monotonous family." He further notes that "at a near view there is a wearisome sameness of attitude" of the trees' branches.

> Close at hand, too, there is a reliefless and relentless smell of pitch and turpentine; there is a ceaseless melancholy in their sighing and complaining foliage; one walks over a soundless carpet of beaten yellow bark and dead spines of the foliage till he feels like a wandering spirit bereft of a footfall; he tires of the endless tufts of needles and yearns for substantial, shapely leaves; he looks for moss and grass to loll upon, and finds none, for where there is no bark there is naked clay and dirt, enemies to pensive musing and clean apparel. (385)

The narrator's objections undercut the common notion that paradise is a place of unchanging peace and beauty by suggesting that part of humankind's doom is an innate restlessness and, consequently, an inborn inability to be content with what it has.

> But the wicked are like the troubled sea, when it cannot rest, whose waters cast up mire and dirt.
> There is no peace, saith my God, to the wicked. (Isaiah 57:21)

Indeed, the narrator himself is the best example of this in the entire book. He suffers from an internal hell and is never satisfied. An archetypal man, he leaves home because he finds it boring and is attracted by the variety of travel, but once he gets to some place that seems idyllic, he soon tires of its monotonous perfection. The unpleasant reality of where the narrator is always contrasts to the attractive but illusory aspect that was lent to it by distance. Hence, from a railroad car approaching California from the snows of the Sierras, he looks down "as the birds do, upon the deathless summer of the Sacramento Valley, with its fruitful fields, its feathery foliage, its silver streams, all slumbering in the mellow haze of its enchanted atmosphere, and all infinitely softened and spiritualized by distance—a dreamy, exquisite glimpse of fairy-land, made all the more charming and striking that it was caught through a forbidding gateway of ice and snow and savage crags and precipices" (56:390). Insofar as the long-range view through "a forbidding gateway" suggests either the gates of Eden—from which Adam and Eve were expelled—or the pearly gates of heaven—which forbid them entrance—the stage is set for the ironic contrast which follows between the remembered or imagined ideal and the earthly reality. The romantic vision uses such loaded words as "deathless," "enchanted," "spiritualized," "dreamy," "fairy-land," "charming," and "striking" to set up the reader for the ensuing disillusionment. In the next sentences, a close-up view of the Sacramento Valley shows the ravages of gold-mining operations: "its grassy slopes and levels torn and guttered and disfigured by the avaricious spoilers of fifteen and twenty years ago. You may see such disfigurements far and wide over California—and in some such places, where only meadows and forests are visible—not a living creature, not a house, no stick or stone or remnant of a ruin, and not a sound, not even a whisper to disturb the Sabbath stillness" where only shortly before stood a "fiercely flourishing little city" (57:390). In the first sentence the distant vision "charm[ed]," "enchanted," and spiritualized like a dream, but close up one is struck by the realization that what was seen was "fairy-land," an illusion. In the second sentence "fiercely flourishing" is oxymoronic except in an ironically hellish sense. The towns flourished by bustling with activity, noise, and commerce, but were fierce by consisting of "gambling hells crammed with tobacco smoke, profanity" and "labor, laughter, music, dancing, swearing, fighting, shooting, stabbing—a bloody inquest and a man for breakfast every morning—*everything* that delights and adorns existence" (57:391). After the Fall, all succumbs to ruin, and existence is hellish.

This is literally demonstrated in the narrator's experience in San Francisco. Following the familiar pattern we have seen in this book of initial ecstasy followed by crushing letdown, his sojourn there begins on a high note: "After the sage-brush and alkali deserts of Washoe, San Francisco was Paradise to me" (58:396). Immediately, however, he began to live like a "butterfly." He stayed at the best hotel, "exhibited" his clothes in the most "conspicuous" places, attended private parties in "sumptuous evening dress, simpered and aired my graces like a born beau," "infested" the opera, and "learned to seem enraptured with music which oftener afflicted my ignorant ear than enchanted it" (396). This chapter, written from the perspective of the older narrator, is clearly condemnatory of the profligacy and affectation of his younger self and sets him up for the fall that was not long in coming. Motivated by greed, the younger self held on to stocks that had zoomed to insupportable levels. "What a gambling carnival it was!" is the narrator's last judgment of the general folly before "all of a sudden, out went the bottom and everything and everybody went to ruin and destruction" (397).

Repeating the pattern established in chapter 28 of learning moral lessons but being unable to take them to heart, Twain has the narrator castigate himself: "I, the cheerful idiot that had been squandering money like water . . . thought myself beyond the reach of misfortune," and the narrator is forced to go to work and live humbly. But immediately after this admission, he confesses, "I was not entirely broken in spirit, for I was building confidently on the sale of the silver mine in the east" (58:397). The speculative spirit was so strong in him that the lessons of the present were ignored, and he continued to live prospectively for a future of rosy dreams that the older self knew would not come to pass.

The narrator also finds the climate of the San Francisco region hellishly monotonous. At first it is described as "as pleasant a climate as could well be contrived . . . and is doubtless the most unvarying in the whole world." He explains that "[d]uring eight months of the year . . . the skies are bright and cloudless, and never a drop of rain falls. But when the other four months come along, you will need to go and steal an umbrella. Because you will require it" (56:388). In other words, change hardly ever comes, and when it does it simply brings something else that also becomes tiresome. The narrator later puts it more vividly. In the middle of the "dismal monotony" of the quiet rains of the rainy season, "[y]ou would give *anything* to hear the old familiar thunder again and see the lightning strike somebody. And along in the summer, when you have suffered about four months of lustrous, pitiless sunshine, you are ready to go down on your knees and plead for rain—hail—snow—thunder and lightning—anything to break the monotony—you will take an earthquake, if you cannot do any better. And the chances are that you'll get it, too" (388).

What appears to be the narrator's indulgence in hyperbole turns out to be prophetic shortly thereafter in chapter 58 when he recounts how he "enjoyed" his first earthquake, which came without warning on a bright October day in San Francisco, when "all was solitude and a Sabbath stillness" (398). The seemingly offhand details that one will "need to go and steal an umbrella" and that the earthquake comes in a moment of "Sabbath

stillness" are subtle hints, repeated throughout the book, of Twain's belief
that human nature is inclined to break the commandments and that the
Sabbath is associated with the punishment of the community rather than
its refreshment.[21] Twain later links the monotony of weather and the deceptive character of the Sabbath in his 1897 story, "The Enchanted Sea Wilderness," when the ship *Adelaide* enters upon the region of the Everlasting
Sunday, a doldrums contrast to the stormy region of the Devil's Race-Track
which surrounds it.[22] The narrator therefore indicts the deception of California when he describes its weather in ironically ambiguous phrases: the
"endless winter of Mono," the "eternal spring of San Francisco," and the
"eternal summer of Sacramento" (389). It looks like paradise but it feels
like hell.

The pattern of deceptive appearances continues in the book's section on
Hawaii. Far from being a tacked-on section discontinuous with the chapters on the West, the Hawaiian part is only an extension of the book's almost systematic exposure of prevailing romantic conceptions: of the West,
of unspoiled nature, and of Pacific island paradises. The narrator's first,
romantic, impression of Hawaii, of "a summer calm as tranquil as dawn in
the Garden of Eden" (63:433), is typically followed by a realistic undercutting. "It was tranced luxury to sit in the perfumed air and forget that there
was any world but these enchanted islands. It was such ecstasy to dream,
and dream—till you got a bite. A scorpion bite" (434). Eden had its snake,
and Hawaii has its equivalent, the scorpion. And mosquitoes, tarantulas,
and a centipede in bed that had "forty-two legs on a side and every foot
hot enough to burn a hole through a raw-hide" (434). As before, romantic words like "tranced," "enchanted," "ecstasy," and "dream" set up the
reader for a fall.

Unobtrusively, also, the narrator has gotten into the habit of lavishly
praising his new location at the expense of his former one, which he had
earlier exalted. So, walking through the "white town of Honolulu," he ad-
miringly describes its "luxurious banks and thickets of flowers . . . glowing
with the richest dyes, in place of the dingy horrors of San Francisco's pleasure grove" (63:431). How quickly the paradise of San Francisco became a
place of "dingy horrors," and how quickly the Edenic beauties of Hawaii
turned out to be deceptive. The early chapters about Hawaii thus continue
the patterns found in the rest of the book, and subsequent chapters continue the references to a ruined Eden and to hell.

Even the volcanic origin of Hawaii is fraught with opposing double meanings of picturesqueness and ominousness. The narrator walks on a layer of "lava and cinders overlying the coral, belched up out of fathomless perdition long ago through the seared and blackened crater that stands dead and harmless in the distance" (63:433). But in chapter 74, on a trip to the volcano Kilauea and viewing close-up a crater that is neither dead nor harmless, the narrator sees perdition in action, boiling lava with scattered fountains of fire ejecting "a shower of brilliant white sparks—a quaint and unnatural mingling of gouts of blood and snow-flakes! We had circles and serpents and streaks of lightning all twined and wreathed and tied together" (511). When the narrator comments at the end of the chapter that "[t]he smell of sulphur is strong, but not unpleasant to a sinner" (512), this is also an admission that he is a sinner, for he is not alarmed at recognizing the presence of hell by its smell.[23]

Indeed, wherever he has traveled the narrator has never been far away from the wreckage of Eden and the reminder of hell. Although Twain does not admit it in the book, his narrator self fled the incipient hell of the Civil War for the supposed peace and prosperity of the Far West. Instead of prosperity he found himself immersed in situations where wealth seemed imminent but vanished into illusion just as he tried to grasp it, but where toil—"slavery" he called it—was always interposed between his present situation and his dream of the future. Instead of peace he found a lawless society where vice and violence were rampant; where murder and other crimes were frequent occurrences; where charm, enchantment, or dreaminess also signified an illusion; and where the beauty of distance was always undercut by the ugly or monotonous reality of what was close up. In other words, he was not meant to escape the common doom of humankind, nor did he for more than an occasional moment of illusion. *Roughing It* looked at from a distance is an extremely funny book about the illusory attractions of travel, but regarded close-up it is a tour of ruined Eden overlooking hell. It is proof that the deep Calvinism that drove Mark Twain's art in *Huckleberry Finn* and *A Connecticut Yankee* was alive and well in this early masterpiece and shapes ironically its conception of existence.

Not just during his traveling days, but all of his life, Mark Twain was haunted by a sense that life was comprised of hoaxes and practical jokes. Early, middle, and late, his work teems with the ironies, surprises, reversals, unexpected twists, and tricks that are associated with hoaxes. "The

Celebrated Jumping Frog of Calaveras County" (1865) is a veritable nest of hoaxes, one inside the other. *Roughing It* contains the famous image of the trickster coyote which slyly induces a dog to follow him, draws the dog farther and farther from his base by pretending to be near exhaustion, and then puts on a burst of blinding speed and leaves the dog alone in an unfamiliar wilderness, tricked and baffled by the unexpected turn of events. In *Huckleberry Finn* Tom Sawyer's unexpected announcement at the end of the book that Jim was free means not only that Jim and Huck had been put through idiotic and humiliating rituals just to satisfy Tom's appetite for romance, but that the reader had also been deceived. As a matter of fact, Huck has been doubly misled, because Jim finally reveals that Pap Finn, from whom Huck had been fleeing, had in reality been dead since chapter 19. In "The Man That Corrupted Hadleyburg" (1899) the mysterious stranger plays a diabolic practical joke on the town in order to avenge some unspecified slight he had received in the past. And in "Letters from the Earth" (1909/1962) Satan gleefully describes how humankind is doubly deceived, first by the "Law of God"—the built-in limitations of imperfect human nature, which can never avoid running afoul of God's moral law, and then by its own foolish insistence on piously maintaining that God is benevolent in the face of overwhelming evidence that he is not. But whereas those who have read widely in Twain's later works especially are able to see that he did not then regard God as benevolent, it should now be evident that even from his early career, Twain regarded God as the greatest trickster of them all. It was never a compliment.

Despite his explicit claims at various times in his life that he regarded the God of the Bible as a patently ridiculous superstition, that he himself was a deist (in his early years) or a determinist (in his later years), Twain retained a suppressed belief in God. His works are saturated with religious imagery, religious allusions, and religious ideas and attitudes. This was the case in his later years, when he wrote so bleak a deterministic view of humankind's inherent nature as *What Is Man?* (1906), while in other works of the same period he reverted to explicit considerations of God, Satan, supernatural messengers or agents, predestination, and notions of heaven or hell. Twain's early indoctrination into Calvinism was ineradicable. He would differ with it, oppose it, and detest it, but he could never quite extirpate it from himself. The main reason for this was that it made sense to him. Calvinism preached the corruption of human nature, and this teaching was reinforced empirically for Twain almost every day of his life. Calvinism affirmed predestination, and Twain saw freedom as a mirage. Calvinism preached a stern, angry, and vengeful God, and insofar as Twain observed what might be called God's providence at work, it was apparent to him that Calvinism was right again. In one main matter only did Twain break with Calvinism sufficiently to be heretical. Calvinism viewed God as omniscient, omnipotent, and benevolent. Twain would have agreed with the omniscience and omnipotence, but he early came to regard God as malevolent. Twain saw the world and humans as the victims of a God who did not mean them well. God played tricks on creation, and the tricks were not funny. In his later years, after he became established, Twain was fairly direct about describing God as maliciously whimsical in works such as "Letters from the Earth" that he set aside to be published after his death. But in his earlier career, while he was still anxious to ensure that his books sold well, he was more devious or circumspect about hiding his targets and beliefs beneath dark hints and veiled clues, usually by means of humor and ironic levels of language in his layered style. This can be seen in the carefully indirect way he criticizes the Bible in *Roughing It*, making light of some of its almost incredible details while stopping just short of sacrilege. He puts readers in the position of having to choose between a religious belief and the mockery of it.

Twain begins mildly in *Roughing It* with a short sequence of observations on how it is now possible to move quickly across what were formerly regarded as great distances. In chapter 4 an impressed young narrator reports that a stagecoach had traveled three hundred miles in only fifty-six hours. A page later the narrator, now older, is impressed by the fact that it is possible to travel the same distance in luxurious comfort in a railroad coach in only fifteen hours and forty minutes. But in chapter 6 the older narrator recounts an episode from his travels in the Holy Land during which an elderly "pilgrim" tried to instruct Jack, a religiously ignorant nineteen-year-old member of the group, about Moses. When the old man praised Moses for guiding the children of Israel for forty years across three hundred miles of the Sinai desert, Jack retorted: *"Forty years? Only three hundred miles? Humph! Ben Holladay [a famous stagecoach driver] would have fetched them through in thirty-six hours!"* (39).

The older narrator pretends to defend Jack on the ground that he meant no irreverence, but Twain did. A pious readership accustomed to accepting Bible stories at face value and idealizing them might never question what was so great about taking forty years to cross a three-hundred-mile desert at the rate of seven and a half miles a year when a stagecoach driver could do it in a matter of hours. So Twain becomes tactfully circumspect by employing a technique that may be called the "diverted target," which substitutes for a target too socially sensitive to attack directly another parallel one that is hidden by "acceptable" social prejudice. Because it is too risky to criticize the Bible openly he does it circumspectly, venturing upon the higher criticism by concealing his purpose with humorous-seeming naïveté. Indirectly, by the use of humor, he makes his readers complicit in the ludicrous irreverence, and thus plants the seed of religious skepticism in them.

That skepticism is nurtured in chapter 16, where the text seems to be largely devoted to a mocking overview of the Mormon Bible. Twain quotes liberally from it and gives special attention to the episode that "travestied Noah's ark" by quoting how Nephi built in one day a ship that was spacious enough to accommodate his entire nation. Once everyone got on board they began to make merry and tied him up. In punishment, God interfered with the working of their compass so that they were disoriented, and he caused a great storm to threaten the vessel. Not until the people released Nephi and he prayed to the Lord did the storm subside and the effectiveness of the ship's compass became restored so that the ship could safely reach its destination. To most readers of his time, this would indeed seem like an obvious "plagiarism of the Old Testament," especially of the stories of Noah and Jonah.

But if the account of Nephi building a ship large enough to hold all his followers seemed ridiculous, what of the original, the story of Noah who built an ark large enough to hold two of every kind of animal? And if the Lord stopped the storm on the supplication of Nephi, what of the account of God's causing a storm to rage for days until Jonah was put overboard from his ship? The satire of the *Book of Mormon* is thus also a thinly disguised satire of the Bible. Here again Twain employs the technique of the diverted target. In this case, he pretends to ridicule the incredibility of the *Book of Mormon* and its quaint wordiness, whereas it is evident that the same charges can be leveled at the Bible. Twain's point may well be that his readers laugh at miracles and customs they find in other scriptures but swallow without thinking details no less questionable that appear in their own.[24] Further, by having started gently the process of undermining the believability of the Bible, he prepares his readers for the escalation to his more important target, Christian doctrine based on the Bible.

We have previously demonstrated incidents in which signs of Calvinism not only appear in abundance in *Roughing It* but also combine to unify the book around a central theme. These were fairly obvious examples of human deceit and trickery, and there are many more of them, but perhaps Twain's most skillful examples of the divine trickster's handiwork are the deftly subtle ones that illustrate the corruption of human nature and that function in such a way as to include the readers in the human tendency to misinterpret sins as virtues and to regard real virtues as folly. The potentially controversial character of such moral inversions is typically concealed under a thick sugarcoating of humor.

The account in chapter 34 of the elaborate practical joke played on General Buncombe is justly regarded as one of Twain's most inspired flights of humor, but it also works as a third example of the diverted target, this time as it applies to Christian doctrine. The practical joke *is* brilliantly funny as a hoax, but it additionally has a serious dimension in its connection to Twain's countertheology. When looked at closely, Buncombe, though naïve and slow to catch on to the fact that he is being strung along, does struggle rationally for justice and order in a situation controlled by a heaven run on the principle of might makes right. Ex-governor Roop as a Lord of Misrule functions as an agent of the irrationality and arbitrariness of heaven. The outcome of the trial is fixed, a point Roop does not even try to soften. His decision is fundamentally Calvinistic: what happened was in accordance with the prerogative of heaven and, "worms as we are," we must not question the inscrutable wisdom of heaven. "The plaintiff... has been deprived of his ranch by the visitation of God! And from this decision there is no appeal" (225–226). If this decision is judged by legal standards, it is ridiculous; judges cannot block the right of appeal. In real life, however, and especially from a Calvinistic perspective, there is no appeal from the dictates of heaven. Roop was only having fun, but Twain's humor, typically, was edged; there is an ulterior purpose to his joke.[25]

Another famous specimen of Twainian humor, chapter 47's delightful narrative of Buck Fanshawe's funeral, is yet a fourth example of the diverted target technique, and it also functions as an application of Twain's countertheology. On its face it is one of the richest examples of humor in the book. The humor is apparent even in paraphrase. Scotty Briggs, a Comstock miner, asks a clergyman to officiate at the burial of his friend, Buck Fanshawe. Scotty, however, is incapable of speaking in correct conventional English; his first language is mining jargon largely made up of colorful metaphors that are incomprehensible to someone from the outside. The clergyman is that someone, but he also speaks in his own professional ecclesiastical diction, which is equally incomprehensible to Scotty. After a number of hilarious false starts, the two finally understand each other, the minister accommodates Scotty's request and officiates at the funeral, and Scotty eventually is converted and henceforth teaches the Bible to the local Sunday school children using the lingo they all understand.

The episode takes on a deeper and ironic level, however, when we shift our perspective from plot to language. These two aspects of the narrative are at deliberate cross-purposes with each other, with language sabotaging plot. Buck Fanshawe is disarmingly categorized as "a representative citizen," but that distinction has to be understood ironically in the context that his town is described as a violent and lawless place. By way of illustration, ensuing details further undercut this seeming compliment. "He had 'killed his man,'" "kept a sumptuous saloon," "been the proprietor of a dashing helpmeet whom he could have discarded without the formality of a divorce," "been a very Warwick in politics," and been a favorite of "the vast bottom-stratum of society." Subsequently, under the influence of typhoid fever, he "had taken arsenic, shot himself through the body, cut his throat, and jumped out of a four-story window and broken his neck" (308). The introduction of these latter details enables Twain to employ diversion, one of his favorite techniques, to protect his use of ironic language from easy detection. He then further diverts his readers to yet another target, the coroner's jury, which incredibly "brought in a verdict of death 'by the visitation of God'" (47:308). This is a superb example of how the whole can be greater than the sum of its parts, for the different layers of the episode are all dimensions of the same chapter yet are at odds with each other.

The ironies escalate once the language is inspected more closely. Most readers pay scant attention to the minor detail that Buck had a mistress ("a dashing helpmeet whom he could have discarded without the formality of a divorce"), but the text's description of him as the "proprietor" of his mistress is a strong implication that Buck was a pimp as well. Nor is the funeral itself as innocent as it seems at first glance. It is a lavish affair,

and the clergyman delivers an impressive eulogy, for which he is well paid.
But in the final analysis the minister hires out to praise a brawler, a killer,
a saloon-keeper, the pimp of a mistress who was probably a whore, a devious politician, and a suicide. Is this serving his religion, or selling it for his
own profit? Twain has daringly taken the chance that his readers will have
been so sanctimoniously lulled by the surface story of godless miners at
last seeking support from the offices of religion that they will miss the basic
immoralities of the deal. This episode, therefore, is yet another illustration
of the Calvinist principle that even what seem like good deeds are tainted
by human corruption.

Furthermore, the chapter ends with two seemingly warmhearted sentences:

> It was my large privilege, a month before he died, to hear him [Scotty] tell the
> beautiful story of Joseph and his brethren to his [Sunday school] class "with-
> out looking at the book."[26] I leave it to the reader to fancy what it was like, as
> it fell, riddled with slang, from the lips of that grave, earnest teacher, and was
> listened to by his little learners with a consuming interest that showed that
> they were as unconscious as he was that any violence was being done to the
> sacred properties. (47:317)

Twain generally uses sentiment ironically, and the details of phraseology in
these sentences point to the conclusion that this is no exception. Although
the narrator appears to approve of Scotty, Twain does not; he is satirizing
Scotty. This may be deduced from the textual hints that Scotty is "unconscious" of the "violence" caused by his rendition of the Bible story, and
the pregnantly ambiguous phrase that the story "fell, riddled with slang,"
from Scotty's lips. The "violence" referred to can be understood when it
is remembered that the kind of slang Scotty typically indulges in includes
complimenting someone for being "white" or because "[h]e warn't a Catholic," referring disparagingly to people as "Greasers" or "niggers," and using the slogan "no Irish need apply." Such prejudice-loaded slang would,
of course, violently taint the "beautiful" story of Joseph or any other uplift-
ing Bible text. Conforming the Bible to local slang brings down (that is,
fells) the moral lessons of the Joseph story by riddling it (that is, shooting
it full of holes) with the biases of the mining camp. The main point of this
episode, however, is not to ridicule what may be fictional characters, or
even to suggest that Bible lessons might be undesirably altered by reducing
them to vernacular, but to illustrate that human nature is so thoroughly

debased that neither the characters in the story nor the readers of the book recognize the signs of moral corruption in Scotty's well-intentioned lesson, let alone are aware of the degree of it. Indeed, we are misled by the author's consummate skill into believing that we are reading a benevolent tale of the goodness of human nature when what underlies the text is the cynical moral that the innate viciousness of human nature is concealed from us by a depraved conscience and an innate tendency to moral blindness. As Mary Richards of "The Man That Corrupted Hadleyburg" said, "Lord, how we are made—how strangely we are made!" (Budd, *Collected Tales* 2:398).

Implicit in that comment, however, is a criticism of the maker. Twain's references to the Bible and religion in *Roughing It* are not gratuitous. While the book's surface level humorously de-romanticizes the naïve and popular expectation that wealth and happiness awaited the adventurous, its deepest level de-romanticizes the naïve and popular belief in a benevolent deity. Unlike Twain's writings in the last decade of his life, he stops just short of explicitly blaming God for making humankind incurably foolish, unbalanced, and hobbled; for deceiving it into believing it can do more than it was made to do; for depriving it of true choice; and for then holding it to impossible standards. But the book's disenchanting view of the promises and opportunities of the new world of the West and, beyond that, of Hawaii and the easy life in close contact with nature uniformly implies a trickster maker who has a wicked sense of humor.

In the eighteenth century, citizens of London used to visit Bedlam (the Bethlehem hospital for the insane) to be entertained by the delusions and antics of the inmates.[27] But their infirmities of mind were not matters of fun to the inmates; their fancies were their realities. So, too, while on one level *Roughing It* may be a hilarious book for unreflective readers, for the narrator it is a record of mounting frustration and profound disappointment that transforms him from an eager optimist in chapter 1 into a gloomy pessimist at the end. For him, the constant experience of being forever led on by what always turned out to be delusory dreams and vain hopes is akin to the torments of Sisyphus. If not actually hell, life for the narrator often seems hellish.

Twain in *Roughing It* was already a consummate master of both language and irony. He was able to effect extended connections of different levels of meanings of words and, similarly, to build levels of coherent quasi-narratives out of levels of irony. It would be a mistake to assume that the wordplay and ironies that are so common in his novels are always prodigal offthrowings of his creative spirit. Often they are component elements of quasi-narratives—seemingly thematically autonomous, self-contained elements within the larger story—that when tracked and plotted lead to alternate and consistent interpretations. This phenomenon may help explain why divergent interpretations are possible of *Roughing It* and other works. It does not follow from this, however, that Twain is indeterminative, but it does emphasize the importance of prioritizing the levels of interpretation.

Some levels of quasi-narratives are deeper than others, "deeper" meaning more powerful and wide-ranging in consequence, and more central to the author's basic values. Unless an author undergoes a dramatic conversion in his or her life, the author's basic values will remain more or less intact, constant and unique fingerprints that recur in all his or her main works and enable us to identify him or her and also establish connections between works written over the span of the author's career. The "dark side" of *Roughing It* we have explicated is the deep side of Twain, that introspectively honest and intensely private "dark" half of the moon which he seldom showed to anyone but which underlays and gives unity to all his great works.

Although *The Innocents Abroad* (1869) preceded *Roughing It* by three years and was extremely popular, for the reasons made obvious in our analysis of *Roughing It*, we regard the later book as the first of Twain's major works. Because its novelistic characteristics and its serious aspects have not before now been treated this extensively or closely, here they have been emphasized in order to establish their existence and reveal their functions. In detailing how subtly Twain cloaked his deeper and unifying themes, how many passages are unexpectedly ambiguous, and how skillful is the tension between the humorous and the serious, we have also given reason to reevaluate the book as a brilliant artistic success, the work of a newly mature author in the full powers of his craft. *Roughing It* breaks thematic ground for the novels *The Adventures of Tom Sawyer* (1876), *Huckleberry Finn*, *A Connecticut Yankee*, and *No. 44, The Mysterious Stranger* (composed between 1902 and 1908), and for a number of his short stories. As will be seen in the following chapters, the distinctive stylistic and, most especially, the thematic fingerprints of Twain's countertheology that it introduces will recur repeatedly in his later works.

The Adventures of Tom Sawyer

Peradventure there shall lack five of the fifty righteous: wilt thou destroy all
the city for lack of five? —Genesis 19:28

The reputation of Mark Twain's *The Adventures of Tom Sawyer* (1876) as
a "hymn to boyhood" was established in both the popular American consciousness and American literary history soon after the novel's publication and prevailed throughout much of the twentieth century. In the early
1970s, however, a new scholarly trend emerged as critics began to recognize the novel's darker undercurrents. Hamlin Hill, Judith Fetterley, Tom
H. Towers, and Forrest G. Robinson, for example, all concluded that *The
Adventures of Tom Sawyer* possesses dimensions that do not accord with
the work's reputation for idyll and nostalgia.[1] And while scholarship of the
last forty years indicates that *The Adventures of Tom Sawyer* is generally
regarded as a more serious book than was once assumed and as one whose
themes are more aligned with its better-praised companion, *Adventures of
Huckleberry Finn* (1885), no comprehensive study has yet ventured to read
the novel's more somber designs in the context of Twain's Calvinist vision.

Tom H. Towers's 1976 essay "'I Never Thought We Might Want to
Come Back': Strategies of Transcendence in *Tom Sawyer*" was among the
first analyses of *The Adventures of Tom Sawyer* to explore the degree to
which Twain embedded his 1876 novel with recurring patterns of violence,
horror, and despair. Towers argues persuasively that the major episodes
of *Tom Sawyer*—the graveyard scene, the escape to Jackson's Island, the
quest for treasure in the haunted house, and the adventure in MacDougal's
Cave—all exhibit variations on a single theme: the effort of the individual
"to exchange the deadening actuality of everyday life for a more intense,

62

spiritually informed reality" (510). Despite the suggestive nature of this description, however, Towers limits his definition of the "more intense, spiritually informed reality" that Tom and other characters seek to that of a social construct, explaining that "opposed to that sought-for world is the town, which represents everything that inhibits the realization of freedom and selfhood" (510). Fetterley, Robinson, and others who have also treated *Tom Sawyer* as a more serious book have similarly tended to interpret the novel principally as a work of social criticism. Communal issues are certainly at stake in *Tom Sawyer*, but Twain's concerns here apply to more than mere cultural forces of St. Petersburg that seek to repress and control. While the novel is definitely preoccupied with the social issues of freedom and the self, in *Tom Sawyer* Twain also wrestles with freedom and identity as metaphysical concerns.

The first seven chapters of *Tom Sawyer*, nearly one-quarter of the entire novel, serve generally as expository material, mapping the town of St. Petersburg, identifying the principal characters and their manners, and establishing motifs that will develop and resonate more deeply later in the story. In a larger sense, however, the opening chapters of *Tom Sawyer* represent, as Henry Nash Smith observed nearly fifty years ago, Twain's first attempt in fiction to employ the "Matter of Hannibal," which he had recently "discovered" in the process of writing "Old Times on the Mississippi" (1875).[2] Smith's argument has generally been taken to mean two things. First, that with *Tom Sawyer*, Twain began to mine the "Matter of Hannibal" in novel form, to shift his artistic gaze to the characters and the region that he would eventually become most identified with and most celebrated for. Second, that *Tom Sawyer* represents something of what Gary Scharnhorst calls a "dress rehearsal" for the materials that would eventually find fuller expression a decade later in *Huckleberry Finn* (*Critical Essays* 8). Certainly few would take issue with the general assertion that *Tom Sawyer* does not achieve what *Huckleberry Finn* accomplishes. But the tendency to regard *Tom Sawyer* as mere context for the "discovery of the unexpected possibilities" of Huck, Tom, and the Mississippi River, which Twain would not make complete use of until the masterpiece that is *Huckleberry Finn*, has both contributed at times to its underappreciation as a serious work of fiction as well as allowed some of its deeper thematic currents to go unnoticed (Smith, *Development of a Writer* 91).

Another phenomenon in Twain criticism of the last fifty years is the way in which the "Matter of Hannibal" has been generally thought of. Smith and subsequent generations of critics have employed the term essentially to describe three major elements in Twain's art: the inhabitants of St. Petersburg, the Mississippi River valley as a region, and the Mississippi River itself. There is no question that the characters of Huck and Tom, the landscapes of Twain's adolescence, and the river as symbol lay at the heart of the "discovery of river and town" in *Tom Sawyer*. That said, comparatively little attention has been paid to the town of St. Petersburg as a physical space in Twain's canon. This is not to argue, of course, that scholars have not discussed the setting of *Tom Sawyer* and the first few chapters of *Huckleberry Finn*. Indeed, they have focused on the citizenry of St. Petersburg— Tom, Huck, Aunt Polly, Miss Watson, Widow Douglas, Pap Finn, Injun Joe, Jim, Judge Thatcher—and the manner in which these characters contribute to the thematic designs of *Tom Sawyer* and *Huckleberry Finn*.[3] Yet St. Petersburg as a setting in *Tom Sawyer* is foundational, too, for it thereafter becomes among the two or three most identifiable features of his art. This small-town milieu is not only reprised in *Huckleberry Finn* but also figures in many of Twain's most significant works of fiction after 1876. St. Petersburg is Offal Court of *The Prince and the Pauper* (1881); it is Pokesville, Bricksville, and Pikesville from *Huckleberry Finn*; it is Camelot of *A Connecticut Yankee in King Arthur's Court* (1889); it is Dawson's Landing of *The Tragedy of Pudd'nhead Wilson* (1894); it is the setting of "The Man That Corrupted Hadleyburg" (1889); it is Eseldorf of *No. 44, The Mysterious Stranger* (composed between 1902 and 1908). It is heaven itself as represented in "Letters from the Earth" (1909/1962).

This is all to say that with his depiction of St. Petersburg in *Tom Sawyer*, Twain discovered more than simply a locale for his characters to reside within and a stretch of shoreline for his symbolical river to flow beyond. St. Petersburg and its later incarnations function metaphorically in Twain's work as a cosmos writ small, invoked in work after work and embodying a relatively consistent vision of human experience. And exactly what, then, does the setting of St. Petersburg signify? To begin, St. Petersburg, particularly in the opening chapters of *Tom Sawyer*, is the quintessential portrait of repressive small-town life. It becomes, as Fetterley, Towers, Robinson, and others have pointed out, among the earliest expressions in American literature of the "revolt from the village." We agree. The citizens of St. Petersburg are vain and hypocritical; they take great satisfaction from enforcing strict communal hierarchies; they derive a warped sense of delight in adhering to constricting cultural conventions. Again, there is little question that elements of social critique abound in *Tom Sawyer* or that the novel can be read satisfactorily from this perspective—as it has been for decades. Additionally, however, Twain might have also been operating simultaneously at far deeper levels of analysis throughout the novel that both point to the Calvinist sources of his cynical views of humankind and complete the circuit between those sources and the social commentary for which the novel has been recognized.

Consider, for example, the ways in which Twain's choice of the name "St. Petersburg" establishes a basis for reading the setting of *Tom Sawyer* as a repressive environment. It ought to be acknowledged right away, of course, that Missouri is rife with saint-towns (St. Charles, St. Thomas, St. Louis) and place-names from around the world (Troy, Lebanon, Milan), so Twain's selection of "St. Petersburg" does in fact fit inconspicuously with the geography of the novel. Nevertheless, the most famous "St. Petersburg"—and presumably the most immediate register for that name—in the nineteenth century would have been the capital of czarist Russia, which as the seat of that government had a long-standing reputation for the vigorous suppression of individual liberties at home and its oppressive authoritarian policies abroad.[4] And whether Twain's decision to use the name "St. Petersburg" is to be taken humorously as if from the perspective of an overly punished adolescent boy or more seriously as commentary on the restrictive cultural milieu of small-town America, there can be little question that Twain, well-read and -traveled by the early 1870s, would have at least been cognizant of the implications of his choice for the setting of *Tom Sawyer*. This is but one of several connotations into which Twain shrewdly taps in *Tom Sawyer*, as he does in numerous other texts, via nineteenth-century name associations.

Certain scholars have also argued that "St. Petersburg" operates as a subtle reference to heaven. The manner in which this allusion has been thought to operate has evolved over time. On the one hand, John C. Gerber, coeditor of the Mark Twain Library edition of *Tom Sawyer* (1982), maintains that Twain used the name St. Petersburg ("St. Peter's place") to reflect the ways in which the novel's setting is "like heaven for boys and girls" (xiii). On the other hand, Kent Rasmussen and other recent commentators, taking into account more skeptical readings of *Tom Sawyer*, have pointed out that the allusion to heaven probably operates as ironic commentary on the setting of the novel rather than attempting to draw any direct comparison between St. Petersburg and paradise. Twain, they argue, appears to criticize the narcissistic river town at the center of *Tom Sawyer* by contrasting it to heaven (and, by extension, according to some, the idyllic village of his youth).[5] But the logic of this latter reading would require that Twain held a sufficiently affirming view of heaven (not to mention of his boyhood home) for the allusion to operate in such ironic fashion. He did not hold that affirming view, and that opens the way for a potential third way to read the allusion to heaven. Twain's lifelong view of heaven and its sovereign were, as we have argued, actually more analogous to the conventional nineteenth-century opinion of czarist Russia. And one need only consult Twain's largely unflattering sketch of his hometown "Villagers 1840–3" (1897/1969) to appreciate his private opinion of Hannibal and its citizens. Thus, rather than force irony onto Twain's naming of St. Petersburg in *Tom Sawyer* and *Huckleberry Finn*, it appears equally if not more fruitful to read his allusion to heaven more straightforwardly in the context of his heretical countertheological vision. A compression of all three locations—St. Petersburg, Missouri; St. Petersburg, Russia; and heaven—in direct relationship to each other leads to a unified and consistent association that for Twain operates simultaneously at multiple levels, including the local, historical, and cosmic: that freedom is an illusion and that the true state of the human condition, from which there is no escape, is to suffer. Put another way, Twain's St. Petersburg is the metaphorical home of his damned human race.[6]

The central authority figures of St. Petersburg in *Tom Sawyer* affirm this multilayered reading of Twain's setting. Rev. Sprague, minister of the town's Presbyterian congregation, represents an especially subtle but pervasive brand of oppression throughout the opening scenes of the novel. Consider again the content of his sermon described in chapter 5 (which begins with a ridiculous invocation pleading for a laundry-list of people and things, including, interestingly enough, "the oppressed millions groaning under the heel of European monarchies"):

> The minister gave out his text and droned along monotonously through an
> argument that was so prosy that many a head by and by began to nod—and

yet it was an argument that dealt in limitless fire and brimstone and thinned the predestined elect down to a company so small as to be hardly worth the saving. (40)[7]

Sundays are the only days when—and church is the only location where—the characters of the novel, young and old, regularly gather as one. Consequently there is great thematic import in what takes place there. At their core, Rev. Sprague's sermons characterize the cultural milieu of St. Petersburg—whether individuals in the novel are fully aware of it or not—as governed by a Calvinist sense of doom. It permeates everything, including the implications embedded in the name "St. Petersburg." Even though church appears to offer occasional relief for Tom from the rigors of home and school with its diversions of flies and pinch bugs and howling dogs, Sundays present their own variety of subjugation. The description of Tom's contemplation of snatching a fly that lands in front of him during Sunday services is just one such example: "For as sorely as Tom's hands itched to grab for it they did not dare—he believed his soul would be instantly destroyed if he did such a thing while prayer was going on" (40). The most obvious similarity between church and other principal settings in the novel in which Tom is depicted, school and home, is the omnipresent threat of violence; however, here that threat of violence rises to a spiritual level. And if Tom's behavior that morning is any indication, the congregation has internalized everything embodied by Sprague's sermons: a brand of spiritual repression that induces and perpetuates the domestic and public forms of tyranny in St. Petersburg throughout the novel.

Aunt Polly obviously represents the most immediate threat to Tom's sense of freedom throughout the novel. Cynthia Griffin Wolff puts it most plainly, perhaps, when she counts Aunt Polly as among the novel's "matriarchy . . . that holds small boys in bondage." But Aunt Polly's presence in Tom's life signifies much more than an impediment to playtime with friends. Significantly, associations with harsh religious theology exist throughout Twain's portrayal of Aunt Polly. Consider, for example, the frequency with which she justifies her treatment of Tom based on scripture. In the novel's first chapter, Aunt Polly distills her entire philosophy of child-rearing into the notion of "spare the rod and spile the child" (3). Additionally, note the way in which Twain contextualizes Aunt Polly's spare-the-rod parenting logic in her notions of human nature in the same scene:

"Well-a-well, man that is born of woman is of few days and full of trouble, as Scripture says, and I reckon it's so. He'll play hookey this evening, and I'll just be obleeged to make him work, to-morrow, to punish him. It's mighty hard to make him work Saturdays, when all the boys is having holiday, but he hates work more than he hates anything else and I've got to do some of my duty by him, or I'll be the ruination of the child." (3)

There is no question that Aunt Polly's is a time-honored disciplinary philosophy, but its sources are biblically stern, and it promotes the idea that a severe parental attitude is an obligation. Placed in the context of the passage above, it resonates with broad theological implications. Note, for example, Aunt Polly's dour notion of humankind expressed in her belief that "man" is "of few days and full of trouble," an expression that comes from Job 14:1. Taken literally, the belief that "man" is "full of trouble" echoes a conventionally Christian but distinctly pejorative view of the human condition. It especially accords with the vision of corrupt human nature that Twain received from his Presbyterian catechism, held throughout his life, and eventually developed into his philosophy of the damned human race.[8] It leads Aunt Polly to prejudge Tom in the last two sentences of the passage. She has already decided—before the fact—that Tom will misbehave. Further, her punishment is formulated—again, far in advance of any misdeed—not from what would be just, but that which would inflict the greatest degree of misery on Tom.

It is entirely possible, of course, to argue here that in his characterization of Aunt Polly, Twain simply drew from his experience with his own mother, herself a stern, God-fearing woman.[9] It might also be claimed that Aunt Polly operates from a conventional mid-nineteenth-century cultural perspective in her reliance on selectively stern scriptural passages for guidance in dealing with her mischievous nephew. However, neither rationale necessarily precludes the likelihood that Aunt Polly, like other characters in Twain's writing who function simultaneously at multiple levels of meaning, might also operate in more profound ways in *Tom Sawyer*. The same potential for multiplicity of meaning extending beyond the superficial and the literal is likewise potentially embedded in Twain's presentation of many characters in the novel. Injun Joe, for example, also has a source in Clemens's biography (Hannibal's Joe Douglas) as well as in mid-nineteenth-century American cultural history (the image of the displaced Native American). These two explanations for Injun Joe's characterization, however, have not prevented scholars from arguing that his portrayal additionally resonates at the deeper levels of philosophical romanticism (an indictment of the trope of the Noble Savage) and myth (the malevolent figure of the underworld).[10]

Twain's description of Aunt Polly in the novel's opening chapter offers additional basis for a generally darker and potentially more theologically freighted interpretation of her role in the novel:

> While Tom was eating supper, and stealing sugar as opportunity offered, Aunt Polly asked him questions that were full of guile, and very deep—for she wanted to trap him into damaging revealments. Like many simple-hearted souls, it was her pet-vanity to believe that she was endowed with a talent for dark and mysterious diplomacy and she loved to contemplate her most transparent devices as marvels of low cunning. (3–4)

Both the insights into Aunt Polly's behavior and the mature tone betray a far more sophisticated awareness than that of an adolescent boy. Indeed, the voice that passes judgment on Aunt Polly and her treatment of Tom here is omniscient and largely detached. As a result, the analysis of Aunt Polly embedded in the passage comes off as more reliable and fundamentally more penetrating than Tom's would have been. Admittedly, on the surface, references to Aunt Polly and her child-rearing in the context of "guile," "dark and mysterious diplomacy," and "low cunning" might be read as mere hyperbole crafted in part for humorous effect. However, such descriptions also render a largely unflattering portrait of Aunt Polly as a deceptive authority figure. That said, Twain's presentation of Aunt Polly here and throughout the novel is that of a victim of prevailing cultural attitudes. She is a person who loves Tom but has been transformed by an environment that promotes and practices an uncompromising brand of theocratic hegemony. Like Huck Finn in his dealings with Jim on the river, Aunt Polly is a person whose compassionate instincts have been warped by the obnoxious moral codes of her culture.

Throughout the first half of *Tom Sawyer*, Aunt Polly, despite her harsh treatment of Tom, suffers pangs of guilt for the way that she believes she is compelled to deal with her sometimes mischievous nephew. Moments like these in the novel serve to humanize Aunt Polly as well as to point out the degree to which St. Petersburg's culture of repression and cruelty has distorted her judgment. Aunt Polly, like Huck Finn during his adventures on the river, suffers whether or not she follows her intuition to act with mercy.

In chapter 3, for instance, after learning that Tom was not responsible for breaking the sugar bowl, the narrator reveals that Aunt Polly's "conscience reproached her" (22) for unjustly cuffing Tom. Importantly, before Aunt Polly feels remorse for wrongly blaming Tom, she justifies her rush to judgment, ironically, with another indictment: "Umf! Well, you didn't get a lick amiss, I reckon. You been into some other owdacious mischief when I wasn't around, like enough" (22). Tom, whom we are told "looked for healing pity" (22) from Aunt Polly after she slapped him, finds himself in an impossible situation: not only is he punished for something he is literally not responsible for, he is presumed to be so bad that he inevitably merits the punishment for something else he has done—or doubtless will do in the future. That Aunt Polly experiences such momentary fits of remorse is not as significant as how she reacts to them. Aunt Polly, even after an attack of conscience, refuses to apologize to Tom because, she concludes, "it would be construed into a confession that she had been in the wrong" (22). Twain's irony here is cutting. Aunt Polly, of course, *was* in the wrong and ought to have apologized to Tom, but her refusal to do so showcases two significant elements of Twain's thematic design: first, the scene highlights that side of Aunt Polly that has been disfigured by the culture of St. Petersburg; second, it underscores the fact that Tom exists under conditions—whether at church, home, or school—in which there is little hope of being treated fairly.

Twain introduces additional authority figures in the opening chapters of *Tom Sawyer* in his efforts to establish St. Petersburg as metaphor for autocratic rule. Schoolmaster Dobbins, in particular, is a portrait of outright tyranny. Dobbins's accusatory nature, his vindictive temperament, and his merciless punishments also provide for Tom a public complement to Aunt Polly's sometimes overly stern treatment at home. The parallels in Twain's portrayal of Dobbins and Aunt Polly can be taken even further. Dobbins and Aunt Polly, for instance, are both characterized by their acute sense of vanity. Dobbins's wig is every bit as ridiculous as Aunt Polly's spectacles are useless. And both individuals are more concerned with not being personally humiliated than with actually dealing with the rightness or wrongness of Tom's behavior. Dobbins's reaction to the torn page in his anatomy book is less a function of his being angry at the destruction of his property than it is a result of his fear of exposure for his own lurid fixation on the nude diagrams in the anatomy textbook. Similarly, Aunt Polly is furious with Tom not for lying to her about his "dream" after running away to Jackson's Island, but because he allowed her to make a fool of herself before Joe Harper's mother. In the depiction of Tom's daily routine throughout the opening chapters of the novel, Twain presents it—whether at church, home, or school—against the backdrop of looming authority figures.

Given the conditions under which Tom lives, it is little wonder that he repeatedly runs away from St. Petersburg. In fact, Tom's cycles of flight and return so dominate the action of the novel that, as Towers has pointed out, they define the fundamental structure of *Tom Sawyer*. But what is to be made of this motif? Again, at its most literal Tom's running off from the village—and its authority figures—reflects, as Towers argues, his desire to exchange the deadening reality of small-town life for experiences that more closely match those of his romantic imagination. He is an adolescent boy, after all, who simply wants to get away from the rigors of church, home, and school. However, Tom's flights also symbolize an attempt to escape the harsh vision of human nature Twain represents in his portrayal of St. Petersburg throughout the novel. But none of Tom's attempts to flee from St. Petersburg's oppressiveness—whether considered literally or metaphorically—succeeds in providing him with any real or sustained sense of freedom. These experiences either offer only temporary relief (as when he is playing Robin Hood in the woods) or, if intended seriously, are largely untenable (as in the case of running away to Jackson's Island).

One of the first depictions of Tom running off from St. Petersburg comes in chapter 8, and it serves as a general template for subsequent flights in the novel. After a difficult morning marked in swift succession by Aunt Polly's somewhat spiteful tooth extraction (she pulls Tom's tooth even though she realizes that he fabricated the tooth pain to get out of going to school), Dobbins's schoolroom beating, and Becky's rejection, Tom decides to skip afternoon classes and run off to the woods beyond the outskirts of town. As Tom reaches his destination, the narrator begins to set a tone that characterizes the rest of the episode:

> He entered a dense wood, picked his pathless way to the centre of it, and sat down on a mossy spot under a spreading oak. There was not even a zephyr stirring; the dead noonday heat had even stilled the songs of the birds; nature lay in a trance that was broken by no sound but the occasional hammering of a woodpecker, and this seemed to render a pervading silence and a sense of loneliness the more profound. The boy's soul was steeped in melancholy;

his feelings were in happy accord with his surroundings. He sat long with his elbows on his knees and his chin in his hands, meditating. It seemed to him that life was but a trouble, and he more than half envied Jimmy Hodges, so lately released; it must be very peaceful, he thought, to lie and slumber and dream forever and ever, with the wind whistling through the trees and caressing the grass and the flowers over the grave, and nothing to bother and grieve about, ever any more. (63)

With its references to nature, the melancholy sentiment, and the suggestions of Tom's isolation, and his communing with his pastoral surroundings, the passages establish a conspicuously (if excessive) romantic mood for the rest of the scene. Further, references to death are abundant in chapter 8, even framing the episode, and are designed to invoke a graveyard-school brand of romanticism. Joe Harper soon appears on the scene, and the two boys briefly enjoy themselves by reenacting scenes from Robin Hood, but Tom eventually returns to St. Petersburg not revived by his afternoon diversion but "grieving" (69) because their playtime is over and he must go back to the realities of life in the village below.

On the one hand, there seems little out of the ordinary here: a young boy plays hooky, has fun with his best friend reenacting scenes from their favorite story, and is disappointed that he has to return home when all is said and done. On the other hand, the scene represents Twain's satiric treatment of romantic literature—in particular, his assault on the trope of the romantic cycle and its assurances of deliverance. The descriptions of nature, the overdone melancholic tone early in the chapter, and the boys' by-the-book reenactment of scenes from Robin Hood are all examples of Twain's mild burlesques of romanticism. Tom's afternoon on Cardiff Hill also follows the general pattern of the romantic cycle: he retreats into nature, communes with the natural world, and then returns from nature to rejoin his community. Of course in romantic literature the protagonist who withdraws to nature ideally returns permanently enlightened and renewed. Tom's excursion into the natural world here, however, provides none of the sustained relief promised by romanticism. Instead, the retreat into nature leaves Tom no happier about his life in St. Petersburg than before he ran off. The importance of this scene lies ultimately in the way that it establishes the fundamental pattern for the rest of Tom's attempted flights: every escapade is a romantic delusion and is always concluded by a return without renewal or reprieve.

At first, Tom's flights from home take the form of playing hooky during the day or slipping out his bedroom window at night. Eventually, however, Tom's attempted escapes increase in duration, distance, and degree. But whether Tom is merely sneaking off to the graveyard with Huck (in chapter 9) or descending into the depths of MacDougal's Cave with Becky (in chapter 29), three constants run throughout each of the novel's major episodes. First, the destination of each escape is a distinctly romantic setting; second, each experience is marked heavily by death; third, Injun Joe or some symbolic representation of his presence figures prominently in the scene. Ultimately, the cycles of flight and return that define the action of the novel point to the larger thematic purpose of these episodes. Insofar as St. Petersburg serves as metaphor for Twain's countertheological vision of the human condition, Tom's hope that he can flee the oppressive environment of the small village and what it represents is but a romantic delusion.

The major scenes of *Tom Sawyer*—the graveyard scene, the escape to Jackson's Island, the quest for treasure in the haunted house, and the adventure in MacDougal's Cave—all begin by repeating the basic patterns established in chapter 8. For example, the graveyard incident in chapter 9 commences with Tom's sneaking out to a distinctly romantic setting beyond the limits of St. Petersburg, this time an overgrown country cemetery possessing many of the most obvious stereotypes of gothic literature (for example, a pervading sense of the supernatural, the Byronic hero, superstition, ritual, ruins, decay, darkness, and so forth). It is not surprising, too, that given this particular location, images of death are present everywhere throughout the scene. And like the earlier incident on Cardiff Hill, the graveyard scene begins innocuously with Tom's pursuit of adventure in an attempt to displace the constricting reality of life in St. Petersburg. However, both episodes also present Twain's efforts to put the lie to romance, generally, and to the promises of the romantic cycle, specifically, with all of its implications of healing and deliverance. There is nothing romantically ideal about how Tom and Huck witness Doc Robinson's grave robbing and his murder at the hands of Injun Joe or how Tom and Huck's oath to each other not to reveal the details of the crime afterward results not in personal enlightenment, communal growth, or any of the other results assured by romance, but rather in a deepened sense of torment for the two boys within their community.

Twain's introduction of Injun Joe to the narrative in this scene reinforces and extends the novel's major themes.[11] But Twain's handling of Injun Joe is ultimately more complex than most scholars have apparently acknowledged. At the heart of the depiction of Injun Joe in *Tom Sawyer* is Twain's attack on the trope of the Noble Savage of romantic literature. Twain begins his critique by embracing the logic of the Native American as an image of the "natural man": that is, human nature in its most unaffected state. He then inverts the romantic assumptions of nobility, virtue, and goodness embedded in the notion of the Noble Savage to reflect simultaneously the falsehood of romance and humankind—at least in his opinion—as it truly is. Twain's characterization of Injun Joe indeed dramatizes a vision of human nature in its "natural" state: corrupt, violent, and predisposed to evil. In his depiction of Injun Joe, Twain showcases a vision of human nature consistent with his heretical countertheological views. Importantly, however, Twain casts Injun Joe as a "half-breed," which precludes the position that Injun Joe's natural state of corruption is an exclusive function of his Native American lineage. That Injun Joe is half white actually universalizes his corrupt nature. There is, after all, little real difference between Injun Joe's tendency toward violence and that of the citizens of St. Petersburg who are eager to tar and feather, even lynch, individuals without the benefit of a trial.[12] At its most fundamental level, the depiction of Injun Joe is as efficient as it is brilliant, a compression of Twain's counterstatement to romantic literary conventions and his deepest convictions about humankind's corrupt state.

The image of Injun Joe works in even more practical ways here and throughout *Tom Sawyer*. In the process of fleeing from St. Petersburg, Tom runs directly into Injun Joe in the graveyard. Inasmuch as St. Petersburg and Injun Joe represent similar visions of human nature from which Tom attempts to escape throughout the novel, Twain suggests that though Tom runs from home, he will ultimately find, no matter in which direction he flees, that human nature is the same everywhere. Like the protagonist-narrator of *Roughing It* (1872), who expected that the West would provide a hopeful alternative to the weariness of life at home but instead found human behavior the same no matter where he traveled, Tom and his experiences lead to the inevitable conclusion that there is no escaping one's fate as a member of the damned human race. Injun Joe and the vision of universal corruption he represents will be waiting ready to greet Tom every time and wherever he attempts to run.

The Jackson's Island episode, which takes place in chapters 13–17, is the most important in the novel, for not only does it echo the patterns found in the graveyard scene in more sustained ways, it also represents something of a transition between the first and second halves of *Tom Sawyer*. Like the graveyard scene, this episode begins with Tom's midnight getaway from St. Petersburg. This time, however, Tom's running off carries with it the suggestion of his attempting to get away permanently. The destination of Tom's flight is a singularly romantic setting, a deserted island reminiscent of those found in the pirate adventure stories of Ned Buntline and others.[13] Here again, however, rather than offering communion and relief, nature actually conjures up a hostile threat in the form of a dangerous storm that leaves the boys feeling lonely and afraid. While there are moments during the episode when Tom, Huck, and Joe appear to be enjoying themselves, the joy their playtime provides is fleeting and devolves by the end of the episode into what the narrator describes as "savagery": "By and by they separated into three hostile tribes, and darted upon each other from ambush with dreadful war-whoops, and killed and scalped each other by the thousands. It was a gory day. Consequently it was an extremely satisfactory one" (127). As the final image of the boys on Jackson's Island, their playing "Indians" is significant for a number of reasons. First, the image of violent Native Americans here echoes Injun Joe's vicious murder of Doc Robinson in the graveyard. Second, it once again puts on display Twain's counter-theological vision of the "natural man" and represents a symbolical reversion of the boys to their "natural" state while on the island, à la William Golding's *Lord of the Flies* (1954). As with the other episodes, Tom finds no relief from St. Petersburg—and what it represents in terms of human nature—on Jackson's Island.

Also significant is that the end of the Jackson's Island episode occurs almost exactly at the physical midpoint of the novel. Chapter 18, which features the boys' dramatic return to St. Petersburg by appearing at their own funeral, likewise marks a transition in Tom's characterization. Symbolically, the incident represents Tom's rebirth into St. Petersburg. Prior to Jackson's Island, Tom's behavior is guided by his desire to variously rebel against and escape from St. Petersburg and its agents of repression. After the Jackson's Island incident, Tom's conduct shifts from outright rebellion to gradual acceptance of the status quo. It could be argued, of course, that

Tom simply begins to "grow up" after his dramatic homecoming. Consider, for example, the fact that following the funeral, Tom in quick succession recommits to his pursuit of Becky in a way that mimics all the features of a conventional adult courtship. But at the same time, Tom also embraces the conformist pieties of his community by joining the Cadets of Temperance and grows increasingly eager to perform the hypocrisies of "civilized" society, particularly in his dealings with Huck. Neither course of action can be said to represent Twain's view of responsible mature behavior.

In fact, Tom's evolving attitude toward Huck serves as an index to just how much Tom's sensibilities change over the course of the narrative and increasingly begin to resemble those of the general population of St. Petersburg. Early in the novel Tom, like the other boys, "envied" Huck and "played with him every time he got a chance" (48). Tom looks up to Huck throughout the first half of the narrative as an icon of rebellion and treats him as a kindred spirit. After the funeral, though, Tom's interest in associating with Huck wanes considerably. Indeed, the farther we go into the second half of *Tom Sawyer*, the more it seems that Tom and Huck pursue their somewhat related interests separately, mostly because Tom distances himself from Huck in order to align himself with the more "respectable" members of the community and their cultural practices. All of this is to say that in the second half of the novel, Tom behaves more and more like the citizens of St. Petersburg he resisted and defied earlier in the story. Put another way, Tom's rebirth in chapter 18 represents the beginning of his impersonation of a "respectable" member of St. Petersburg society. Tom's continued impersonation throughout the later chapters is subtle and certainly unwitting, but it is no less transformative and significant.

The motif of impersonation is fundamental in Twain's writing. But scholarly discussion of Twain's use of impersonation has generally focused on works such as *The Prince and the Pauper* and *Huckleberry Finn*. However, Twain's portrayal of Tom in the second half of the novel appears to possess all the characteristics of impersonation as a motif found in novels written and published just a few years after *Tom Sawyer*. Take, for example, the ways that Tom's "rebirth" in chapter 18 and subsequent transformation over the course of the second half of the novel anticipate Huck's "rebirth" in chapter 32 of *Huckleberry Finn* at the beginning of the Phelps farm incident and his subsequent regression throughout the "evasion" chapters. Just as circumstance intervenes with Huck at the Phelps farm and dictates to him that he "is" Tom Sawyer, the circumstance of Tom's environment in *Tom Sawyer* likewise dictates Tom's identity: rebel and resist as he may, St. Petersburg coaxes Tom into conforming to its superficial sense of respectability. Moreover, in both situations neither character protests the imposition of an identity from the outside. Indeed, both seem to embrace their new personas with enthusiasm. Their acceptance of them, however, does nothing to mitigate the destructive nature of those new identities. Practically all critics recognize, for instance, the devastating consequences of Huck's impersonation of Tom at the Phelps farm, both in terms of his own development and the direct impact it has on Jim's well-being. The same can be said for Tom throughout the second half of *Tom Sawyer*. Tom's acquiescence to the cultural hegemony of St. Petersburg following his "rebirth" is every bit as self-destructive in terms of his independence as Huck's impersonation and is similarly not without collateral casualties: Huck could be said to suffer in the late chapters of *Tom Sawyer* because of Tom's impersonation of a respectable citizen of St. Petersburg in ways that anticipate Jim's suffering under Huck at the end of *Huckleberry Finn*.

There are also numerous parallels between Tom's gradual and unwitting submission to the values of St. Petersburg and David Wilson's ultimate embrace of Dawson's Landing's status quo in *Pudd'nhead Wilson*. Like Tom Sawyer, David Wilson is introduced by Twain as an individual set in opposition to the conformist tendencies of the rest of his village. Wilson's fatal remark in chapter 1 about killing half a dog demonstrates not only intelligence and a capacity for complex thinking but also his truly independent nature at the beginning of the novel. The irony at the center of Wilson's observation shows him to be a capable intellect, and his total lack of self-consciousness as a newcomer to the village about commenting aloud among strangers identifies him as a true individualist. By comparison, the incident exposes the people of Dawson's Landing as collectively dim-witted and small-minded. The village, of course, is intellectually incapable of appreciating Wilson's irony, and its reaction as a group to the remark (and later to Wilson's acerbic maxims) is to ostracize him socially and to ruin him professionally. But just as Tom Sawyer slowly and unknowingly conforms to the repressive sensibilities of St. Petersburg, David Wilson over time inadvertently gives in to the moral hollowness of Dawson's Landing; the proof of this is that Wilson is honored by Dawson's Landing by being elected its mayor. Thus his antislavery inclinations are co-opted by a slaveholding town, and he thenceforth presumably serves, as indeed he has since the trial, to uphold laws and customs he had earlier opposed.

The final two major episodes of *Tom Sawyer*, the search for treasure in the haunted house and the adventure in MacDougal's Cave, again follow all of the patterns established earlier in the novel. Both begin as boyhood excursions designed in large part to escape from the harshness of life in St. Petersburg; both begin at midnight;[14] both are marked throughout by suggestions of death; both involve unexpected run-ins with Injun Joe; and both turn dangerous very quickly. And just as important, Tom and Huck grow increasingly farther apart during these two incidents. At the beginning of the haunted house incident, Tom and Huck pursue their hunt for treasure together. By the end of the scene Huck is keeping watch by himself because Tom has placed his pursuit of Becky above everything else. With the MacDougal's Cave episode, Tom and Huck literally do not come into contact with each other even though their experiences during these chapters parallel one another. Both boys' respective involvement in the episode, for example, begins at about the same time (Huck overhears Injun Joe threatening the Widow Douglas just as Tom realizes that he and Becky are lost in the cave), both run into Injun Joe (Huck in chapter 29 and Tom in chapter 31), and both are rescued, fed, and housed by strangers following their ordeals (Huck by the Welshman and his sons in chapters 29 and 30 and Tom by the men on the skiff in chapter 32).

The final two chapters of *Tom Sawyer* provide a logical climax for the trajectory of Tom's characterization in the second half of the novel. Chapter 34 begins with Huck and Tom alone in a bedroom in the home of the Widow Douglas as representative citizens of St. Petersburg, characters whom the narrator describes as "everybody that was of any consequence in the village" (248), wait downstairs for the boys to return. Huck assumes that he and Tom will take the opportunity to escape out the window and run, but Tom reveals that he has other plans:

> "Tom, we can slope, if we can find a rope. The window ain't high from the ground."
> "Shucks, what do you want to do that for?"
> "Well, I ain't used to that kind of a crowd. I can't stand it. I ain't going down there, Tom."
> "O, brother! It ain't anything. I don't mind it a bit. I'll take care of you."
> (250)

Tom and Huck appear to be faced with a decision that is simultaneously literal and metaphorical: do the boys run and continue to rebel against St. Petersburg, or do they return to the party downstairs and accept a place within their community? Tom, of course, has already made his decision to return to the party and in doing so his impersonation of a "civilized" member of St. Petersburg reaches its full development. Tom is able to persuade Huck to follow. As such, the scene completes Tom's unwitting transformation from tireless rebel to contented apologist for everything that St. Petersburg stands for. And not only does Tom refuse to run, he appears satisfied enough with the values of the village, represented in the people gathered below in the Widow Douglas's drawing room, that he is now willing to act as its chief enforcer. As Forrest G. Robinson puts it, Tom has become by the end of the novel "St. Petersburg's preeminent gamesman" ("Social Play and Bad Faith" 176). Twain's irony embedded in Tom's promise to "take care" of Huck could not be any more pointed, for "take care" of Huck, Tom will. From this point forward—and continuing throughout *Huckleberry Finn*—Tom will work to repress the independent-minded radical in Huck in ways that go beyond anything the authority figures of St. Petersburg employed in dealing with Tom. But none of this is to say that Tom realizes he has actually embraced the status quo by refusing to run in chapter 34. To the contrary, Tom continues to think of himself as the chief enemy of St. Petersburg by maintaining his gang of make-believe robbers and murderers. Like Hank Morgan in *A Connecticut Yankee in King Arthur's Court*, Tom is oblivious to the fact that he no longer fights power but has become an elite powerbroker himself. And Tom's manipulation of Huck in chapter 35 only intensifies as the two boys are introduced in the opening chapters of *Huckleberry Finn*.

Mark Twain famously maintained to William Dean Howells that he originally thought he wrote *The Adventures of Tom Sawyer* as a book intended for adults. Scholarship of the last several decades has gradually uncovered and identified elements of the novel that would tend to corroborate that claim. Behind its affectations of nostalgia and pretense at the boy's book genre resides an unsettling vision of humanity. Yet Twain's critique with this novel is not limited to merely pointing out the hypocrisies of civilized society. Through his portrayal of Tom, Twain depicts the hopelessness of escaping one's destiny as a member of the damned human race, and in his depiction of St. Petersburg Twain constructs the metaphor of that condition that would come to reside at the center of much of what he would write over the next thirty-five years. Indeed, with *The Adventures of Tom Sawyer,* Twain provides a link between the early accomplishments in theme and form of *Roughing It* and the artistic maturity of *Adventures of Huckleberry Finn* and beyond.

Adventures of Huckleberry Finn

Thus saith the Lord, Let my people go, that they may serve me. —Exodus 8:1

For a book generally believed to affirm freedom, *Adventures of Huckleberry Finn* (1885) features a plot that makes this goal incredibly difficult to attain. First, Huck and Jim undertake their voyage to freedom on a raft of logs lashed together that is minimally navigable and essentially controlled by the current of the river.[1] They float between shores which are hostile to them, and meet with perils both on the river and on its shores. After they encounter fog, they miss the critical juncture at Cairo, Illinois, of the Ohio and the Mississippi rivers. It had been their plan to discontinue rafting at Cairo and find a steamboat that went up the Ohio River to Cincinnati, a safe city at which Jim could connect with the Underground Railroad and be conducted to freedom and security in Canada. But having missed that transfer point, they are committed to continuing to drift south—exactly the wrong direction. Each mile they drift from then on takes them farther away from any practical hope for freedom, deeper into slave territory, and closer to New Orleans, the largest slave-trading market in the country and the place all slaves dreaded the most. Stops on both sides of the Mississippi are frightening and literally dangerous. Once Jim and Huck arrive at the Phelps farm in Arkansas, they are so deep in slave territory that it is almost inconceivable that they still have any reasonable chance of achieving freedom. Either a divine or romantic miracle would have to occur, or readers would be left with the realization that from the first, Huck and Jim never had a hope for freedom. And Twain placed no stock in divine miracles, and his hostility to romanticism is well documented.

This situation sets up the general nature of the main hoax of the novel. Despite the surface appearance of its conclusion, the novel does not have a happy ending. Readers (almost all of us, initially) who believe that, at the end, Jim is free, that Huck can go back to being a boy again with his chum Tom Sawyer, that all is well, and that the novel ends on a positive note have fallen for the hoax and have consequently missed a great deal in the novel. To believe the novel ends happily it is necessary to downplay all the serious adventures Huck and Jim have undergone and the perils they survived as having been entertaining but inconsequential episodes. It is to misinterpret as benign or neutral the function in the novel of the river itself, to ignore the implications of the fact that the raft is being swept along passively and inexorably southward by its current. It is to underplay the importance of the way that Jim and Huck have grown on the raft, and have grown together, and to dispose of three-quarters of the novel as merely a backdrop for the superficially happy ending. And for readers who claim to admire the book but are dissatisfied with the last ten "evasion" chapters, it is to praise the novel as one of the great works of American literature while maintaining at the same time that Twain bungled the whole last quarter of the novel, that he was not a skillful enough author to unify the whole work and make it fully believable.[2]

There is no other author in all of world literature whom we call great even though he or she could not write a book that hung together and continued to gain significance up to the end. Why make an exception for Twain? Would it not be simpler and more honest to take Twain off his pedestal and regard him simply but sadly as an author who shows signs of genius, but who lacked the disciplined artistry to ever justify his prospects? In order to justify the claim that Twain is a great author, a straightforward way has to be found of reading his literature so that thematic consistency and artistic strengths can be seen. Fortunately, that avenue exists. It takes the form of accepting the position that Twain's main theme is *not* an affirmation of freedom but rather its opposite: a tragic denial of any hope for freedom in human life. This interpretation does not require any special pleading or selective reading; on the contrary, in *Huckleberry Finn* the whole novel supplies abundant evidence for it, especially the evasion chapters.

While our attention is on Huck's resourceful and valiant efforts to achieve freedom for Jim and himself, the entire rest of the novel steadily and undeviatingly builds a context in which freedom is impossible, and which subtly but surely manipulates Huck and Jim toward an illusion that only deepens the tragedy of what increasingly becomes clear is their destiny. Their seeming escape from obvious human bondage and danger is ultimately only a transference to a condition of stricter but more insidious divine control. Not only are they unaware that they are being manipulated, but so are all casual readers unaware that Twain is manipulating them as well. He offers them a choice between a romantic and highly engaging surface-level narrative with major structural flaws, and a less obvious but fully coherent story driven at a deeper level by his countertheology, and he bets that his readers will choose the more accessible alternative and fall for his hoax. It is a bet he has won by a large margin in every generation. As decades of literary scholarship have demonstrated, the novel's claim to aesthetic unity has been sacrificed by most commentators. We argue that it is not necessary to pay this price; the novel as it stands can be viewed as an outstanding success from both thematic and formal perspectives.

The main obstacle to adequately appreciating the novel is an old one but one which still governs most interpretations: it is Leo Marx's bold and thoughtful charge that the novel fails to perform satisfactorily as an affirmation of freedom. In response to the challenge of Marx and subsequent critics who agree with him, a series of scholarly and critical investigations have been undertaken which have discovered depths and nuances in the book that were not apparent earlier. These appraisals have all been partial defenses of the book as having some important or unifying feature; however, our discussion is intended to fully meet Marx on his fundamental point, that *Huckleberry Finn* is a fatally flawed novel. Marx's objection has three interrelated parts to it: the main theme of the book is freedom; this theme is not sustained to the conclusion, a failure of nerve having afflicted Twain; and the last ten chapters, lacking the theme which informed the preceding thirty-three, specifically fall short of the novel's impressive achievements in its earlier parts. Structurally, in other words, the evasion chapters are not unified in form or thought with the earlier ones and cause the book at the end to revert to the level of children's literature. As Marx interprets the book, therefore, Twain failed in his apparent purpose to carry through to completion the bold and mature conception of freedom which he steadily promoted until the evasion chapters.

If the novel's purpose were to promote a conception of freedom, then we would have to agree with Marx; but we do not find that it was. While *Huckleberry Finn* is fundamentally concerned with freedom, in conjecturing that Twain *affirmed* freedom Marx overlooked significant textual evidence pointing to the contrary conclusion. On the basis of such evidence, and with the additional support of literary history showing Twain to have denied the possibility of freedom before as well as after *Huckleberry Finn*, and legal history which shows Jim's manumission to be, in reality, a grimly ironic ending, we propose that *Huckleberry Finn* is best read as a novel which depicts the impossibility of any meaningful measure of freedom for any of its characters and, in moving to this end, is consistently unified in both theme and structure.

Let us begin by defining what is meant by freedom. Though it is agreed that freedom is a basic theme in the novel, it is not necessary to accept Marx's statement that "freedom in this book specifically means freedom from society and its imperatives" (436). This definition of freedom is over-restrictive both in its purely negative quality (freedom *from*) and in its limitation to social morality. Twain in *Huckleberry Finn* considers freedom in the broad philosophical sense (under which category social freedom and political freedom are subsumed) of being able to exercise choices toward realizing one's individuality, and the final chapters, far from being flawed or "fainthearted" in respect to this theme, are in fact the deepest and most pointed in the book. The function of those concluding chapters is to drive home the central lesson of the book, a lesson which Twain constructed carefully from the first chapter to the last: there is no freedom; all human life in the final analysis is subservient; whether humans realize it or not, without agreeing to their roles or even sensing what they might be, all are in a state of servitude to God. Through an examination of one recurring literary device, impersonation, and three recurring motifs—romanticism, destiny, and the hoax—we will demonstrate how Twain drives inexorably to this conclusion.

The literary device of impersonation is the most important single technique that Twain uses in *Huckleberry Finn*. Basically, this consists of a person's taking on a new identity. It is not necessary to the technique that the person be aware of the conversion; it is not necessary that any special conditions or reasons be operant; all that is necessary is that a change of identity take place. Twain practiced his use of this technique in *The Prince and the Pauper*, published in 1881, just three years before *Huckleberry Finn*. Of *The Prince and the Pauper*, Gladys Bellamy says: "This book was Mark Twain's first full-length study of the power of determining environment and circumstance. The transformation of beggar into prince and vice versa was effected by a mere 'change of clothes'" (310).³ Although those impersonations begin consciously and innocently, it develops that neither the prince nor the pauper is able to stop them. When destiny finally intervenes to rectify the situation, both boys have become captives of their new identities and are beginning to submit to them. The use of impersonation in *The Prince and the Pauper* is simple and obvious; in *Huckleberry Finn*, as in *Roughing It* and *The Adventures of Tom Sawyer*, it is more subtle and complex. Not only is it repeated, with variations, in almost every important incident, but it forms the very structure of the novel. Frank Baldanza came very close to realizing this when he identified the principle of repetition and variation as the main structural technique of the novel and cited specific examples of its use: change of identity, superstition and prophecy, and lying (354). But he dismissed these as "minor correspondences" and "exuberant impulses" (354–355). The term "correspondence," however, is singularly apt and too relevant to our discussion to be dismissed lightly, for essentially *Huckleberry Finn* is a novel of corresponding impersonations, each related to the other, and all to a fundamental pattern.

The fundamental pattern in the book is that no human is free to create his or her own identity; each is given an identity by one of a hierarchy of concentric, progressively superior forces—family, environment, and destiny–and each person in fact plays out an assigned role. Most conventional Bible-centered religions would find little to be upset about this situation, because all of them already regard God as the master of destiny and believe that whatever God decrees for us has an ultimately benevolent purpose. Twain, however, did not. He regarded God as a cruel trickster, an omnipotent and malevolent divine puppeteer who managed events not for the benefit of humans but for his own inscrutable pleasure. Therefore, because every human life is predestined, but no one knows what that destiny is, "reality" is an illusion, and life at the core is humanly hollow and meaningless. It is impossible for humans not to impersonate the identities that Providence gives them, and though they may at times sense uneasily that they are being manipulated, and though they may have intended different courses of action, in the final analysis they have no choice.

Students of Twain will, of course, recognize this seemingly deterministic view of life as that which informed some of the pessimistic works of his later years, most notably *What Is Man?* (1906). But there is no reason to limit Twain's pessimistic negation of freedom to his later years. It began with the pessimism of his boyhood Calvinism, and he never discarded its legacies, even after he apparently ceased believing in God. These ideas appeared previously in various writings of his in the 1860s and 1870s, and on February 19, 1883, only one year before *Huckleberry Finn* was published, he revealed in a speech before the Monday Evening Club how prominent these ideas were in his current thinking: "I observed that the human machine gets all its inspirations from the outside and is not capable of originating an idea of any kind in its own head; and . . . that no man ever does a duty for duty's sake but only for the sake of avoiding the personal discomfort he would have to endure if he shirked the duty; also I indicated that there is no such thing as free will and no such thing as self-sacrifice."[4] It would have been strange had Twain disavowed free will so soon before *Huckleberry Finn* and so frequently and forcefully afterward and yet had affirmed a meaningful idea of freedom in it—but such is not the case. Through his device of impersonation in *Huckleberry Finn*, he demonstrates in literary terms the validity of the thesis of the denial of free will that he advanced to the Monday Evening Club.

Impersonation is a manifestation of Twain's countertheological theme of dreams because impersonations are not only by definition a form of unreality but, additionally, a veiling of that fact. The idea of impersonating—in the form of acting—was on Twain's mind during the critical years 1883–1884. Albert Bigelow Paine said that Twain "had a lingering attack of dramatic fever that winter" (439). He and William Dean Howells completed a play about Colonel Sellers, and Twain dramatized both *The Adventures of Tom Sawyer* (1876) and *The Prince and the Pauper*. Even a cursory glance at the characters in *Huckleberry Finn* reveals how common a device impersonation is throughout the book and how deeply most of the characters are involved in impersonations. The book begins with two instances of impersonation:

> The Widow Douglas, she took me for her son, and allowed she would sivilize me; but it was rough living in the house all the time, considering how dismal regular and decent the widow was in all her ways; and so when I couldn't stand it no longer, I lit out. I got into my old rags, and my sugar-hogshead again, and was free and satisfied. But Tom Sawyer, he hunted me up and said he was going to start a band of robbers, and I might join if I would go back to the widow and be respectable. So I went back. (1:1–2)[5]

It is significant that Huck's very first attempt to achieve freedom was his escape from an impersonation of a "sivilized" boy, the Widow Douglas's son. Even more significant are the terms of Tom Sawyer's bribe: if Huck returns to his impersonation of a respectable boy, he can join a gang organized for the purpose of impersonating robbers. Beyond the humorous irony of the juxtaposition of a robber gang and respectable society is the more serious irony of the suggestion that both respectable society and robbers are impersonations and that the free human is lost in either role. Also important is the romantic character Tom Sawyer gives his gang; his inspirational models obviously include *Don Quixote* and *The Arabian Nights*. It will be seen henceforth that most impersonations in the novel partake to a greater or lesser extent of romanticism. Furthermore, there is a tendency for the impersonators to get carried away by their impersonations, to become what they impersonate, and therefore to live in a world of illusion.

Tom Sawyer himself, of course, is at once the arch-romantic and the arch-impersonator. This is almost a cause-and-effect relationship. Tom can hardly impersonate enough; acting is his very nature. Huck notes this in his description of Tom's arrival at the Phelps farm: "Tom had his store clothes on, and an audience—and that was always nuts for Tom Sawyer" (285), and immediately posed as a stranger from Hicksville, Ohio, by the name of William Thompson. Inspired by, or imitating, works of romantic literature, Tom impersonates only a robber chieftain at the beginning of the book, but by the end he simultaneously impersonates Sid Sawyer, a "nigger-stealer," and a variety of captive heroes found in the pages of romantic fiction. Not content with arranging impersonations for himself, Tom causes others to impersonate. At the beginning, he persuades his gang to consider themselves robbers. At the end of the book, he obliges Huck to impersonate him, and makes Jim impersonate storybook captives. An ominous significance thus attaches to Tom and hence to romanticism, of which he is the chief exemplar. The ultimately deadly nature of romanticism is symbolized in chapter 40 by Tom's deliberately creating a dangerous situation, then getting caught in it. By that juncture Tom has utterly lost contact with reality. He is so glad that he has been wounded in an evasion, in the best romantic tradition, that he is completely oblivious to his medical condition. It is Huck and Jim, clear-sighted and practical, who value life. Were it left to Tom, he would willingly embrace death. "He had a dream,"

Huck says tellingly of Tom near the end of the novel, "and it shot him" (41:343).

The Grangerfords and Shepherdsons impersonate cavaliers out of a Sir Walter Scott romance. The aristocratic bearing of Colonel Grangerford; the exaggerated respect of the Grangerford boys for their parents as shown in the morning ritual of formal greeting and the toast, "Our duty to you, sir, and madam" (18:243); and the ridiculous sense of honor which nurtures a fatal feud—these are all affected behaviorisms. This point is made even more explicit in chapter 46 of *Life on the Mississippi* (1883), written at the same time as the Grangerford chapters, in which Twain denounces Sir Walter Scott for infecting the South with "the sillinesses and emptinesses, sham grandeurs, sham gauds, and sham chivalries of a brainless and worthless long-vanished society . . . the duel, the inflated speech, and the jejeune romanticism of an absurd past that is dead" (327).[6] When we read, a little farther along, that "Sir Walter . . . made every gentleman in the South a major or a colonel" and that "it was he that created rank and caste down there, and also reverence for rank and caste, and pride and pleasure in them" (328), we can be certain that we have encountered in those lines the Grangerfords and the Shepherdsons.[7]

The citizens of Colonel Sherburn's one-horse Arkansas town—all of them—are impersonators and connoisseurs of impersonation. When Boggs, ordinarily "the best-naturedest old fool in Arkansaw" (21:184), rides into town transformed by drink into a different man, an angry avenger, the townspeople are pleased by his romantic new role and look forward to some entertainment. And when Colonel Sherburn shows himself governed by the same deadly code of honor that the Grangerfords and Shepherdsons followed, the townspeople's first reaction is that of having enjoyed a well-acted drama. This is clearly shown by its approval of one man's reenactment of the tragedy the townspeople had just witnessed:

> One long lanky man, with long hair and a big white fur stovepipe hat on the back of his head, and a crooked-handled cane, marked out the places on the ground where Boggs stood, and where Sherburn stood, and the people following him around from one place to t'other and watching everything he done, and bobbing their heads to show they understood, and stooping a little and resting their hands on their thighs to watch him mark the places on the ground with his cane; and then he stood up straight and stiff where Sherburn had stood, frowning and having his hat-brim down over his eyes, and

sung out, "Boggs!" and then fetched his cane down slow to a level, and says "Bang!" staggered backwards, says "Bang!" again, and fell down flat on his back. The people that had seen the thing said he done it perfect; said it was just exactly the way it all happened. (21:187–188)

The people who had watched the actor then become fired up to participate in the drama around them. The spectators suddenly become actors themselves: they try to impersonate heroic avengers—lynchers—until they are disheartened by the shotgun and scathing ridicule vented upon them by Colonel Sherburn. Having participated in two dramas already that day, the townspeople disperse, but shortly reassemble at a circus, where they watch a clown impersonate a drunk on an uncontrollable horse. That night they watch yet another impersonation, the Dauphin playing the Royal Nonesuch. And they leave the performance pretending pleasure but plotting vengeance.

The Duke and the Dauphin, for that matter, have no identities apart from whom or what they impersonate. We meet them in their grandiose roles of phony royalty and watch them as their scoundrelly natures lead them to impersonate yet other identities, including the actors David Garrick and Edmund Kean, also impersonators. But never do we learn their true identities. These they never reveal, not even to each other.

The device of impersonation might be applied to practically every individual and to every group of people in the book; young and old alike, each segment of society accepts some image (with its connotation of pose, "image" is the exact word for the situation) of itself fostered by society or seeks to change one image for another. Up to this point, Leo Marx's definition of freedom ("freedom from society and its imperatives") is valid, for social rank and status are obviously determined by society. Insofar as society also determines mores and laws, it is able to induce or compel the individuals who comprise it to seek or to accept given identities with definite associated values and behavior patterns. No one involved in society, therefore, is truly free, for instead of following one's own bent, of being "oneself," an original, each instead must act out one or more social roles. There is no alternative for anyone who is involved in society; society cannot consist of originals and therefore is intolerant of nonconformists.

Our attention, then, must turn to Huck and Jim, the two nonconformists of the book, the only individuals in the novel who seem to stand a chance of attaining real freedom—and this by virtue of their leaving society for an isolated and seemingly free existence on the raft. In Marx's comment on this situation, "Yet freedom, in the ecstatic sense that Huck and Jim knew it aboard the raft, was hardly to be had in the Mississippi Valley in the 1840s, or, for that matter, in any other known human society" (437), it is obvious that he considers the quest for freedom the intention of the book, life on the raft the implausible outcome of the quest, and the chapters after the passing of Cairo, Illinois, a disappointing anticlimax. To consider the "ecstatic sense" of freedom on the raft as a high point in the book, however, is to confuse the sense of freedom for the real thing. It may be true, in a manner of speaking, that Huck and Jim are freer on the raft than they were back in St. Petersburg, but they are not truly free. Marx himself admits a major qualification—"the circumscribed nature of the raft as a means of moving toward freedom." The raft lacked "power and maneuverability," could move only with the current, was drifting southward into slavery, and "patently was not capable of carrying the burden of hope Clemens placed on it" (438). If Twain had, indeed, placed a "burden of hope" upon a raft with such a "circumscribed nature," then Marx is right; the book does fail in its ending.

But if we do not demand a paradox from the situation, and instead read the chapters after the passing of Cairo at face value, as a steady progression, literally as well as figuratively, into slavery, the ending of the book can be seen as an integral part of a unified whole. The novel is unified not around the subissue of freedom from social morality but around the grander issue of free will versus predestination. Humans are allowed to yearn for freedom, Twain shows, to struggle for it, and even to believe they have achieved it—but it is an illusion. Freedom is not allowed by the inscrutable and cruel force that oversees us. To see how Twain arrives at this conclusion, we have to observe how he applied the literary device of impersonation to Huck and Jim.

We have already looked at one incident at the beginning of the book in which Huck simultaneously attempted two impersonations: he tried to appear to be a respectable boy to the Widow Douglas and a bold robber in the heroic tradition to Tom Sawyer (significantly, the two impersonations overlap). But at least ten other impersonations take place in Huck's career over the course of the book.[8] In addition to the two just mentioned is the occasion in chapter 11 when Huck dresses as a girl and tries to convince Judith Loftus that his name is Sarah Mary Williams. When she sees through his disguise, he quickly invents a fourth identity, George Peters. A fifth impersonation occurs in chapter 13 when he poses as the son of a boatman whose trading scow collided with the wreck of the *Walter Scott*.

Three more impersonations take place in chapter 16. Two of them occur on the long raft Huck swims to in order to hide on it and get information about Cairo. When he is discovered and asked his name he is caught so unawares that he blurts out "Charles William Allbright," an obvious lie because the men on the raft had just been listening to a ghost story about Dick Allbright and his dead son, Charles William. Asked again for his name, Huck calls himself Aleck James Hopkins. The raftsmen accept the story he builds around this name and let him off their raft to swim back to his. The eighth impersonation, the third in chapter 16, occurs a little later and after Huck had returned to the raft. Attempting to paddle to shore in a canoe in order to get information about Cairo, he is intercepted by two men in a skiff looking for runaway slaves. To keep them away from Jim, Huck successfully convinces them that he is the son of a smallpox victim on the raft.[9]

Huck invents his ninth impersonation, the character of George Jackson, when he is discovered by the Grangerfords. Then when the Duke and the Dauphin come aboard the raft in chapter 20, Huck begins the role of the orphan of a Pike County farmer, a tenth impersonation.[10] An eleventh impersonation, as the English valet of the Duke and Dauphin masquerading as the Wilks brothers, is one which he is forced to accept. He is similarly handed a twelfth role, that of "Tom Sawyer," when he arrives at the Phelps farm.

In addition to these twelve examples of assumed identities we could include a thirteenth, the role that went along with his own name, Finn. By the mere accident of birth, Huck is expected by society to emulate his father, the town drunkard and ne'er-do-well. In *Tom Sawyer* pious parents forbid their children to play with him, and in *Huckleberry Finn* the Widow Douglas undertakes not merely to raise him but to "sivilize" him, and Aunt Sally Phelps prepares to continue this effort. *Huckleberry Finn* can be read as Huck's doomed attempt to remain what he yearned to be: free, and his own person. Two obstacles barred his path. One was the unsuitable identity assigned him by birth—his father's name and reputation. The other was the set of impersonations just enumerated. The first he overcomes—

temporarily—in chapter 7 by rigging his own "murder." With the old Huck Finn dead, the way is cleared for a new Huck to develop and become free. At this point, however, the impersonations begin.

Huck's impersonations fall into two categories: those which he invents himself and those which he has to accept. The ones he makes up are all on-the-spot inventions, designed to serve some clear purpose as efficiently as possible. Although he is quick-witted and resourceful about creating impersonations, he is not always successful with them. Judith Loftus, for example, saw through both of his impersonations, and in the raft passage in chapter 16, Huck at first tries to assume the patently absurd identity of Charles William Allbright but quickly invents a more plausible one, that of Aleck James Hopkins. These occasional failures at impersonating disclose a vein of basic honesty in Huck. He does not impersonate or lie wantonly; he acts out of necessity. He is most successful when he impersonates defensively. When his impersonation involves imposition, as it does with Judith Loftus, the raftsmen, Joanna Wilks, and Levi Bell, he blunders. Furthermore, Huck does not try to protract his own impersonations any longer than is absolutely necessary. Possibly this is because while he is acting he cannot be himself; he cannot be free.

The impersonations that he has to accept have a demoralizing effect upon him. He simply cannot stand being "respectable"; he infinitely prefers freedom in his rags and sugar-hogshead to a "cramped up and smothery" environment, even though riches accompany it (18:155).[11] Ultimately, Tom Sawyer's robber band disgusts him. He scorns it as "just one of Tom Sawyer's lies. . . . It had all the marks of a Sunday school" (3:17). From the first, he is an unwilling accomplice of the Duke and the Dauphin in their attempt to swindle the Wilks girls. This impersonation is a lengthy one— Twain devotes six chapters to it—and it is obvious toward their end that Huck is on the verge of breaking under the prolonged strain. He despises the Duke and Dauphin for their imposture; he despises the townspeople for their romantic credulity, which puts them at the mercy of the impostors ("it was enough to make a body ashamed of the human race" [24:210]); he despises himself for passively fulfilling his role. When Huck temporarily escapes from the situation, reaches Jim and the raft, and shoves off into the river, he capers from pure relief. Then he discovers that the Dauphin and the Duke are overtaking them in a skiff. "So I wilted right down onto the planks, then, and give up; and it was all I could do to keep from crying" (29:260).

In Huck's own opinion, his forced impersonation with the Duke and Dauphin "was the most awful trouble and most dangersome I ever was in; and I was kinder stunned; everything was going so different from what I had allowed for" (29:257). This episode, as we have seen, demoralized Huck and drained him of spirit. He was no longer the captain of his own raft, the master of his own future. His happy companionship with Jim, who, left with the raft, had been disguised outrageously and instructed to act wild if anyone approached, had come to an end, and Jim was in imminent danger of losing what little freedom he had tasted. To appreciate the significance of this episode and the next, it must be kept in mind that Huck is jeopardizing himself for Jim's sake. Huck can shift for himself, Jim cannot. Huck is vulnerable only through Jim and then only because he has willingly undertaken the responsibility for Jim's freedom. But if the old Huck Finn could have been free without Jim, the new Huck Finn cannot. Jim provided the original motive, and remains the inspiration for Huck to formulate and abide by his own principles and to escape the bondage of his impersonations, invented or imposed.[12] As Huck and Jim had broken down social, legal, and moral barriers to become friends and equals, a free Huck had begun to evolve—practical, nonconformist, and resourceful, and a humane individual unencumbered by romantic theories. But now as Jim begins to lose his hold on freedom in the Wilks chapters, so does Huck for the first time feel that his own identity as a free individual is affected. In the next episode, the correspondence between the destiny and freedom of Huck and Jim will appear even more sharply than it does in the Wilks chapters.

Jim loses his freedom on Silas Phelps's Arkansas farm in Pikesville and so does Huck, but Huck's loss is more insidious.[13] It is accomplished by another impersonation. This impersonation, like the last, is forced upon him. In this case, moreover, as a close reading of chapters 32 and 33 will bear out, Huck is literally manipulated. The agent is predestination, disguised here as fate but which will soon emerge more recognizably as Providence.

Chapter 32 opens with a paragraph of unusual somberness.

When I got there [the Phelps farm] it was all still and Sunday-like, and hot and sunshiny—the hands was gone to the fields; and there was them kind of faint dronings of bugs and flies in the air that makes it seem so lonesome and like everybody's dead and gone; and if a breeze fans along and quivers the leaves, it makes you feel mournful, because you feel it's spirits whispering— spirits that's been dead ever so many years—and you always think they're talking about you. As a general thing it makes a body wish *he* was dead, too, and done with it all. (276)

The expectant quiet, modified only slightly by faint droning, thoughts of spirits, death, and fate—an important mood has clearly been established in this paragraph, a mood that suggests doom. Two paragraphs beyond, the mood is intensified:

I went around and clumb over the back stile by the ash-hopper, and started for the kitchen. When I got a little ways, I heard the dim hum of a spinning-wheel wailing along up and sinking along down again: and then I knowed for certain I wished I was dead—for that *is* the lonesomest sound in the whole world. (277)

What is especially significant in this paragraph is the spinning wheel, the classical Grecian symbol of fate. Its "dim hum" incorporates the "faint dronings" of the first paragraph and reinforces Huck's apprehension.

Two paragraphs farther along, in an astonishing stroke of audacious artistry, Twain repeats, transforms, and interprets the wheel image into a terrifying omen of danger. As Huck steps along, the hounds that were sleeping in the yard suddenly awaken and converge on him. "I was a kind of a hub of a wheel, as you may say—spokes made out of dogs—circle of fifteen of them packed together around me, with their necks and noses stretched up towards me, a-barking and howling, and more coming; you could see them sailing over fences and around corners, from everywheres" (277). For an instant, the reader glimpses Huck ringed by what could be hellhounds straining toward him. Then, equally suddenly, a woman appears from the kitchen and rapidly disperses the circle of dogs, half of which immediately return in a friendly mood, wagging their tails. "There ain't no harm in a hound, nohow," says Huck, unthinkingly dismissing the portent (277). In this paragraph, Twain summons and dispels in an eye-blink an alarm of danger that Huck neglects but the reader may respond to. This is the second time in the novel when Huck misinterprets and dismisses warning signs (the first—soon to be discussed—occurs in chapter 1 when Huck in his bedroom experiences a series of bad luck omens but puts them out of mind).

Having established the background against which the drama is to be played, Twain in the next paragraph allows Huck to enter the trap. "I went right along, not fixing up any particular plan, but just trusting to Providence to put the right words in my mouth when the time come; for I'd noticed that Providence always did put the right words in my mouth, if I left it alone" (277). Historically, this statement is contrary to fact. It is one of the clearest examples in the novel that show Huck to be an unreliable narrator. Twain did not make him unreliable in the sense that he deliberately lies to the reader, but in the sense that his statements are not always accurate. As much as readers like Huck and want to depend upon his observations, it must be kept in mind that he is a boy of only twelve to fourteen years of age, with minimum education, almost totally lacking both a sense of irony and of humor, and being pushed to and beyond his limit trying to manage both Jim's and his own survival. It is not surprising, therefore, that Huck occasionally overlooks, misinterprets, or forgets details which Twain intended, and attentive readers may remember, to be significant. In this case, Huck's forgetfulness about his past uniformly negative experiences with Providence is in keeping with his immaturity and his weariness at the long strain of coping with a string of emergencies.

Even before chapter 3, when Huck first conjectured that "there was two Providences, and a poor chap would stand considerable show with the widow's Providence, but if Miss Watson's got him there warn't no help for him any more" (14), it is apparent that the current of events is strangely running against him. He is always finding bad luck signs or precipitating bad luck through some inadvertent action. At the end of chapter 1, for example, after listening to a series of ominous night sounds,

> an owl . . . who-whooing about somebody that was dead, and a whippowill
> and a dog crying about somebody that was going to die; and the wind was
> trying to whisper something to me and I couldn't make out what it was, and
> so it made the cold shivers run over me. Then . . . I heard that kind of a sound
> that a ghost makes when it wants to tell about something that's on its mind
> and can't make itself understood. (4)

Huck killed a spider that has crawled upon him, an action that he knew would bring bad luck, and braced himself for what will follow. At the stroke of midnight, he heard a familiar call, climbed out of a window, and happily found Tom Sawyer waiting for him. But Twain did not put together an elaborately constructed pattern of omens only to disprove superstition; on the contrary, the whole point of the passage is to establish that the omens were correct and that Huck had misinterpreted them: Tom Sawyer is, or will soon become, the incarnation of genuinely bad luck for Huck. The end of the novel, which repeats Huck's "finding" of Tom after a stressful situation, will make this clear.

In chapter 4 Jim's hair ball tells Huck to let Pap have his way and warns him to stay away from the water. That night Pap comes to his room. In chapter 10 a rattlesnake bites Jim—a possible consequence of Huck's having attracted bad luck by bringing back a snakeskin he had found the day before. In chapter 16 Jim attributes the bad luck of having passed Cairo in a fog to the same snakeskin.

The fog that blinds Huck and Jim to the confluence of the Ohio River is another case of coincidence. It is the only time in the novel when a fog appears, and it could not have occurred at a worse time. It destroys the reasonable hope of Huck and Jim of recognizing the junction with the Ohio (a large river), landing at Cairo, and getting Jim on a boat to Cincinnati, and it dooms the pair to drifting south toward New Orleans, the slave center of the country. Again using the common literary device of coincidence, Twain cloaks his own belief that nothing occurs by coincidence, chance, or accident; everything, properly understood, shows the hand of an unsympathizing God in it.

Huck seems marked out for bad luck, and he only avoids it when Jim advises him or when he leaves nothing to chance: "I got to thinking that if I could fix up some way to keep Pap and the widow from trying to follow me, it would be a certainer thing than trusting to luck to get far enough off before they missed me; you see, all kinds of things might happen" (28).

If Huck's luck is bad, he has even less occasion to think well of Providence, which in his experience is always malign.[14] Early in chapter 24, for example, when the King announces that he is going to a nearby village "without any plan, but just trust Providence to lead him the profitable way," Huck's reaction, "meaning the devil, I reckon," is surprisingly pointed. Later, as the Duke and Dauphin gloat over the buried gold which the duped Mary Jane Wilks had told them how to find, the Dauphin says, "Thish-yer comes of trust'n to Providence. It's the best way, in the long run. I've tried 'em all, and ther' ain't no better way" (25:214). Here, Providence would seem to dictate that the Wilks girls and some of their friends were going to lose their money to a pair of impostors; moreover, it also seems to favor Jim's return to slavery. Just before he reaches the Phelps farm, Huck is struck with an attack of conscience: "it hit me all of a sudden that here was the plain hand of Providence slapping me in the face and letting me know my wickedness was being watched all the time from up there in heaven, whilst I was stealing a poor old woman's nigger that hadn't ever done me no harm" (31:268–269).

The topic of conscience and its relationship to Providence leads us to a critical, deep, and controversial aspect of Twain's countertheology. Although his own description of *Huckleberry Finn* as "a book of mine where a sound heart & a deformed conscience come into collision & conscience suffers defeat" has enjoyed wide currency and has been frequently used as an element of interpretation of both the novel and Twain's own philosophy, carefully considered it is of very little value in either function. Its origin is a penciled comment Twain made in 1895—eleven years after the novel was first published—in a copy of *Huckleberry Finn* that he used for his public lectures.[15]

While Twain's statement represents a condensation of his openly professed attitude in 1895, it is ultimately unreliable as an indicator of the source and nature of conscience in the novel. Twain's 1876 short story "The Facts Concerning the Recent Carnival of Crime in Connecticut" establishes that when he wrote both that story and *Huckleberry Finn*, he believed—in accordance with Calvinism—that conscience is innate. The 1895 comment, moreover, is less understandable than it appears. Both conscience and "heart" are innate qualities, and because the issue is not nomenclature but the source of morality, and the crux of the matter is whether morality is innate or assimilated from outside, the distinction between them is problematical. Furthermore, inasmuch as the adjectives used in the 1895 statement appear to be essential, and the statement would make virtually equal sense if recast to read that a sound conscience was better than a deformed heart, Twain seems to have set forth a tautological distinction without any difference. Therefore, both from the standpoint of Twain's attempt, nineteen years after writing that part of the novel and eleven years after publishing the book, to retrofit a latter-day reading on the text, and from the statement's radical confusion, it is almost useless for purposes of interpretation.

Finally, as the first chapter of this book explains Twain's attitude toward conscience, Twain did not regard conscience as either basically benevolent or dependable.[16] Its main function was to make its possessor uncomfortable, and it never acts in opposition to an individual's predestination. In this instance, conscience, in league with Providence, is working to persuade Huck to surrender Jim. No comfort would come to him if he followed either the promptings of conscience or his decision to oppose them. As is stated explicitly in "Carnival of Crime," the function of conscience is not to serve as a moral guide but simply to make its possessor uncomfortable, whatever course of action is chosen. Huck is in a lose-lose situation; hence, the despair of his conclusion.

In both of the preceding incidents—the King's intention to dupe the Wilks girls and Huck's struggle with conscience on the raft—Huck acts in opposition to Providence and saves the victims. Thus it is apparent throughout the book that despite the operation of forces which seem intended to oppress other innocent people as well as himself, Huck is able to check these forces by maintaining his unique combination of nonconformity, his awareness of what is happening to and around him, and above all his self-reliance. As we have seen, however, his association with the Duke and Dauphin has tried him to the limit. His impersonation as an orphan from Pike County is successful in protecting him from the two, but it is no longer efficacious for Jim once Pikesville is reached. Shaken and desperate when he arrives at the Phelps farm, Huck is no longer thinking clearly. His sudden decision to throw himself on the mercy of Providence, a decision that clearly contradicts his previous experience and opinion, is a sign of his confusion. More important, it is a sign of his regression to that earlier Huck Finn whose "murder" he had so carefully managed: the naïve, credulous Huck who tried the widow's respectability, Tom's romanticism, and Miss Watson's Providence. The Huck striving for freedom had rejected all of them. Respectability, romanticism, Providence—in *Huckleberry Finn* they are all related. All three delude their victims, blind them to their own situations and to the true state of affairs around themselves, and ultimately lead them to error, sorrow, or untimely death. As Huck, therefore, regresses to an earlier identity, he begins to give up his uniqueness—and his freedom. When he trusts himself to Providence, he puts himself into the power of a force which means him no good.[17]

This is immediately apparent in the sequence of subsequent events. As soon as Aunt Sally Phelps spots him, she asks, "It's you, at last—*ain't* it?" It is a disarming question, and Huck admits, "I out with a 'Yes'm,' *before*

I thought" (32:277, emphasis added). Huck easily invents answers to her questions until she asks about his family.

> Well, I see I was up a stump—and up it good. Providence had stood by me this fur, all right, but I was hard and tight aground, now. I see it warn't a bit of use to try to go ahead—I'd got to throw up my hand. So I says to myself, here's another place where I got to resk the truth. I opened my mouth to begin; but she grabbed me and hustled me in behind the bed. (280)

If we accept the supposition that Twain intended for Providence to be more than a mere word in his book, then it appears that Providence brought Huck to the Phelps family and engaged him in a conversation which delayed his establishing an identity for himself. At the very moment when he decided to set matters straight, he is again forestalled. The next step in the process occurs when Aunt Sally supplies Huck with an identity when she announces to her husband, "It's *Tom Sawyer!*" (282).

Inasmuch as no two characters are farther apart in this novel than Tom Sawyer and the new Huckleberry Finn, the danger of Huck's entering upon this new impersonation is evident. James M. Cox states the case exactly when he says: "There is bitter irony in Huck's assumption of Tom's name because the values of Tom Sawyer are so antithetical to the values of Huck Finn; in the final analysis, the two boys cannot exist in the same world" ("Remarks" 401). Cox's observation has long since been generally accepted. Tom Sawyer is vivacious, imaginative, mischievous. Huck is practical, unimaginative, humorless, the only and mostly abandoned child of an alcoholic, ignorant, bigoted, and abusive father. Tom is the willing disciple of his reading of a diet of romantic novels and is eager to live in the world of his reading, whereas Huck is only marginally literate and finds close to incomprehensible what attraction anyone would find in unreal worlds depicted in works of fiction. As Pascal Covici Jr. points out, Tom is the creature of society, tied to it by many bonds (*Mark Twain's Humor* 172–173). Huck is a social pariah and exists on the margins of society, surviving by his own resourcefulness. Although the two boys get along as friends, in an adult frame of reference they are mutually exclusive, antitheses of each other.

If Huck *has* to impersonate Tom Sawyer, his own achieved personality will be destroyed. Huck's joyful exclamation at learning that he was believed to be Tom Sawyer, "it was like being born again, I was so glad to find out who I was" (32:282), is rich in irony. In a sense, it is literally true.

The Huck Finn who was to all intents and purposes "murdered" back in chapter 7 has indeed been reborn. The free Huck is dying, however; he will not survive this next impersonation.

The irony of the phrase "born again" extends beyond the narrative to the countertheological level. Being born again, as Twain saw it, always involves surrendering or losing one's distinctive character and personality and having it replaced—temporarily or permanently—by an impersonation of virtue, but it does not mean that one will be saved. Orthodox Calvinism itself guards against false "conversions" (such as the one Huck's father claims to have in chapter 5) by its doctrines of unconditional elections of the saved to their destinies and the perseverance of the saints in life paths that justify their election. In other words, God's predestination for individual souls is not affected by conversions that are either staged or are the products of wishful thinking; those who are saved will live lives that are ultimately acceptable to God, and those who are damned will not be redeemed by a life that merely looks virtuous. In Huck's case, being born again as Tom Sawyer is, so far from being a blessing, a punishment that puts an end to his independence and his resourceful dedication to achieving freedom for Jim and himself. Furthermore, as the last chapter makes clear, Huck does not persevere in his born-again status but reverts to his condition at the beginning of the novel. Everything that he had learned, resolved, and achieved will be wiped out.

Huck does not yet consider this imminent impersonation of Tom Sawyer to be forced. He credulously believes he will be free, at least, to determine what he as Tom will do. However, this happy state of mind comes to an abrupt end just a few lines farther on, in chapter 33, when Huck unexpectedly encounters Tom Sawyer himself on the road to town.

At least as important as what happens in this chapter is the way it happens. Every escape route is swiftly and smoothly blocked off. When Huck informs Tom of his determination to steal Jim out of slavery, Tom says "What! Why Jim is—" The word that fits the space, of course, is "free," but Tom never utters it. Instead, "providentially," he pauses. Huck uses the pause to ask Tom not to stand in the way. Being asked to cooperate apparently gives Tom an idea how to gratify his romantic appetite for adventure: to seem to take on the role of a "nigger-stealer" while actually remaining within the limits of respectability. Covici describes the situation perfectly when he points out that anyone who thinks that Tom Sawyer would actually consent to help an escaped slave has succumbed to Twain's hoax (*Mark Twain's Humor* 176). For Tom, the whole escapade is only a romantic and highly entertaining adventure. In contrast, Huck commits himself, soul as well as body, to freeing Jim. In chapter 31 occurs one of the novel's most dramatic moments, where Huck tremblingly makes the momentous decision to help Jim instead of turning him in. He believed he had "got to decide, forever, between two things." He decides: "All right, then, I'll go to hell," and tore up the letter he had written to turn Jim in (270–271).

Modern readers tend to cheer Huck at this point, but if they do so they underestimate the gravity of Huck's decision from his point of view. Huck, having absorbed some of the teachings of St. Petersburg's frontier Calvinism, really believed in hell, and believed he had damned himself to it forever by his choice. His decision, therefore, is more powerfully an expression of despair than of resolution. He has abandoned hope for himself—in itself an unforgivable sin against God because it implies that it is beyond the power of God to help him. In microcosm, this is the essence of the lose-lose choice that Twain conceived was posed by the biblical God. Resistance means eternal punishment in hell, but obedience to this God means surrendering freedom and suppressing one's humanity.

When Tom offers to help Huck steal Jim, he not only astonishes Huck, but he heads off any intention Huck might have had for going ahead on his own with the escape, and he also takes over the plot. Huck surrenders control of the situation with his assent; he also gives up the incentive to think for himself. At this point, however, there is still a chance that should Huck tire of the romantic antics that had characterized Tom's robber gang adventures and will characterize the escape adventure, he might pull out of the agreement. But this loophole is sealed off when Tom separately appears at the Phelps farm, his wagon "spinning" up the road (the spinning wheels of the wagon recall the spinning wheel of fate in the previous chapter), and begins an impersonation of his brother Sid. The trap is now closed upon Huck. He is bound to the farm because Jim is imprisoned there. He will not try to free Jim by himself because he believes that Tom will help him. He has turned over the initiative for action to Tom and rapidly regresses to his St. Petersburg self, which regarded Tom as a leader and generally superior individual. He is forced to impersonate Tom Sawyer to the hilt, for Tom is now there to ride herd on him and prevent any possible break for freedom, and Huck has no defense against Tom, as he did against the Duke and Dauphin with his protective impersonation of a Pike County orphan. Under Tom's direction and oversight, Jim is made to perform a series of arbitrary and ridiculous tasks all inspired by Tom's reading of romantic "authorities" while Huck is sidelined to look on helplessly and assent to them as necessary because they are proposed by Tom, the leader he looks up to. The acts demean Jim and reaccustom him to following orders like a slave, and bring Huck and Jim's heroic bid for freedom to an adolescent conclusion, which disappoints Marx and practically any one else who reads that part of the novel literally.

The ending of the book, however, is neither unsuccessful nor flawed nor flat—all adjectives applied to it by Twain admirers who otherwise approve the book. Victor Doyno has persuasively argued, based on acute analyses of Twain's processes of composition and on literary history, that the evasion chapters can be read as a sharp attack on the convict-lease system then spreading throughout the South and especially notorious in Arkansas, which perverted the justice system into a means to effectively reduce the freedmen of the post–Civil War years into free men of color (f.m.c.) or worse, into slaves (*Writing "Huck Finn"* 229–239).[18]

While Doyno's reading of the novel's ending rescues it from the charge that it is a reversion to children's literature, it does not provide a solution to the objection that there is no unifying theme to the book. But there remains an interpretation that overcomes both objections: the one of a denial of freedom. In this reading the ending does not burlesque the book's plot or themes but perfects them. The concluding episode is in keeping with Twain's structural pattern of recurrent impersonations and can best be described as deliberately grotesque. It is a special characteristic of the pattern of Huck's impersonations that they grow increasingly dangerous for him to maintain. In his impersonation as the valet of the imposturing Duke and Dauphin, his personal safety was endangered. Now, in this last impersonation, his soul is at stake.

As a lackey of the arch-romantic Tom, whose behavior becomes insane rather than funny as he heaps impersonations upon himself and drives his overawed and helpless followers to extremes of absurdity, Huck is steadily debased and forced to relinquish the maturity, humanity, and independent personality he had begun to achieve in his life with Jim upon the river. He protests less and less and resigns himself to do whatever Tom says. By the end of the book, when he resolves to light out for the Territory so that Aunt

Sally cannot "sivilize" him, he has been beaten back all the way to where he had been at the beginning of the book, stripped of the freedom and manliness he had achieved, and is once again the Huck Finn of yore, son of the town drunkard and ne'er-do-well. In place of the freedom of mind he had once owned and exercised, he is reduced to believing in a childish fantasy. The very idea of finding freedom somewhere out in the West is in itself a romantic idea, as Twain knew very well from firsthand experience.[19] The tragedy of the conclusion at last emerges clearly: in his forced impersonation of Tom Sawyer, Huck essentially loses his soul. Before he could become a man, he has been "born again" as a child.

But, it can be argued, Jim became free. This point, in fact, is central to Marx's objection to the conclusion. He finds that the family reunion and the proclaiming of Jim's freedom create a mood of "unclouded success," a mood which he thinks symptomatic of Twain's failure of nerve. It is true that Jim was freed, but Jim did not become *free*. If we assume that Huck's St. Petersburg was Hannibal of the 1840s or 1850s, then legally speaking, Jim as a manumitted slave had become only a free man of color, a very different thing from a free man. It is true, in a manner of speaking, that Jim owned himself, as he proudly noted at the end of chapter 8 ("I owns mysef, en I's wuth eight hund'd dollars"), but even as a free man of color he did not own his wife and two children.[20] They were still slaves; they would have to be bought, and Miss Watson was not their owner. In chapter 16, speculating on what he would do when he got to a free state, Jim said that he would save up enough money until he could buy his wife. They then "would both work to buy the two children, and if their master wouldn't sell them, they'd get an Ab'litionist to go and steal them" (124). There would have been no difference in alternatives to Jim as an escaped slave or as a free man of color. If their master refused to sell them, Jim would have no recourse but to try to have them stolen. Though a free man of color, moreover, Jim's very marriage would not have been recognized by law, and his wife's master would have been legally able to "marry" her to another black male, sell her, or both.[21] In any case, Jim would not be free in the political sense that he would be equal to the whites, with the right to vote and hold public office, and, as Henry Farnam summarizes the situation, even Jim's social and economic activities would have been severely limited by the laws of Missouri.

> Particularly prominent were laws relating to the immigration of free Negroes; laws prohibiting meetings and association with slaves without the consent of

the owner; laws limiting the liquor trade among them [free Negroes], either by prohibiting the sale of liquor to them, or by prohibiting them from selling liquor; and finally laws creating such disabilities as to put them almost on a level with slaves in respect to the criminal law or other matters. . . . Free Negroes residing in Missouri had to procure a license to remain in the State, and in 1847 they were required to give a bond on going from one county to another. In 1857, those going into a free State or territory, and returning, were subject to a fine of not less than $500, or imprisonment for one year, or both. (200, 202)[22]

Jim's freedom, in other words, would consist mainly of his right to return to St. Petersburg and work like a slave at a severely restricted number of jobs to earn at a pitiful daily wage the staggering sum he needed to buy his wife and children—*if* their master would consent to sell them. Jim's "freedom," then, corresponded to Huck's—both are more fictitious than real.[23] As a free man of color Jim would only be impersonating a free man. There is a profound irony, therefore, in Tom's statement: "They hain't no right to shut him up! Shove!—and don't you lose a minute. Turn him loose! he ain't no slave; he's as free as any cretur that walks this earth!" (42:356). This is one of the most important passages in the novel, but in light of the foregoing information its absurdity, while subtle, is nonetheless undeniable.

With those words, Tom reveals at last what he had held himself back from saying in chapter 33: that Miss Watson had manumitted Jim and he was now "free." Upon this revelation, the novel can conclude "happily." But if the secret that Jim was "free" is all the surprise there is to the ending, waiting until chapter 42 to reveal it means that Tom had hoaxed Jim and Huck, (just as Jim hoaxed Huck about his father), and that Twain had hoaxed the reader with the use of the common and crude O. Henry technique of withholding essential information until the end. It is a simple trick requiring no skill at all to use, and is scarcely worthy of a great author or a masterful book.

Tom's statement, however, is not literally true. Jim is not free, but only a free man of color, a major difference, as we have seen, from being a free man. So that part of Tom's claim is not true. But in the next clause Twain states his true theme: "he's as free as any cretur that walks this earth!" In terms of the novel, that part of the statement is ironically true. Jim *is* as free as any other creature that walks this earth—but only because none are free. In Twain's view, every human being, sooner or later, is forced by family, by society, and ultimately by predestination to impersonate a role and to become the prisoner of that role. Life, as Twain depicts it, is a great drama made up of lesser dramas. It has sound and fury, but it is without significance for the poor players, who lack freedom to exercise any choice in the play of life, which has already been written. When *Huckleberry Finn* ends, Tom is to return to respectable society, Jim to his family in St. Petersburg and the illusion of freedom, and Huck to his pursuit of freedom—avowedly in the Territory. These are three dreams. Their destinies have forced them into final impersonations and final impressions of freedom. Tragically, the characters do not even sense that they are impersonating, let alone how they got that way.

As a Southerner who grew up in Missouri, a slave state, Twain had firsthand knowledge of the condition of free men of color. The very next book he attempted, "Huck Finn and Tom Sawyer among the Indians" (1884), was never completed, but it shows explicitly that he knew of the precarious status of the free men of color and that Huck's ambition to "light out for the Territory" was a romantic dream, for life in the territories was dangerous and not likely a place where a boy like Huck could survive, let alone become free.

Strange as it may seem, though legal slavery is an issue in the novel, it probably played only a small part among Twain's reasons for writing the middle and concluding sections of *Huckleberry Finn*. In 1884–1885, when the book was published, slavery had been illegal since 1865, when the Thirteenth Amendment to the Constitution was ratified. It was a dead issue, and good writers do not waste ammunition on dead targets. A much stronger reason for Twain's writing the novel was that he saw that with the end of Reconstruction, the South had begun to put Jim Crow laws into place, and that freedmen were consequently being "legally" deprived of their freedom and reduced if not back to slavery, to something like f.m.c. status.

Twain was not the only Southern writer who saw what was happening. In 1880 George Washington Cable, a Confederate veteran who had come to detest slavery, wrote *The Grandissimes*, a novel about two sons of the same white father, one the son of a white mother and the other, dark complected, the son of a slave woman. To protect his dark son, the father made him an f.m.c. The white son went on to marry well and live a good life; the free man of color encountered only frustration and tragedy. Cable intended his novel as an allegorical exposé of what was happening to the freedmen as a result of the "New South's" Jim Crowism. The South understood Cable's attack and shunned him. Cable counterattacked in plain prose, and then eventually had to leave the South.

In the November 1884 issue of the *Century* magazine, Joel Chandler Harris published "Free Joe and the Rest of the World," a beautiful and poignant short story about a free man of color who had none of the advantages of such legal freedom as his status purportedly conferred, and none of the protection slaves received from their masters. The story was largely regarded as a sentimental tale of the pre–Civil War days, but Harris, who two years earlier in a review had defended Cable's *The Grandissimes*, also meant his tale as an allegorical attack on the de facto reduction of freedmen to f.m.c. status that was taking place in the post–Civil War South. In December the same *Century* published the first of three installments of *Huckleberry Finn*. And in January 1885 the *Century* printed "The Freedman's Case in Equity," a stinging indictment by Cable of the South.[24]

Although Twain resolved to join Cable and Harris in their criticisms, it is most probable that Cable's ostracism persuaded Twain to be circumspect, a tactic he had used skillfully in *Roughing It* (1872). Accordingly, *Huckleberry Finn*'s evasion chapters, though seemingly a burlesque of romantic evasion narratives, were written at one level to be, like the works of Cable and Harris, allegorical attacks on the resuppression of the South's blacks. It is no coincidence that the common motif that binds *The Grandissimes*, "Free Joe," and *Huckleberry Finn* together is that of the f.m.c. Both Harris and Twain recognized Cable's genius in seizing upon it as the perfect symbol of empty freedom, the role without the reality. Cable later considered himself the godfather of *A Connecticut Yankee in King Arthur's Court* (1889); with justice he could have added *Huckleberry Finn* as well.

Thus the three most important authors of the South at the time all recognized the tragedy in the making that was unfolding in the South, and all attacked it. Cable's attack was the most forthright, and he suffered for it as a consequence. Twain risked the same reaction that Cable had encountered and for the same reason; in the 1880s a large part of the reading public still remembered the status of the free man of color and how hollow it had been, and the South was sensitive to being accused of a de facto revival of it. Twain took risks, but he was not reckless. Twain's attack was potentially more devastating than Cable's and Harris's, but much more subtle. There is no defter example in all of Twain's writings of his distinctive technique of daring exposure by taking a controversial stand but concealing his motives by hiding them in plain sight. He disguised his intention by attacking the target without naming it, and he made himself appear to be innocent of any ulterior purpose by the consummate artistry of his irony and by disguising the novel as a work of romanticism with a happy ending.

While Doyno's detailed argument about the relevance of the evasion chapters to the convict-lease system supports our contention that Twain used the novel—and especially the evasion chapters—to attack the process of reenslavement that was taking place in the South after the Civil War, we go further in maintaining that Twain objected not only to black slavery but to any slavery in any form. In *Roughing It* he had exposed how white Americans had delivered themselves to something like f.m.c. status in the futile quest to earn their bread without the sweat of their brow, and how prospectors had as much as sentenced themselves to hard labor, a solitary and wandering existence, and cruel living conditions in the illusion that they might soon strike it rich.

In a chapter in *A Connecticut Yankee* ironically titled "Freemen!" as Hank Morgan observes a group of "ragged poor creatures" who had been assembled by the local lord to do menial work repairing a road, he remarks, "By a sarcasm of law and phrase they were freemen" (13:109). Here the f.m.c.-type workers were technically free white Englishmen, yet their freedom was merely nominal. Twain's hatred of slavery was as boundless as it was intense. He did not restrict himself to race, nationality, class, or gender. A slave was a slave, no matter what softer name was given slavery, and no matter whether the slave owner was a lord, a plantation owner, a business owner, society, or God. As Twain saw it, God was the ultimate slave owner, and he ruthlessly exercised absolute control over his subjects. In *Huckleberry Finn*, as we have seen, Twain implies that God insinuates impersonation to deceive humans, white as well as black, rich as well as poor, as to their true status, to think themselves better off than they really are and not to question closely how their lives are manipulated to serve their slave owner master's purposes, and his alone. The evasion chapters only sugarcoat the hard reality. Despite all their adventures and efforts, from the time they left St. Petersburg Huck and Jim made little real progress toward freedom. The main difference at the end is that their illusions are deeper; they have no idea how hollow their "victory" is and how much more solidly they have been reinstated in their status ante quo.

Twain himself does not appear to be without compassion for his protagonists, and it may be that this quality is responsible for a general tendency to underestimate the novel's complexity and subtlety. In reading it as a structural and thematic whole, it is still possible not to go far enough with the reading and so overlook Twain's characteristic tactic of misleading his audience. In his insightful study of Twain's humor, Covici was among the first to discover that *Huckleberry Finn* is organized around a pattern of hoaxes Twain plays upon the reader. He finds, for example, that Twain conditions the reader to dislike romantic ideals, and hoaxes the reader "into believing that Tom Sawyer is going to triumph over the romance pattern," go against his own character, free Jim, and effect "a significant rupture with society" (*Mark Twain's Humor* 176).[25] Covici makes inescapable the conclusion that readers who nourished this hope have deluded themselves with a romantic daydream. He finds the concluding chapters of the novel to be a well-organized and deliberate series of hoaxes, most of which are perpetrated by Tom and Huck against other characters in the book. In Covici's view, the main one, however, is aimed by Twain "at the reader's opinion of himself when the author deliberately withholds and then reveals his—and Tom's—mendacity in fooling the reader, along with Huck, into thinking that Tom Sawyer will help to free a slave" (*Mark Twain's Humor* 160–161). This powerful insight is liberating and opens the way for our own.

Applying Covici's insight to other works in Twain's canon, it is possible to see that *Huckleberry Finn* is one in a long list of Twain works that trick the audience with a central as well as subordinate hoaxes. That he uses hoaxes in no way implies that he is not advancing a serious theme. On the contrary, once discovered, his hoaxes, by their intrinsic nature of falsifying reality, intensify the central and serious thrust of his works: the advancement of his countertheology. In *Huckleberry Finn*, in fact, Twain extends himself to guide his readers. Before any can be tricked, they must first disregard the series of warning hints that Twain places in the way. To believe that Tom will suddenly reform at the end, for example, one must first ignore the whole pattern of Tom's character and actions. Similarly, Huck's uniformly unpleasant experiences with luck, Providence, or fate—all manifestations of the same inscrutable, sinister predestinating force—constitute a more than adequate reason to doubt that Huck will be benefited when he trusts himself to Providence. As a consequence, the appearance of any sign of romanticism ought to wave a red flag, for all such signs end in difficulty or danger.

Finally and most tellingly—and here we return to our opening description of the structure of the novel—in order to conclude that the novel ends happily, it is necessary to overlook the extreme improbability of a successful outcome to Huck and Jim's attempt to find freedom. This interpretation, therefore, takes heed of all these formidable reasons that combine to make a highly convincing argument *against* the novel's affirmation of freedom, and simply goes with the abundant and unforced pattern of excellent reasons in the text, in biography, and in literary history that lead to the conclusion that the novel *denies* the possibility of human freedom. Once the central hoax is discovered and thought through, thematic difficulties about the novel's consistency recede, and the book's inherent unity and power become manifest.

Like other famous low-keyed satires in our literary tradition—*Gulliver's Travels* (1726), for example—*Huckleberry Finn* can have the effect of startling readers into a sudden realization that the author has been aiming at them and their own weaknesses all along. Despite his fame, Mark Twain has been underestimated, even by many of his admirers and advocates. Criticism should not take him to task for a "failure of nerve" in *Huckleberry Finn* or for a lapse in moral vision. The novel is a consummate work of art: understatedly subtle, masterfully ironic, intricate in design, and unexpectedly daring, powerful, and poignant. The countertheology which is at its core functions like a masked foil: concealed but deadly. In its refined and original use of the hoax, none can compare to it, except other of his own books. Using all that he had thought and learned in his life and previous literary career, Twain in *Huckleberry Finn* achieves an artistic highpoint in his lifelong pattern of devising warnings to all thoughtful readers to be aware of how shockingly far they are from any condition deserving the name of freedom.

A Connecticut Yankee
in King Arthur's Court

The thing that hath been, it is that which shall be, and that which is done
is that which shall be done, and there is no new thing under the sun.
—Ecclesiastes 1:9

Where dissatisfaction with *Adventures of Huckleberry Finn* (1885) has
largely centered on the "evasion" chapters, *A Connecticut Yankee in King
Arthur's Court* (1889) is typically criticized as a disjunctive novel in which
major sections are considered to be divided between fiction and autobiography, humor and tragedy, historical parody and social criticism. The most
obvious evidences of these supposed disjunctions have been the contrasts
between the abundantly humorous early chapters and the undeniably bleak
conclusion, as well as Twain's seeming alternating uses of the protagonist
Hank Morgan as a fictitious character and as an alter-ego or autobiographical spokesman for his own views. *A Connecticut Yankee* has consequently
been treated as another fatally flawed novel by Twain, one containing some
brilliant and gripping episodes and memorable passages, but on the whole
a work that fails to measure up even to *Huckleberry Finn*. But these views
sell it short. *A Connecticut Yankee* is in fact an extraordinary novel with a
deeper organizing design than has been noticed, and is close if not actually
equal to *Huckleberry Finn* in depth, power, and artistry. Like the other
works we have already discussed, *A Connecticut Yankee* has at its heart
Twain's countertheology disguised by hoaxes to which everything else relates, but it does not merely repeat his "gospel" in a different setting. By
1889 Twain's beliefs had developed beyond what they had been in *Huckleberry Finn*, for in *A Connecticut Yankee* Twain advances his themes and
their implications to starker depths.

Twain's skill with the technique of narrative indirection had also grown by this point in his career. He recurs notably in *A Connecticut Yankee* to the method he adapted from Artemus Ward for use in *Roughing It* (1872), of creating a surface appearance of seemingly incongruous segments while all the while subtly underlaying the whole with a common theme. The well-known episode involving Hank's discussion of economics late in *A Connecticut Yankee*, for instance, is evidence of both the novel's profound artistry and its thematic consistency centering around its use of the hoax. Chapters 31 to 34 focus on the subject of sixth-century political economy and constitute an excellent example of how Twain could construct a narrative in layers that seemingly tell different stories and move in various directions yet share a unifying underlying theme. From very different perspectives than the one we use, Henry Nash Smith devoted an entire book to the political and economic theories which appear in it, and Alan Gribben recognized the novel as "the *locus classicus*" for Twain's use of economic imagery.[1] Other studies have pursued particular sources in Twain's reading or experience for the historical or biographical origin of various political and economic views which Hank—or Twain—advocates.[2] Here scholarship comes close to regarding Hank as an autobiographical surrogate for Twain's own views. These studies have brought to light valuable information about Clemens's interests and activities, but, for the most part, they have left undiscovered that distinctive feature of Twain's thinking which enabled him to assimilate the material turned up by these studies yet subordinate it artistically to his creative purposes. The operative assumptions used by most interpreters of *A Connecticut Yankee* are that the novel was intended to favor progress, and that Hank Morgan is the hero who represents Twain's values.

But it is the holocaust of the Battle of the Sand-Belt that is fatal to all attempts to interpret the novel as an artistically successful presentation of the progressive ideas about politics and economics that occur in the earlier parts. As a consequence, Smith, for example, explains the apparent disunity of *A Connecticut Yankee* by his concluding observation that although Twain began the novel with the intention of promoting the progressive ideals of American industrial democracy, in the course of his writing he "lost his faith in the value system of that society. Henceforth he worked as a writer in a kind of spiritual vacuum" (*Fable of Progress* 107). Stanley Brodwin argues a complicated interpretation of the novel as reflecting a "'law' of eternal tension between 'good' and 'evil' impulses" ("Wandering" 69) that depends on a two-God theory. Despite the extensive knowledge of Clemens the biographical individual who is behind these two interpretations, they apply imperfectly to Twain the author and fail to do justice to the novel.

Much confusion has been caused by misplaced confidence in the reliability of Hank. Whereas early critics typically viewed Hank either as the hero of the novel or as Twain's mouthpiece, or as both, a few later critics came to recognize Hank as an unreliable narrator, one who does not really understand what is happening, although he is certain that he does.[3] Preferring the novel's final text over Twain's occasional statements of intention in letters and in journal entries, these latter critics, in presenting the case that Hank does not represent Twain, open the way to approach the novel from the perspective that it denies a belief in progress. This insight in turn is compatible with the interpretation that the novel is a hoax—but a serious one. As is the case with *Huckleberry Finn* and Twain's other previous novels, the problem is less with the novel than the approaches to it. *Huckleberry Finn* also appears flawed if one insists that the novel affirms freedom. As we have demonstrated above, when it is instead recognized that it embodies a hoax that *denies* freedom, then the novel can be seen as succeeding. Much the same rationale applies to *A Connecticut Yankee*. Like *Huckleberry Finn*, it, too, embodies a central hoax that denies freedom. Chapters 31 to 34 provide powerful support for this position. Indeed, unless the hoax they contain is recognized and its thematic implications are appreciated, these chapters are likely to be read as relatively unimportant.

In this group of chapters Hank undertakes to teach the villagers of the hamlet of Abblasoure the principle of political economy—as he understands it. He states the principle succinctly: "It isn't what sum you get, it's how much you can buy with it that's the important thing" (31:303).[4] The idea is so simple and fundamental as to seem self-evident. But his misplaced confidence that he understands the basic principle of economics exposes Hank's fatal limitations. One component of the hoax is revealed only when it is understood why Hank does not and cannot represent Twain. Hank's confidence that he can explain the fundamentals of political economy to the men of the hamlet is almost as misplaced as his brash assumption, repeated throughout the novel, that he is so wise and so superior that there is almost nothing that he can learn from sixth-century England.

The pride that blinds Hank is not malicious, but it blinds him neverthe-less. Chapter 31 opens significantly with Hank's ruminations about caste. He observes with democratic scorn how humble each man in the kingdom is toward those above him and how disdainful to those beneath. Typi-cally, Hank's reflections do not include himself or recall his resentment, repeated several times in the novel, that he is not "reverenced," that de-spite his outstanding "natural gifts" he is eclipsed by the king, who has not the substance of power—like Hank—but only the shadow (8:63). These contradictory attitudes lead Hank to the misanthropic thought that "there are times when one would like to hang the whole human race and finish the farce" (31:302). Hank, presumably regarding himself more naturally elevated than the rest of the race, thinks as one of the judges and not as one of the victims.

Ironically, just as this notion is expressed, Hank and the king encounter a mob of panicked children who have hanged one of their friends while playing at "imitating their elders." Hank and the king are able to save the boy, and the incident subtly reinforces Hank's sense of being loftier than the rest of humanity. But, completely unnoticed by him, it also contradicts his previous thought. Twain therefore arranges for Hank to continue to think of himself as a kind of deity while readers are mainly attracted to Hank's humanity. This contrast is a purposeful pattern throughout the novel and a necessary part of the developing hoax. Up to this point in the novel, Hank has been allowed to enjoy an unbroken string of successes and has been kept likable. Readers have therefore been set up to side with Hank. Despite a few foibles (which only make him more human), he is a winner and has been invincible. He can be excused for having a few extravagant notions about himself; it is only "natural." While all this has been happening, how-ever, a despotic streak with hubristic overtones has also been emerging, but it is masked by the dominant appearance of Hank's positive features. In chapters 31 to 34 Twain uses the issue of political economy to overtly ex-pose Hank as the dangerous person he has quietly become, to demonstrate how limited his understanding really is, to indicate how serious hubris is and what the penalty for it is, and to turn the tide against Hank.

Another essential component of the central hoax is the mistaken as-sumption that Twain believed in progress. Hank believed wholeheart-edly in progress, but Twain did not. Biography does not present us with a simple and harmonious picture of Clemens but, rather, with a complex and seemingly contradictory one. On the one hand, we learn that Clemens enjoyed the benefits of prosperity and advances in knowledge, advocated democracy, and upheld human progress. On the other hand, he developed what Susan Harris calls a "progressive disdain for human stupidity" (*Mark Twain's Escape* 58). He became increasingly distressed over the way humankind in general, and America in particular, was mismanaging the material and commercial power it was rapidly amassing, and he was notoriously pessimistic about the human race. Both positions are biographically factual; both occurred, in fact, at the same time.

Both positions, however, are not of equal importance. Smith posits a dichotomy in Twain between his "conscious endorsement of progress" (that is, overt purposes) and his "latent" (that is, covert) values—a "revulsion of the non-human imperatives of the machine and all it stood for in the way of discipline and organization" (*Fable* 105).[5] Smith concludes, therefore, that the overt purpose and covert values cancel each other out and that *A Connecticut Yankee* is at cross-purposes with itself and thus forfeits artistic stability; but his analysis can also lead to a different conclusion: an affirmation of deeply ambivalent attitudes in Twain that permit the coexistence of an overt purpose and a different—even contradictory—set of covert values. We agree, therefore, that a hostility to technology can be discerned in *A Connecticut Yankee*, but we think that it is evidence of the deeper and more apposite set of covert values of Twain's countertheology because the cost of advancement in material progress in the novel is a corresponding loss of security and a step deeper into the hell of humankind's age-old abuse of knowledge. As Gladys Bellamy put it, "Instead of pitying man for his failure to develop his latent [that is, undeveloped reserve] capacities, Mark Twain pitied him because he possesses no latent capacities. Thus is all power of growth denied to the human race. Futility and worthlessness of man—indifference or malevolence of the cosmic powers—'It is like the sky,' he once said, 'you can't break through anywhere'" (332). Twain planted himself squarely in agreement with both the classical tradition of recognizing humanity's limitations and Calvinism's corresponding stand not only on human imperfectibility but also on its corruption. As Twain's countertheology saw it, not only would any human conception—however philanthropic in its intent—have a fatal flaw in it, but the fact that humans supervised its employment would guarantee its misuse.

In *A Connecticut Yankee* a conflict of convictions occurs between Twain's conscious endorsement of progress and his suppressed counter-theological opposition to it, but the conflict occurs in a way that adds depth and richness to the novel. The suppressed values are the ones that represent Twain's deepest and most powerful insights and feed his imagination. These suppressed but potent values co-opt his conscious purposes and subordinate them artistically to the beliefs that he held all along: life was a delusion, and humans were damned. Hank's intentions might represent that part of Twain which wanted to believe in progress, but the deeper part of the author was convinced that it could not be, and *A Connecticut Yankee* is the inevitable, remorseless, and tragic victory of that conviction.

The issue of political economy is highly appropriate to the central hoax because it is one of the key ideas to the realization of Hank's dream of a progressive republic, democratic and prosperous. Ironically, as chapters 31 to 34 reveal, it is not the importance of political economy which Hank advocates that undoes him but his limited understanding of it. In these chapters, Twain reduces Hank to being just another fallible and vulnerable mortal, ironically equal to the villagers he undemocratically patronizes as his inferiors. Simultaneously, Twain affords the reader a clearer understanding of political economy but also the ironic possibilities of hell it contains. The way the hoax operates is best observed in chronological sequence, beginning with Hank's arrival in the village.

Hank's downfall begins with an apparent whim. In retrospect it can be seen that the whim was fatal, but it is significant that when it occurs it is typical of Hank and of a piece with his whole scheme to reform and reshape all of sixth-century England. The whim is his sudden decision to confer a benefit upon Abblasoure's villagers: he will teach them about political economy. They had not asked for instruction; there was no particular need or obligation for Hank to explain anything to them. He undertook the task of instruction solely for self-gratification and self-glorification. His stated purpose in visiting Abblasoure was to "dispose of" some leisure time by inquiring about wages (31:303).[6] Typically, however, he begins his inquiry with a flamboyant gesture, asking for change for a twenty-dollar gold piece when he knew that the effect would be "the same as walking into a paltry village store in the nineteenth century and requiring the boss of it to change a two-thousand dollar bill for you all of a sudden" (31:304–305). His real intention is made evident when, immediately after becoming the object of questioning, he reflects that his questioner "*had* to respect a man of my financial strength." Afterward, Hank notes smugly, the proprietor followed him to the door and stood gazing after him "with *reverent* admiration." Next, when a villager named Marco introduces Hank to Dowley, the blacksmith, obviously a bit higher in the social hierarchy than Marco, Hank's liking for Dowley clearly reflects his own sense of hierarchy: "Dowley and I *fraternized* at once; I had had just such picked men, splendid fellows, *under* me in the Colt Arms factory" (31:305, emphases added).

Hank clearly enjoys the attention he is getting, and seeks to further impress his new acquaintances by arranging a sumptuous feast for them at Marco's house. When he selects a store for his supplies, he makes his purchases in a way "to corral the shopkeeper's respect." Hank admits that "I never care to do a thing in a quiet way; it's got to be theatrical or I don't take any interest in it" (309). It may now be seen that, without realizing it, Hank is demonstrating his principle of political economy: it isn't what sum you get; it's how much you can buy with it that's the important thing (31:303). This is being applied, however, in a slightly extended sense. What Hank is buying, or at least is trying to buy, is the reverence of the villagers. He has no taste for democratic fraternity; he wants to be looked up to—and from a great distance.

That is the point of chapter 32, "Dowley's Humiliation." To get this reverence, Hank sets a trap for Dowley, the most affluent guest at the feast. Led into thinking himself the object of admiration, Dowley condescends to inform "brother Jones"—the disguised King Arthur's alias—that the two of them are "equals—equals." Considering Arthur's aristocratic hauteur, this is a humorous and richly ironic scene, but it is immediately followed by a sardonic description from Hank that might be applied with even more appropriateness to his own efforts to establish democracy in Arthur's England: "He [Dowley] smiled around on the company with the satisfaction of a god who is doing the handsome and gracious thing and is quite well aware of it" (316).

Dowley's sense of largesse and magnanimity is shaken, however, as course after course of Hank's feast is laid on the new and richly appointed table. Hank receives his first reward when the mason mutters, "There is that about earthly pomps which doth ever move to reverence" (316). Then Hank destroys what is left of Dowley's esteem by ostentatiously letting everyone know that he paid four dollars for the feast, a stupendous sum when contrasted to Dowley's annual expenditure of just under seventy cents for expensive provisions for his family of three. At this disclosure, Dowley is humiliated, and Hank hugely enjoys appearing far superior to his rival and usurping the reverence of the villagers. He might have bought this reverence for less, but Hank craves it so badly that price is no object to him. He does not understand, however, what the chapter's title implies, that he becomes superior to Dowley not by rising above him but rather by making Dowley appear inferior.

Thus far, Hank has demonstrated the validity of his principle in its extension into social relations. He is satisfied that it applies to other men but is clearly unaware of any application to him. But there is an unexpected one. Chapter 33 begins with some of Hank's typically sour meditations on human development in an undemocratic society. As always, much of Hank's resentment derives from his own feelings of unrecognized merit. In Abblasoure, he believes, he has an opportunity of rectifying this inequity. Hence, "I had the smith's reverence, now, because I was apparently immensely prosperous and rich; I could have had his adoration if I had had some little gimcrack title of nobility" (322–323). The first part of this sentence criticizes the system for what it does to others, but the second part expresses his own resentment at being deprived of his just deserts.

But in what way is Hank being deprived? Much earlier in his career, when he first accepted the fact that he was in Arthur's England and decided to adjust to the situation, Hank was able to see himself as having an advantage. He understood that being back in the sixth century was preferable to being ahead in the twentieth.

> Look at the opportunities here for a man of knowledge, brains, pluck and enterprise to sail in and grow up with the country. The grandest field that ever was; and all my own; not a competitor nor the shadow of a competitor; not a man who wasn't a baby to me in acquirements and capacities; whereas, what would I amount to in the twentieth century? I should be foreman of a factory, that is about all; and could drag a seine down street any day and catch a hundred better men than myself. (8:63)

But by chapters 31 to 34, Hank appears to have forgotten that he was not exceptional in his own time, and he frets only that he is not sufficiently valued in Arthurian England.

It is not enough for him that he has risen in Arthur's kingdom from the status of a slave—the property of his captor—to second in power. Even reverence is not enough for him; it does not buy *adoration*, and although he does not realize it consciously, he regards himself as being somewhat more than human. "With the spirit of prophecy upon me," he says, "I could look into the future and see her [England] erect statues and monuments to her unspeakable Georges and other royal and noble clothes-horses, and leave unhonored the creators of this world—after God—Gutenberg, Watt, Arkwright, Whitney, Morse, Stephenson, Bell" (33:323). In this statement, Hank disingenuously thinks of himself, explicitly, as a prophet and, implicitly, as one of the "creators" of this world. A vestige of propriety, perhaps, causes him to credit God also—but as an afterthought. In short, Hank is verging upon hubris. Before long, God's church will shatter all his plans with its interdict, but the first step in his humbling will be a lesson in political economy.

Hank spends the first half of chapter 33 futilely trying to convince Dowley and his companions of the sense of his advanced principle of political economy: purchasing power, not the amount of wages, is the true index of prosperity. While that applies to a more sophisticated market economy, Abblasoure's economy was elementary and practical. Even so, it was governed by a basic principle that Hank did not take into account. When one looks at the situation in context, the villagers are reacting sensibly, and it is Hank who is slow. Hank's "lesson" posits a hypothetical and theoretical situation, the existence of what he believed erroneously was a free market— that of his own time and place—but in reality was a protected market. The villagers know that what in fact exists for them is a protected market which sets wages and prices. The villagers have an excellent grasp of their situation, in which money buys status. Hank, on the other hand, neither has an adequate appreciation of the existing system nor knows as much about a really free market as he thinks.

It is not a pedagogical problem that causes Hank's frustration over his failure to convince the villagers, and especially Dowley, that earning twice as much money is less important than the consideration of what the doubled wage would buy. His admission of defeat pinpoints the exact cause: his ego was hurt. "The first statesman of the age, the capablest man, the best informed man in the whole world, the loftiest uncrowned head that had moved through the clouds of any political firmament for centuries, sitting here apparently defeated in argument by an ignorant country blacksmith" (328). Shamed, "smarting," but most of all wounded in pride, Hank attributes his burning desire for revenge to "human nature" and consequently determines to humiliate Dowley by a stroke so sudden and unexpected that Dowley would not be able to tell how it happened.[7] Hank is successful in bringing this to pass, but the same thing later happens to Hank, and he is more taken aback than was Dowley. Dowley's humiliation is the balance point of the novel. From here on, Hank's fortunes sink rapidly.

The surprise attack is stunningly successful. Hank is hardly through congratulating himself when he notices that he had "overdone the thing a little" (333). In the process of defending his preference for the familiar system over Hank's theoretical "free" market system, Dowley had inadvertently admitted that he had on occasion paid higher wages than the law allowed. To humble him Hank seizes upon this slip and observes that if the harsh penalties of the system Dowley preferred were strictly observed, Dowley's life and the life of everyone else at the table who did not inform on him would be in peril. Hank intends by this sally to compel Dowley to recognize how oppressive the protection system is, but instead Dowley and the others interpret this exposure as a betrayal and a threat to their lives.

All of the ironies and all of the force that Twain builds up in the preceding three chapters come to a head in chapter 34. With lightning swiftness, a series of unexpected reactions occurs. Dowley and his friends, fearing for their lives, attack Hank and the king and call for help. Hank and the king narrowly escape, but are trapped and fight for their lives against the mob. When all seems lost, some horsemen appear, as if by deus ex machina, and drive away the peasants. Hank and Arthur are rescued, but not saved, by Earl Grip, the lord of the territory, who quickly has them handcuffed and made slaves, to be sold at auction. In answer to their protests that they are freemen, they are told that the burden of proof is on them and that the lord Earl Grip will not help them prove their case because "it would cost much time" and inconvenience him (346). Hank's adventure with political economy has come to an end without his having taught anything, learned anything, or even recognized that a lesson has been taught him. He has failed both as a teacher and a pupil.

The unrecognized lesson that had been taught is more fundamental than Hank's principle of what money would buy; it is that in a *completely* free market individuals are ultimately worth only what price they will bring. This elementary but fundamental principle of political economy was thoroughly understood by the sixth-century Englishmen Hank patronized. They were not backward; he was. Hank likewise completely misunderstood Earl Grip's motives in saving him and the king. There was no humanity involved, only economics; he and the king were simply unclaimed items with a market value.[8] "King," "Sir Boss," and other such titles, considered in terms of Hank's principle of political economy, may be politically and socially desirable, but ironically, it is only in a protected market, where favored conditions are established and enforced by law, that those titles and the status of freedom have worth.

If those qualities cannot be proven in a protected market, then the market reverts to being a free market. In a completely free and open market, titles and claims of freedom will not be recognized, in which case individuals will be worth only what a buyer is willing to pay for them in the expectation of some capacity for utility. A title is external to an individual, as is even the condition of being "free." And therefore, as there is no utility in a completely free market for titles and status, they will have no value.

The king brings seven dollars in such a market and Hank nine. Taking some satisfaction that the market confirms that he is worth more than the king, Hank still grumbles over the low price. He thinks the king should have brought at least twelve dollars and he fifteen. Thus Hank is humbled, brought down in a matter of hours from thinking of himself as "the first statesman of the age . . . the loftiest uncrowned head" to returning to his original sixth-century status as a slave and to quibbling over his market value.

The shocking and bitter lesson that Twain springs in this group of four chapters was one that was not unknown in nineteenth-century America. Melville showed his familiarity with it in *Moby-Dick* (1851) in Stubb's admonition to the black cabin-boy Pip about his market value.[9] George Washington Cable, in chapters 23 and 29 of *The Grandissimes* (1880), related how the powerful and spirited captive African prince Bras-Coupé is sold and bought solely for his capacity to do work. In an age which had known literal slavery, the phrase "wage slave" also had literal meaning, given a cruel and "free" buyers' market that purchased men for their manpower rather than their manhood. Twain used situations in many of his works wherein a man's worth would be expressed in terms of money: *Life on the Mississippi* (1883), *Huckleberry Finn*, and *The Tragedy of Pudd'nhead Wilson* (1894), to name just three. And in *Roughing It* and *The Gilded Age* (1873–1874), he described how even where people could be happy, proud, and free, the lust for riches and power drove them to enslave themselves, to set a market value upon themselves, and to spend their entire lives seeking not to remain independent but to become "worth more." In his personal life, Clemens himself was not immune from this natural madness. He would have included himself in Hank's last reflection on humanity in chapter 34, "I reckon we are all fools. Born so, no doubt" (347).

It should be startling to think that Twain literally believed that the human race was damned. Too often to discount in his personal life and in his fiction, Twain referred to the world as "hellish." When Hank and Arthur are sold at auction at the end of chapter 34, Hank reflects that in his own time and place, freemen "who could not prove that they were freemen had been sold into life-long slavery without the circumstances making any particular impression upon me; but the minute law and the auction block came into my personal experience, a thing which had been merely improper before became suddenly hellish. Well, that's the way we are made" (346). Among the "freemen" Hank was alluding to were certainly pre–Civil War free men of color, and Twain was also alluding to the black freedmen of the Reconstruction era whose rights had been bargained away by the Compromise of 1877 and who were being effectively returned, in all but a technically legal sense, to slave status.[10] His personal experience shows to Hank for the first time, however, what it means to become subject to the real laws of political economy. The word "hellish" is exact and not restricted by time, place, color, or social status.

Long before Joseph Heller's "catch-22" notion there was a theological equivalent with which Twain was familiar: the Calvinist situation of double damnation. According to it, most humans were predestined to hell, but even if they had not been, their lives would be so sinful that they would go to hell anyway. This idea is at work in *A Connecticut Yankee* and can be clearly seen in this group of four chapters. When Hank says, "that's the way we are made," he speaks more truly than he knows. The sequence of events which in four short chapters topples him from being "Sir Boss" to a slave is anything but coincidental. It is part of the plan of the whole novel, which plots the rise and fall of Hank against the default reality of slavery and the transient and illusory status of freedom. "As sure as guns" (6:47), though Hank does not realize it, his existence in sixth-century England leads inevitably and unswervingly to the Battle of the Sand-Belt and the obliteration of all that Hank thought he had "created." But even if this were not so, human nature as depicted by Twain makes it possible to see that the insatiable natural covetousness for riches, status, and power corrupts people to the point where they create their own hell on earth and lose their freedom. It was not Twain's purpose to represent sixth-century political economy as a primitive, local, and historical notion but, on the contrary, as the naked operation of an elemental, universal, and timeless law.

This can be seen when *A Connecticut Yankee* is regarded as a serious hoax. Hank was set up by his nature to believe in appearances and in the possibility of creating a utopia—a progressive republic ruled by pure principles of democracy and capitalist economics.[11] Hank, however, never understands or follows any of these principles. Being unreflective and uncritical of himself, he never considers that because he regards himself as superior to everyone else, he is not at heart a democrat. He also thinks of a free market relativistically and simplistically, as something resembling what he believed he knew in America. He cannot conceptualize an *absolutely* free market in which nothing is protected: patents, titles, reputation, freedom, or life. The Yankee is well-intentioned, but dangerous nevertheless. Henry Nash Smith says that his "economics resemble Hitler's."[12] Chadwick Hansen calls him a totalitarian and likens him to a Nazi with "a personality capable of the most callous mass slaughter and at the same time full of a vulgar and self-centered *Gemütlichkeit*" (72). Whoever believes in Hank's goodness has been hoaxed by the presence of Hank's self-advertised but small personal virtues into ignoring his major social vices.

The belief in progress, therefore, is an idea Twain uses as a hoax. Material progress is of course possible. In *A Connecticut Yankee* it is present in soap, the newspaper, the telegraph, factories, searchlights, electric fences, pistols, and Gatling guns. Twain does not deny this material progress. But *human* progress? His Calvinistic training rejected the idea. Twain's novel implies that if Hank is an example of progressive man, then God help the world because the more power that material progress puts into his hands, the more dangerous he is.

Finally, Twain treats the very idea of political economy as a hoax because by its means humans are deceived into believing they can rule themselves by some rational or scientific theory. As Twain describes it, human nature, dangerously inconsistent at best and frequently deadly, and perhaps most deadly when humankind does not understand itself, can be reined only by an external force. The theories human beings create to rule themselves are insufficient because humans do not and cannot understand all their ramifications and because even the best, democracy and a "free" market, can be perverted or caused to go out of control.[13] Under these circumstances, Twain implies, only authoritarian and strict governments can rule efficiently on Earth—and behind that despotism of earthly power stands the despotism of heaven.

This conclusion may seem to be challenged by the issue of Twain's determinism, the subject of much of the criticism focusing on *A Connecticut Yankee*. In a passage in chapter 18, Hank Morgan offers a rationale for not attempting to reason with Morgan le Fay:

> Oh, it was no use to waste sense on her. Training—training is everything; training is all there is to a person. We speak of nature; it is folly; there is no such thing as nature; what we call by that misleading name is merely heredity and training. We have no thoughts of our own, no opinions of our own; they are transmitted to us, trained into us. (162)

This is one of a number of examples in the novel where Hank speaks somewhat deterministically.[14] It has been the tendency of previous scholarship to be tempted by such examples to regard Hank as an autobiographical mouthpiece for Twain's opinions. A more promising approach, however, holds that Hank is *always* a fictional creation, and that he speaks in character even when he seems to express views we know Clemens held. Accordingly, there are several valid and satisfactory alternative ways of interpreting the passage.

One is simply to regard it as just another one of Twain's several speculations into the theory of human nature, none of which turns out to be conclusively satisfactory. In chapter 30, for example, Hank suspects that the charcoal burner in whose house he and the king slept knew who killed the baron of the manor house of Abblasoure and burned down his house, and yet joined the locals who hunted down and helped hang neighbors he knew were no more than suspects. Hank leads the man into a confession of his duplicity, and a further confession that he believed the baron got what he deserved. Just a few minutes earlier, Hank—"a man with the dream of a republic in his head" (297)—had been depressed by the charcoal burner's pusillanimity. But after the man's admission, Hank is restored to cheerfulness:

There it was, you see. A man *is* a man, at bottom. Whole ages of abuse and oppression cannot crush the manhood clear out of him. Whoever thinks it a mistake, is himself mistaken. Yes, there is plenty good enough material for a republic in the most degraded people that ever existed. . . . Yes, there was no occasion to give up my dream yet a while. (300)

This speculation, in its emphasis on innate character, contradicts the earlier one about training. It does not prove one right and the other wrong; it only proves that Hank is unreliable as a narrator not because he lies to us but because he is inconsistent. This is a repetition with variation of the technique of the "misleading past tense" that Twain employed in *Roughing It*, in which the narrator recounts an earlier impression as a conclusion even though the narrator knows that subsequent events will contradict that early conclusion. Subsequent events in *A Connecticut Yankee* will include, as a result of the interdict, the almost total desertion of Hank by his followers and the graduates of his Man-Factories, and the return in the final chapters to a dream framework.[15]

As a consequence, another approach recognizes that individual passages cannot be taken out of the context of the entire novel and used to interpret the novel merely because they relate to external biographical information; the ultimately compelling interpretation must be holistic and true to the novel in its entirety. If we do give more weight to the passage about training, then it should become quickly apparent that its drawbacks outweigh its advantages. This passage is no more central than any of Hank's other momentary speculations because little has led up to it and little if anything follows it as a consequence; those opinions are not important enough in themselves to support an interpretation of the entire novel. Even more important, all the themes, motifs, and literary stratagems based on theology that are at play in the novel; all the incidents of supernatural intervention such as "coincidences" and manipulation; and the very idea of tragedy would have to be ignored, discounted, and abandoned as irrelevant to an account of moral mechanism in operation.

Nonfiction in the form of the essay is fully appropriate and efficient to describe the operation of a mechanistic system, but fiction and tragedy create interpretive complications and generally hinder the communication of literal truth. In other words, Twain would have been working against himself most extravagantly if all he wanted to say in *A Connecticut Yankee* was that the human being is nothing more than machinery with metabolism.

By the same token, whatever the ultimate reason is for Twain's undeniable engagement with determinism, and whatever weight is ultimately assigned to it in that yet unwritten definitive biography, *What Is Man?* (1906) is just the most well worked-out of the various inconsistent autobiographical statements of creed he wrote in his lifetime. No doubt Clemens the biographical individual believed whatever he wrote when he wrote each one of them. But against Twain's experimentation with determinism stands an enormous amount of evidence even in biography but especially in his literature that supports his deep, passionate, and painful involvement with religion, and with Calvinism in particular. As was the case with young Sam Clemens, that though he was exposed to several varieties of religious experience in Hannibal, the dominant impression he was left with was that of traditional Calvinism, so might we say of Twain that though in his lifetime he engaged with determinism, the dominant impression that governed the composition of the great bulk of his fictional literature, and probably governed him as well, was the countertheology he derived from traditional Calvinism.

A Connecticut Yankee, accordingly, is a successful novel constructed around a tragic vision of universal damnation. As such it is Twain's bleakest novel and is not only a logical stage of development on the continuum from the antic humor of *Roughing It* to the gloomy bitterness of "The Great Dark" (1898), "Letters from the Earth" (1909), and other works of his late period, but it is also significantly closer to those late, dark works than to *Huckleberry Finn*, published only four years earlier. The novel's integrity is achieved redundantly and in multiple ways by various devices. Among the most important is the novel's pointed use of dreams first to establish the hoax of objective reality and to function as a subtle manifestation of Hank's illusory life, and then to gradually replace what appeared to be objective reality with the growing proposition that this world is already a form of hell.

The idea that one can be in this world and also literally in hell had been previously proposed by other authors, to be sure. As early as Marlowe's *Dr. Faustus*, for example, occurs the following exchange between Faustus and Mephistophilis:

Faust: How comes it then that thou are out of hell?
Meph: Why this is hell, nor am I out of it. (I, i 75–76)

What is striking about the presence of this idea in *A Connecticut Yankee* is that Twain, reared in Calvinism and acutely in mind of its doctrines all his life, has generalized Mephistophilis's condition to all humans. But unlike Mephistophilis, who understands his situation, none of the humans in this novel are quite conscious of the true nature of their existence. All live and struggle in a dream. Some move from one dream to another, but they function in a state of false consciousness and remain deceived about their state.[16] The novel blurs and dissolves first the distinctions beween dream and reality and then between reality and hell. At the end, when Hank Morgan in his delirium speaks of the "strange and awful dreams" that were "as real as reality," he is summing up a main point of the novel: that there is no difference between the nightmare of hell and what is thought of as reality; they are one and the same ("Final P.S. by M.T." 446).

The blurring of the distinctions between reality and dream is an important motif in Twain's writing that grew out of the lifelong importance he attached to dreams and his susceptibility to nightmares. Originally, two different kinds of dreams disturbed Twain: dreams in the night and waking dreams. The night dreams were more obviously alarming,[17] but Twain appears at an early stage in his career to have regarded the waking dreams as both more insidious and more ominous. As discussed earlier, all of the references to the waking dreams of *Roughing It* have some negative connotations. Beneath that book's humorous anecdotal level, the phenomenon of the silver fever's infectious hope of striking it rich is exposed by Twain as only a dream, a mass dream, but a mad one which wasted the lives of the miners deluded by it. And the narrator's experience in the "Eden" of Hawaii is perfectly summed up by his rueful recollection of it: "It was tranced luxury to sit in the perfumed air and forget that there was any world but these enchanted islands. It was ecstasy to dream, and dream—till you got a bite. A scorpion bite" (63:434).

Twain's antagonism to romantic daydreaming appears frequently in his middle period in forms as diverse as his diatribe against Sir Walter Scott in *Life on the Mississippi* (1883) or more subtly as his disparaging characterization of Tom Sawyer in the evasion chapters of *Huckleberry Finn*. The ground of Twain's animosity is not that such daydreaming is immature, foolish, or even unrealistic, but that it is perilous.[18] The great danger of waking dreams consists of their ability to take control of the actual lives of the persons affected and fatally mislead them.

The preoccupation with dreams in the literature of Twain's late period is well known, but the most chilling feature of this motif is its tendency to effect a tangible takeover of reality by dream. In the unfinished tale "The Great Dark," for instance, not only does a dream appear to usurp reality but reality itself is relegated to the insubstantiality of dream. A mysterious and sinister character called the Superintendent of Dreams appears to the narrator Edwards first in a service role, but soon inverts the relationship and dominates him. When commanded by Edwards to end the dream sea voyage, which has become a nightmare, he stuns Edwards with his retort: "The dream? *Are you sure it is a dream?* . . . You have spent your whole life in this ship. And this is *real* life. Your other life was the dream!" (*Which Was the Dream?* 124). Passages like this probably led even so astute a scholar as William Gibson to sum up what he considered to be the central paradox of *No. 44, The Mysterious Stranger*: "Mold your life nearer to the heart's desire; life is at best a dream and at worst a nightmare from which you cannot escape" (33). In interpreting the novel so literally from Forty-Four's final words to August, Gibson short circuits any other literary interpretation by assuming Forty-Four to be a mouthpiece for Twain's inmost views, at least in accordance with the state of conventional biography, and he thereby ignores the need to interpret those fictional words in terms of both the wider contexts of the novel and of Twain's lifelong distrust of waking dreams.

As will be seen in our next chapter, *No. 44*'s particular depiction of the blurring of dream and reality will be a new development in Twain's thought as well as a late manifestation of an entire lifetime of his brooding on the nature of dreams and their portents. Against this background of a distinctive thought pattern that affected Twain even before his writing career began and lasted until his death, *A Connecticut Yankee* can be seen as a natural link in the pattern. The novel's abundant references to dreams are purposeful and crucial parts of both its structure and its themes. It is obvious that the dream motif is the structural frame of the novel. But a close look at almost any episode in which dreams play a part reveals that dreams are even more important as content than they are as structural elements.

By the novel's end, for example, Hank Morgan dreams a final dream— that he is with his wife, Sandy, again and is telling her of some "hideous dreams" he had had of a revolution against him, of his extermination of England's chivalry, and of his flight forward into the "remote unborn age" of the nineteenth century. And that last dream was the most tortuous of them all ("Final P.S. by M.T." 447–448). Given Twain's supposed attack in the novel on the barbarities of the sixth century, one might have expected something different than Hank's total alienation from his real or, rather, his original era, and his preference for the barbarous sixth century. Instead, his apprehension is entirely directed at being separated from his adopted era, and the love he found in it. Hank cannot be looked to for help in understanding what has happened to him. Like the Ancient Mariner, he has had a strange and distressing experience and has brought back a detailed report—but he does not understand the full meaning of it. This is evident from the lack of reflection he gives to the dreams which massively dislocated his existence in the first place and more subtly shaped it thereafter.

Hank's first contradictory impressions of sixth-century England bear this out. He notices that before him was "a soft, reposeful summer landscape as lovely as a dream, and as lonesome as Sunday." This pair of contradictory impressions (reposeful but lonesome) is immediately reinforced when a young girl appears, her head adorned with "a hoop of flame-red poppies"—beautiful but suggestive of opium. "She walked indolently along, with a mind at rest, its peace reflected in her innocent face" (1:10). Again, pairs of contradictory judgments: indolence and innocence, a mind at rest (by implication in a dream state induced by drugs) but peaceful.

Later in his tale, Hank observes how a lack of thought characterized the inhabitants of this dreaming age. Of the knights of the Round Table he notices that "there did not seem to be brains enough in the entire nursery, so to speak, to bait a fish-hook with, but you didn't seem to mind that, after a little, because you soon saw that brains were not needed in a society like that, and indeed would have marred it, hindered it, spoiled its symmetry—perhaps rendered its existence impossible" (3:23). Once again, a contradictory judgment: a brainless society but an attractive one in which brains would have been a blemish. And although the "child-like improvidence of this age and people" (13:106–107) prevented the development of civilization—as Hank knew it—on the other hand, it had a symmetry and a charm that Hank increasingly grew to prefer to his own age. Because these contradictions escape his consideration, or even his notice, Hank is governed by false consciousness and becomes absorbed in developing his schemes to materialize and modernize England. He admits that they are dreams but never suspects that they are just as illusionary as Arthur's dream of a grand invasion of Gaul (31:310) and the dreams of everyone else, whom Hank loftily assumes to be his inferiors in perception and acumen. Thus blinded by hubris, Hank quickly accepts his new situation at face value. Once he does this he unknowingly seals his doom, for by accepting his situation so unreflectively he forfeits his only opportunity of understanding it. Hank also becomes an unreliable narrator when he abandons himself to his dreams.[19] The perceptive reader, therefore, can no longer look to Hank for a satisfactory account of objective reality but must seek it through interpretation, by paying closer attention to Twain's strategies.[20]

At first, Hank does keep in mind that he is dreaming. As he awakens in the dungeon of Camelot he thinks at first, "well, what an astonishing dream I've had," but with the reappearance of Clarence, he resigns himself: "All right, let the dream go on. I'm in no hurry" (5:36–37). However, Clarence brings news that Hank will be burned on the next day and evokes a reaction from Hank that unexpectedly discloses an essential element in common between dream and reality and illuminates how arbitrary and unimportant the distinction between the two states can be. "The shock that went through me was distressing. I now began to reason that my situation was in the last degree serious, dream or no dream, for I knew by past experience of the life-like intensity of dreams, that to be burned to death, even in a dream, would be very far from a jest, and was a thing to be avoided" (5:37). Hank's pregnant realization is paralleled by a comment that Clemens made in an 1893 letter to Mrs. Theodore Crane:

> I dreamed I was born and grew up and was a pilot on the Mississippi and a miner and a journalist in Nevada and a pilgrim in the Quaker City, and had a wife and children and went to live in a villa at Florence—and the dream goes on and on and sometimes seems so real that I almost believe it is real. I wonder if it is? But there is no way to tell, for if one applies tests they would simply aid the deceit. I wish I knew whether it is a dream or real.[21]

However it was in "real life" for Clemens, for Hank at this point the distinction between dream and reality dissolves. Once he boldly steps forward into the dream to defend his existence, the dream becomes his reality from then on and his former reality the dream. He soon finds the exchange gratifying and by chapter 8 "wouldn't have traded it [the sixth century] for the twentieth" (62–63). His optimism, however, is blind. It is one of the major

ironies of *A Connecticut Yankee* that while Hank boasts about his shrewd-
ness and compliments himself on his successes in remaking sixth-century
England into his dream of a nineteenth-century republic, he is at the same
time fatally insensitive to the implications of living in a dream.

In contrast to Clemens, who, inwardly at least, constantly questioned
the accuracy of his perceptions and the truth of his experiences, Hank
never doubts himself or the world of appearances. As a consequence,
Hank chronically overestimates himself and underestimates his situation.
Twain's scorn for this brash cockiness can be inferred from the pattern
of ironies which ultimately turn every one of Hank's "successes" into sad
failures.

A case in point is the old married couple whom Hank releases from Morgan le Fay's dungeon. They had been imprisoned on their wedding night
in separate and lightless cells and kept there for nine years. When they
are at last released from their cells the woman sits dumbly on the ground,
unable to disturb "the meaningless dull dream that was become her life"
(18:165); the man is no better. Then Hank brings them together, rhapsodi-
cally predicting that they will renew their love and lives. But after looking
curiously at each other they resumed their "wandering in some far land of
dreams and shadows that we know nothing about" (166). Hank's naïve but
unintentional cruelty in trying to awaken them from their dream refuges
to sharp and painful reality contrasts strongly with Clemens's very different way of handling a similar situation in his own family. In a letter to his
brother on July 2, 1888, about the care of their aged mother, whose senility
was at least dulling the pains of her infirmities, Clemens chided Orion for
attempting to disrupt the comfort of her "dream" and urged him to take
pity on her and restore it.[22] The incident in the novel represents more than
a chiding of Hank by Twain; it is an ominous exposure of a significant
weakness in a man who would change history. He is not only unable to
awaken the captive couple from their dreams, he is shown as being in the
grip of a dream himself, a dream of his own power and importance.

It is this dream which manipulates Hank through most of the novel, and
it is this dream which is his ultimate undoing. Believing himself free and
powerful, Hank focuses his efforts on realizing his "dream of a Republic"
(42:415) and remains enthusiastically hopeful about it until it collapses
violently in the debacle of the Battle of the Sand-Belt. That this dream was
a delusion and not only could not happen but was never meant to happen

can be demonstrated both by the logic of the dream structure of the novel and by the plot itself. All dreams in the novel lead to the same event: the Battle of the Sand-Belt.

The Battle of the Sand-Belt is central to both the thematic and structural integrity of the novel. The fact that the novel begins at the end has direct consequences for both standpoints. First, the first part of *A Connecticut Yankee* that Twain worked out was the section dealing with the Sand-Belt.[23] It would therefore have been natural and convenient to relate everything he subsequently composed to this climactic event. Second, everything has already happened to Hank Morgan in the sixth century when Clarence takes over the manuscript. Everything has already happened to Clarence when the "reborn" Hank repossesses it in his proper age, the nineteenth century. Almost everything has happened to the reborn Hank when the narrator, "M.T.," takes over, and everything *has* happened by the time M.T. finishes with a P.S. The reader knows, moreover, that the sixth century ran its course without the extraordinary transformation that Hank narrates, and has therefore been induced to get emotionally involved in a novel that essentially demonstrates that history consists of past events that are permanently fixed beyond change—and that implies that present events are also fixed. The point at issue here is a variation of Twain's main theme of universal damnation: *everything has already happened, and the hope that we can by our efforts effect a change is a vain dream.* If this idea sounds hellish, it is no accident.

The inevitability of the Battle of the Sand-Belt and its true meaning are established as early as chapter 10. In a passage dense with ironies, Hank, while bragging about his surreptitious achievements, unconsciously prophesies their frightful consequences, totally unforeseen by him, that would attend England's awakening from its sixth-century dream to Hank's dream of nineteenth-century civilization.

> My works showed what a despot could do, with the resources of a kingdom at his command. Unsuspected by this dark land, I had the civilization of the nineteenth century booming under its very nose. It was fenced away from the public view, but there it was, a gigantic and unassailable fact . . . and as substantial a fact as any serene volcano, standing innocently with its smokeless summit in the blue sky and giving no sign of the rising hell in its bowels. I stood with my finger on the button . . . ready to press it and flood the midnight world with intolerable light at any moment. (82–83)

The passage, of course, conveys Hank's intended meaning that sixth-century England was sleeping or dreaming ("dark land"—"midnight world") and that he was about to awaken it. Hank's boastful pride, however, is undercut by Twain's irony. For one thing, the internal logic of the passage is marred by contradictory impressions of a serene volcano *hiding* the "rising hell" within it, and an *unsuspecting* "dark land" about to be *surprised* by "intolerable light." Although Hank intends to imply that he is bringing progress to Arthur's England, when the passage is compared to the account of the Battle of the Sand-Belt, the ominous connection between Hank's language and the battle is quickly seen. The verbs "booming," "fenced," and "flood" and the adjective "unassailable" anticipate what happens in that awful holocaust, and "flood" even does triple duty, suggesting the "intolerable" fatal spotlights, the surge of current through the electric fences, and the release of the torrent that drowns three-fourths of the besieging army.[24] What Hank reveals when his hand frequently touches the button in chapter 10 is nothing less than the "rising hell" that is the nineteenth century.[25]

Twain's criticisms of the damned human race were expressions of the deeply characteristic gloom that was implanted or reinforced in him by his Calvinistic background. As shown earlier, that outlook is present in the early and middle stages of his writing career, though it tends to be somewhat submerged in them. It surfaces more frequently and openly in the works of the last two decades of his career, and has unmistakably theological associations despite his avowed attraction to determinism. In 1896 he suggested that humans had "no need of any hell 'except the one we live in from our cradle to our grave'" (*Notebooks* 302; also quoted in *Mysterious Stranger Manuscripts* 19). And should anyone believe that Twain fundamentally subscribed to the belief in the progress of civilization, it might be well to recollect a relevant passage in chapter 8 of "The Chronicle of Young Satan" (1897–1900) fragment. It is 1702 in that work, and Young Satan is speaking of the history of the human race:

> It is a remarkable progress. In five or six thousand years five or six high civilizations have risen, flourished, commanded the wonder of the world, then faded out and disappeared, and not one of them except the latest, ever invented any sweeping and adequate way to kill people. They all did their best, to kill being the chiefest ambition of the human race and the earliest incident in its history, but only the Christian Civilization has scored a triumph to be

proud of. Two centuries from now it will be recognized that all the competent killers are Christian; then the pagan world will go to school to be Christian: not to acquire his religion, but his guns. (*Mysterious Stranger Manuscripts* 137)

Twain might have had some illusions, but if he could put a speech like that in the mouth of even a fictitious character, a belief in nineteenth-century life as a cultural high point and the notion of the progress of the human race were not among them.

Hank carried his "dream of a Republic" to Merlin's cave in the midst of the fortifications in the Sand-Belt. One more, and very important, clue to *A Connecticut Yankee*'s essential integration is implicit in the ominous symbolic significance of these fortifications. They are set in the midst of a belt of sand, itself a symbol of the transience of time.[26] They consist of twelve fences around a cave. In chapter 39, "The Yankee's Fight with the Knights," just after he used guns for the first time and killed nine knights with them, Hank crows, "The march of civilization was begun." Hank is not ironic, but Twain is. If the "march of civilization" begins with the shooting of nine knights in a tournament, then the slaughter of twenty-five thousand men in the Battle of the Sand-Belt means that the nineteenth century has arrived in its deadly fullness. Each circle is filled with men; the closer they get to the center, the cave where the future extension of "civilization" is now concentrated, the more their doom is sealed.

One of Dan Beard's illustrations of Morgan le Fay's dungeon shows a barred slit window with an arch over it bearing the inscription "All hope abandon ye who enter here" (18:167). The line, from Dante's *Inferno*, is not in the text. Beard supplied it as part of his graphic illustration of the first edition, in 1889. But Twain knew of Dante (Gribben, *Library* 173), and he certainly approved the illustration. Dante's hell consists of nine circles and is a function of sin. In this novel Twain's hell has thirteen circles and is a function of the human condition and time. Dante's hell is complete; Twain's is not; it is as endless as time; the thirteen centuries represented by the Sand-Belt fortifications and the cave are only a fraction of history applicable to the story.[27] The story begins in the nineteenth century, moves back to the sixth century, then returns again to the nineteenth. In this scheme, there is nothing, there is no time that is outside of hell. All human beings are in it, all are damned, and "progress," therefore, is a delusion. As in the *Inferno*, the closer one gets to the center, the deeper and more awful is the damnation. The innocent little girl with the "mind at rest" whom Hank saw when he first arrived in Camelot is damned and in hell, born into a cruel and barbarous age and destined to a hard life. Her damnation is ameliorated, however, by being in an outer circle and by her inactive—her dreaming—mind. The boisterous joy of the knights of the Round Table in chapter 3 is made possible by their brainlessness. By the same token, the married couple in Morgan le Fay's dungeon have achieved some degree of peace by the escape of their minds into dull dreams; they would have been caused additional torment by being made aware of what had been done to them and what they had become. In Twain's circles, the more humanity is "enlightened," the more it experiences hell; the more it "progresses," the more its corrupt nature paradoxically sinks it deeper into hell.

Mark Twain, like his contemporary Dostoevsky, pondered what hell was. In *A Connecticut Yankee* Twain used a pattern of dreams to intimate, by analogy, that human civilization's nightmarish descent to hell is more plausible as a model of reality than is the familiar daytime world's dream of progress ever onward and upward. Dante described hell as a place where the last kind word that damned souls encounter before entering it is the advice to abandon hope, because in hell hope is a delusion, a burden, and therefore a form of needless punishment. Were Hank not in hell, he would not have suffered such cruel dreams.

Not from the first page of the novel was there ever any chance of his realizing the slightest degree of success in his endeavors to reform society and bring nineteenth-century civilization to the sixth century; it was not meant to be; it had not been predestined; it had not happened. The course of past history is, by definition, fixed beyond change. Thus, when Hank found himself in sixth-century England, he was in an era whose events had already occurred and whose history had already been written and with which he was already generally familiar.

Twain therefore represents the process of time as having been determined by some superior decree, completed in advance, and fixed into an inflexible pattern of eternal repetition. In line with it, at any given moment, an infinite number of historical epochs are being continuously replayed in different time dimensions. Should someone, as was Hank, be displaced from his proper epoch, his person could be transposed to another epoch, one from either the future or the past.[28]

This view of time is shocking in the enormity of its deceit and its remorselessness. But it is a view consistent with the idea that this world in all time dimensions is hell. It is a view, moreover, that could have had its origins in Twain's Calvinist background or, even more basically, in the gloomy reflection of the preacher: "The thing that hath been, it is that which shall be, and that which is done is that which shall be done, and there is no new thing under the sun" (Ecclesiastes 1:9).[29] All Twain had to do to appropriate this idea was to take it literally. The eclipse of the sun, therefore, which Hank "providentially" remembers at the beginning of the novel, is an event doubly ironic and ominous. Humanity's very ability to predict eclipses implies a fixed order in which they are already accomplished facts. And the very existence of such a fixed order of accomplished facts implies that just as to travelers to the past all events are "predictable"—because they had already happened—so are future eclipses predictable because *they have already occurred* at their "appointed" times.[30] Hank knew from the beginning details of the historical period in which he found himself: names, dates, and events—because they had already happened and were fixed. Unlike the time travel stories of modern science fiction, Twain's novel does not allow that the future is open, either totally or even to some significant degree, and that a change introduced into the "past" can radically alter the "future." On the contrary, with the aberration of input from a visitor from the future, the flow of events might experience a minor and temporary perturbation, but the fixed pattern will hold.[31] So when Hank was unable to understand the consequences of his knowledge of the "future"—that he was not free to alter what had been appointed (and also accomplished)—he was doomed to a dream existence, in reality a Sisyphean labor of the damned because all of his labors would fail their intent.

A Connecticut Yankee is the last of Twain's major works in which his artistry veils the deep-rooted and despairing pessimism that was always central to both his inner life and his art. After 1889 the awful dreams which he had hitherto successfully suppressed or contained, and which are still subordinated with brilliant subtlety in *A Connecticut Yankee*, finally began to surface and increasingly become the overt subject matter of his writings. Though Twain fought his countertheology, he did not defeat it. The doubts it implanted in him about the truth of the objective world and the nature and destiny of humanity were supported over the course of his lifetime by his own observations and reflections and became near-convictions. In his inner and artistic life, therefore, Twain was not divided. His distinctive hallmark was the edged jest; it was a peculiarly appropriate talent for one whose deepest and most persistent purpose was to expose life as a cruel hoax.

A Connecticut Yankee, therefore, is not most deeply about Hank, or sixth-century England, or nineteenth-century America either, or about the issue of technology and capitalism versus pastoralism for that matter. Twain projected in the novel a theological and chronological paradigm whose extrapolations bear upon his readers, whose present could be as immutably fixed to the people of "a remote unborn age, centuries hence" as that of the sixth century was to the visitor from the nineteenth century. In a life where true individuality is only a sole "microscopic atom," and experience, in Hank's words, is a "plodding sad pilgrimage . . . [a] pathetic drift between the eternities" (18:162), the one who thinks the most is plunged into the deepest torment. As Mark Twain portrayed hell in *A Connecticut Yankee*, it is the common lot of humanity, and the best that can be done is to submit to it humbly, put one's mind at rest, and perhaps be allowed to dream of life in one of its outer circles.

There are, in addition, other episodes in *A Connecticut Yankee* that reinforce the main theme of universal damnation with subordinate arguments on more limited canvasses. Take, for example, the process in the novel by which Hank comes to think of himself as literally godlike. This process comes to a head in chapter 26, in which readers are treated to a new gospel according to Hank's newspaper. A startling aspect of the chapter is that Hank's account of the newspaper is heavily loaded with allusions to the birth of Christ, as told in the New Testament. There are so many of these allusions and they are so striking that there can be little doubt that Twain wove them into the narrative purposefully. Considered in the context of the novel and Twain's other works, they lead to a series of nesting conclusions: Hank thinks of himself as not just the power behind the throne in King Arthur's court but as a kind of world creator. He manifests hubris when, perhaps half-consciously, he challenges God on the shape of things as they are and as they are to be. The new order that Hank tries to promote by means of the gospel of his newspaper is therefore doomed to defeat.

The newspaper makes its entrance in chapter 26, titled "The First Newspaper," by significantly breaking in upon the droning of a priest with the clarion cry of a newsboy: "Camelot *Weekly Hosannah and Literary Volcano!*—latest irruption—only two cents—all about the big miracle in the Valley of Holiness!" (257). At first glance, everything about this announcement seems humorous. It is an abrupt and incongruous juxtaposition of different centuries and literary styles. "Hosannah" and "Literary Volcano" are both incongruous and hyperbolic terms for a newspaper. "Irruption" seems to be a misspelling. "Miracle" seems an exaggeration for characterizing Hank's patching of a leak in a well, as does "Valley of Holiness" for the name of a place whose monastery and nunnery are filled with superstitiously credulous inhabitants. The announcement, however, is immediately followed by two interesting sentences. "One greater than kings had arrived—the newsboy. But I was the only person in all that throng who knew the meaning of this mighty birth, and what this imperial magician was come into the world to do" (257). The first sentence might appear to reflect some humor from the announcement, but the second has no humor at all. Hank is serious about his statement. What is Twain about with these sudden shifts in tone and these patterns of incongruity? He is enabling his readers first to sense that Hank conceives himself as a sort of divinity, and then that there are problems with this conception.

Whatever humor seems to attend the account of the newspaper in chapter 26 quickly evaporates when it is realized that the account parallels the accounts of Christ's birth in the Gospels of Matthew and Luke.[32] From this perspective, "Valley of Holiness" sounds familiar, and "Hosannah" is appropriate. "One greater than kings had arrived—the newsboy" takes on a deeper and more daring significance once it is recalled that "gospel" literally means "good news" and that according to the Gospel of Luke (2:10–11), the good news about the "newsboy" was that one mightier than kings had arrived. "Irruption" is a correct word, with its meaning of "breaking into" or "intruding" exactly characterizing every one of Hank's innovations, including the "miracle" of the newsboy. The next sentence, however, diverges slightly from the Gospel accounts with some unusual and significant nuances. Most important, instead of a number of people in the room being aware that something extraordinary was happening, only Hank knows the meaning of the mighty birth and what "this imperial magician was come into the world to do." Also, "magician" does not seem to be a suitable designation for Christ, but Hank in chapter 24, titled "A Rival Magician," apparently in competition with Christ, thinks of himself as a magician.[33] Finally, "imperial" connotes more of might and governance than it does of salvation. In Hank's egotistical opinion of himself, the sky is the limit.

Additional allusions to the birth of Christ appear in the last two paragraphs of the chapter, all focused on the manger scene. The passage is so important that we must summarize and quote from it at length. As it begins, Hank purchases a newspaper and shows it to the monks, who are distracted by it from the religious ceremony of the curing of the king's evil. The monks cross themselves, utter a few prayers, and say "Ah'h—a miracle, a wonder! Dark work of enchantment." Then Hank begins to read from it "in a low voice" about the "miracle" of the restoration of the well, constantly accompanied by "astonished and reverent ejaculations" from the monks: "How true!" "Amazing, amazing!" Hank then permits them to take it in their hands.

> So they took it, handling it as cautiously and discreetly as if it had been some holy thing come from some supernatural region. . . . These grouped bent heads, these charmed faces, these speaking eyes—how beautiful to me! For was not this my darling, and was not all this mute wonder and interest and homage a most eloquent tribute and unforced compliment to it? I knew, then, how a mother feels when women, whether strangers or friends, take her new baby, and close themselves about it with one eager impulse, and bend their heads over it in a tranced adoration that makes all the rest of the universe vanish out of their consciousness and be as if it were not, for that time. I knew how she feels, and that there is no other satisfied ambition, whether of king, conqueror or poet, that ever reaches half way to that serene far summit or yields half so divine a contentment.
>
> During all the rest of my séance . . . I sat motionless, steeped in satisfaction, drunk with enjoyment. Yes, this was heaven; I was tasting it once, if I might never taste it more. (26:262)

The existence of a pattern of religious imagery in this passage is undeniable, and it undeniably resembles the account of Christ's birth in the manger with which the Christian world is so familiar. The significance of the chapter's allusions to this scene emerges when we examine them carefully and then link them to related patterns that occur elsewhere in the novel.

It is clear from his point of view that Hank regards the newspaper as his creation. He imagines himself as the mother of his "darling," but in his own person he derives great pleasure out of the expressions of awe, reverence, and adoration that are offered. The desire to become the object of awe, reverence, and adoration is a growing characteristic of Hank's throughout the novel. Although Hank realizes in chapter 8 that while he was talented in his own time, by the twentieth century he would be only average and that one "could drag a seine down street any day and catch a hundred better men than myself." Nevertheless, by chapter 32, "Dowley's Humiliation," he delights when a guest in Marco's house, plainly awed by the splendors of the richly appointed table, mutters, "There is that about earthly pomps which doth ever move to reverence" (316). The word "reverence" sticks in Hank's mind, for he uses it again in the next chapter: "I had the smith's reverence, now, because I was immensely prosperous and rich; I could have had his adoration if I had some little gimcrack of nobility" (323). There is a note of wistfulness in this latter observation.

Throughout much of the novel Hank complains about the nobility, but part of his resentment is that he is not noble and entitled to the "adoration" (the word he uses) that nobles command. Hank angles to become the leading magician of sixth-century England until Arthur, in chapter 27, rates prophecy above magic. Hank thenceforth tries thinking of himself as a prophet, although he began earlier, in chapter 8, by tacitly acknowledging that his prophetic "powers" derive from the uniqueness of his hindsight.

> I stood there, at the very spring and source of the second great period of the world's history; and could see the trickling stream of that history gather, and deepen and broaden, and roll its mighty tides down the far centuries, and I could note the upspringing of adventurers like myself in the shelter of its long array of thrones: De Montforts, Gavestons, Mortimers, Villierses, the war-making, campaign-directing wantons of France, and Charles the Second's sceptre-wielding drabs; but nowhere in the procession was my full-sized fellow visible. I was a Unique; and glad to know that that fact could not be dislodged or challenged for thirteen centuries and a half, for sure. (63)

This passage may seem a little confused, for along with his role as a prophet, Hank, apparently inadvertently, calls himself an adventurer and likens himself to wantons and drabs, all uncomplimentary terms that he will soon earn. In chapter 27, once Arthur praises Merlin for being a prophet, Hank immediately begins to pit himself as a prophet against Merlin and compete for the king's reverence, maybe even adoration. Hank called prophecy a "trade," however, and in the process of answering the king's questions about what was going to occur within the next thirteen centuries, "I proph-ecied myself bald-headed trying to supply the demand" (269) until one day "while striding heedlessly along, with jaw spread and intellect at rest, for I was prophecying, I stubbed my toe and fell sprawling" (270).[34]

By chapter 33 Hank finesses himself from prophet to a yet higher status. "With the spirit of prophecy upon me, I could look into the future and see her [England] erect statues and monuments to her unspeakable Georges and other royal noble clothes-horses, and leave unhonored the creators of this world—after God—Gutenberg, Watt, Arkwright, Whitney, Morse, Stephenson, Bell." Again we have Hank's resentment of nobility, but this time he mixes it with praise for the world's "creators." God is mentioned as an afterthought, the others are human, and one creator—by implication—is missing: himself. As early as chapter 7 Hank resolved that "if I wanted to make life bearable I must do as he [Robinson Crusoe] did—invent, con-trive, create, reorganize things" (54). Looking ahead from this standpoint, we can see that Hank here laid out the plans for all his future activities. From here on, Hank did function as an inventor, although "reinventor" might be a more accurate term, for, strictly speaking, Hank does not in-vent anything. So the patent office he inaugurates is largely a sham, because most of the "new" products that attended his technologizing sixth-century England were items from the nineteenth century that he only had to remem-ber how to build. In effect, he had a near monopoly on patents. He was also adept at contriving, in both the good and pejorative senses of that word. He reorganized England and undertook to reorganize the sixth century and overwrite its history and remake the world according to his pattern. And as his comments on his bringing the newspaper and newsboy into existence indicate, he certainly thought of himself as a creator. After God.

By chapter 10, titled "Beginnings of Civilization," Hank was turning over in his mind what it would be like to be an absolute ruler.

> Unlimited power is the ideal thing when it is in safe hands. The despotism of heaven is the one absolutely perfect government. An earthly despotism would be the absolutely perfect earthly government, if the conditions were the same, namely, the despot the perfectest individual of the human race, and his lease of life perpetual. But as a perishable perfect man must die, and leave his despotism in the hands of an imperfect successor, an earthly despotism is not merely a bad form of government, it is the worst form possible. (81–82)

At first glance, it appears that Hank's musings over his recent accession to power in King Arthur's court end innocently. Attentive readers might have a moment or two of alarm as Hank seems to be flirting with despotism, but the last sentence would probably put them at ease; Hank ends on a democratic note. Hank's reflection, however, is immediately followed by this expression of pride in the next paragraph: "My works showed what a despot could do with the resources of a kingdom at his command" (82). Does Hank consider himself a despot? No. All through his narrative Hank thinks of himself as a democrat, from the first time he criticizes the English nobility until the Battle of the Sand-Belt, when, self-convinced that he is justified by intending to institute democracy, he slaughters twenty-five thousand men of the English army raised to depose him. Does Twain consider Hank to be a despot? The answer must be "yes!" for, as in the examples just cited, Hank's actions consistently contradict his thoughts. Criticism in recent years has recognized that Hank is a disarmingly unreliable narrator; his undoubted sincerity blurs the fact that he projects his good intentions upon actions that are truly despotic. Although Hank at first eases the strictures of monarchical rule, the English common man comes increasingly under Hank's authority in his new "democracy." Hank becomes the only employer in the realm: factories, salesmen, technicians, members of the armed forces—all come under his monopolistic control. By degrees, Hank becomes the new oppressor.

Despite his protestations that he believes in free competition, Hank is a single-minded and often ruthless competitor. Whoever stands in his way is either circumvented and manipulated, like King Arthur; or intimidated, like Morgan le Fay; or humiliated, like the rival magician of chapter 24 and Dowley; or suppressed, like Merlin; or killed, like the two knights errant in chapter 39 and the twenty-five thousand mailed knights in the Sand-Belt. Hank rankles at the thought of a competing power, especially the church, of which he is afraid (10:81). With each success, he becomes more convinced that he is the "perfectest individual of the human race," and more ambitious about the scope of his projected changes. Hank's stated goal is to replace the primitive ways of the sixth century with the "civilization of the nineteenth century" (10:82). Each "improvement" he brings into existence is intended to further that goal: electricity, the telephone and telegraph, factories, a railroad, a patent office, advertising, a West Point and

Annapolis, pistols, Gatling guns, dynamite, Sunday schools, and a newspaper. The last two items on this list are far from being the least of his innovations; in fact, they have the same purpose: to overthrow the rule of the church and to establish a new secular order—with Hank as the boss. Hank does not explicitly challenge God, but he does set out to destroy the power of the church—and the church may be assumed to be headed by God.

Hank's intention in setting up his newspaper is not merely to record news, or even to make the news that the paper records, but to promote himself above all men. The feature story of the first newspaper is about his triumph in the Valley of Holiness. The newsboy will therefore spread the good news—the gospel—about Hank. He is not called Hank, of course, but "the Boss"—spelled with a capital B. A new order is being created by a man—in his own view "the perfectest individual of the human race"— who can perform magic and prophecy, set his chosen people free, and perform wonders and miracles worthy of reverence and adoration. As a consequence of his creations, this extraordinary individual would also create a new history.

Twain's depiction of the "natural" progress of the changes that transform Hank from a democrat to a despot who would write his own gospel is so subtle, so gradual, and so insightful that one must be left with the conclusion that in this novel Twain is at the very peak of his artistic powers, and that his art is that highest kind that conceals itself. Equally subtle is Twain's structuring of the quiet and shadowy events that conspire to bring Hank down. For all his talent, Hank is dreadfully—fatally—nonreflective. He does not recognize the changes occurring within himself, nor, unlike Melville's Ahab, with whom he otherwise shares more than one despotic similarity, does he ever question his motives. He forgets his humble origin and his original recognition that he was not remarkable. He does not notice the contradictions in his musings: that he cannot decide whether he is a magician, prophet, or creator, when none of those three designations properly apply to him; that he has acknowledged himself an adventurer, a wanton, and a drab; that he has admitted that even a perfect man—which he is not—will perish and that human despotism is the worst form of government; and that his newspaper really reports hocus-pocus rather than true magic and that its intention is truly imperial, in the full sense of that word.

Most important, Hank does not reflect upon the significance of the fact that, as we have already explained above, past history, by definition, is fixed and beyond change. Hank's fundamental mistake in all his efforts in sixth-century England, in other words, consists of his presuming to re-write a history which had already happened and was therefore immutable. His opposition to the church, therefore, was a hubristic challenge to God, for the church was committed to the gospel of God's plan, whereas Hank was trying to replace both God's plan and his gospel with his own chain of events and his own gospel.

Even if God may be termed a despot, Hank forgot his own observation that God's immortality ensures that the "despotism of heaven is the one absolutely perfect government." Hank's comment probably referred to the efficiency and perpetuation of a governing system rather than to its justice. Even so, when one considers Hank's ultimate ambition of creating nine-teenth-century civilization in sixth-century England—which insofar as it is realized will culminate in the horrible mass-scale slaughter and material destruction made possible by modern technology—Hank's notion of "be-nevolent" despotism is arguably worse than the despotism of heaven.

One of the seven decks of headlines that trumpet Hank's success in his newspaper reads "The Miraculous Well Uncorked amid/awful outbursts of/INFERNAL FIRE AND SMOKE/AND THUNDER!" The operative word here is "infernal." Hank would not have intended the primary mean-ing of "infernal"—hellish—but Twain must have. It connects with Hank's description in chapter 10 of his "unsuspected" success in introducing the civilization of the nineteenth century into Arthur's England. In the omi-nously ironic passage quoted above, Hank unintentionally predicts the ominous character and effect of this anachronistic transplant: "There it was, as sure a fact, and as substantial a fact as any serene volcano, standing innocent with its smokeless summit in the blue sky and giving no sign of the rising hell in its bowels" (82). By his own testimony, Hank is more in opposition to heaven than he realizes. The *Literary Volcano* promotes a gospel of deceit, self-delusion, power, and hellish destruction. The "Ho-sannah" part of the title (Hebrew "please save us") is not fulfilled until the end, when God's church strikes suddenly and unexpectedly—from Hank's point of view but not God's—and wrests the sixth century back to its ap-pointed destiny. Given an omniscient and omnipotent God, no other outcome is even conceivable. In terms of the epigraph from Ecclesiastes which heads this chapter, Hank's plans are doomed from the first because what God predestines will not be altered.

Though Twain was a heretic to Calvinism in not believing God to be benevolent, he was fully sensitive to Calvinism's warnings that humans served hell more than they realized. Hank Morgan, probably more than any of Twain's other literary creations, exemplifies Twain's awareness of this in the careful and convincing way he depicted the insidious and alarming growth of Hank's megalomania. In the light of this analysis it is very difficult to take seriously the position that Hank serves an autobiographical function in the novel. Furthermore, as much as Twain was critical of the grip that the church could have on people's minds and loyalties, and Hank demonstrates a strong streak of anticlericalism, in chapter 35 even he records the noble act of a kindly priest, and later in the book Twain suggests that the power of the church, cruel and corrupt though it often was, was all that stood between man and a worse master—himself.

Biographically considered, Clemens was usually an advocate of democracy. In his literature, however, and in this novel particularly, Twain was profoundly skeptical of humanity's ability to govern itself. All throughout his narrative, Hank shows his contempt for average people. In chapter 13 ("Freemen!"), for example, he calls them "animals" (109), "modified savages" (108), and "cattle" (109), and only rarely finds an individual whom he considers a man, or who has the makings of a man. From one of his choices, Hank "got him to lend me a little ink from his veins, and with this and a sliver I wrote on a piece of bark—*Put him in the Man-Factory*" (114). Twain's distancing himself from Hank can be recognized once the overlapping ironies of the passage are realized: the simple-minded belief that men can be produced by factories, or even by Hank, presumably by making them over in his own image, and never considering that he is on the way to becoming a despot and that the image of one that requires blood for a message is that of the devil. Hank justifies the Reign of Terror of the "ever-memorable and blessed [French] Revolution" and its "one swift tidal wave of blood" (111), unaware that he is on course to the Battle of the Sand-Belt, at which he will use a similar justification for the bloodiness of his revolution, but will be ironically oblivious to the fact that he is putting down a popular revolution against *himself*. This is the man who is setting himself up to be the savior of sixth-century England!

In the name of democracy, Hank ridicules royalty and the priests who assured the people "that this ironical state of things [royalty and nobility representing themselves as the nation] was ordained of God . . . [the priests] not reflecting how unlike God it would be to amuse himself with sarcasms" (110). Hank then, with angry sarcasm, lists what "freemen" owed their lords: taxes, estate taxes, eminent domain, military service, and permissions for licenses and passports. He does not see, but Twain surely did, that freemen of Hank's America, and indeed of any subsequent democracy anywhere, owe their governments exactly the same obligations. Always in mind of how much more advanced he was than anyone else in the sixth century, Hank intends to lead a popular revolution and remain a leader. After he defeats Merlin once more in a later chapter, "the populace uncovered and fell back reverently to make a wide way for me, as if I had been some kind of a superior being—and I was. I was aware of that" (23:224). Twain's sarcastic depiction of the ambition, overweening self-importance, and self-delusion of a common man from American democracy put into a position of power bespeaks a profound skepticism of the common man, democracy, and the human capacity to improve its damnable situation, let alone to challenge God.[35] In terms of his countertheology, Twain indicts both God and humanity.

Hank Morgan's attempt to use his newspaper and his newsboy as means to spread his own gospel undoubtedly reflected Twain's experience with both newspapers and demagogues and his realization that despite their protestations of truth, virtue, and good intentions, and their pretensions to omniscience and prophecy, they were not only self-serving but also often damnably wrong and dangerous. All things considered, the deceptively humorous episodes,[36] the deceptively disjunctive structure, and the deceptively likeable narrator of *A Connecticut Yankee* are the artistically controlled products of what Twain described in his September 22, 1889, letter to William Dean Howells as "a pen warmed-up in hell" (*Twain-Howells Letters* 613).

From the first Hank hated and feared the church not just because it was authoritarian but because it was his competitor. (So much for Hank's fondness for free markets.) It does not occur to Hank that the church was also teaching the truth about God being the absolute ruler and all humans his subjects, and that he, in his own person, was a testimony to the validity of the church's teachings. The novel, for example, begins with Hank a free man in nineteenth-century America. When he comes to in England, he is immediately captured and made a slave. Shortly thereafter his fortunes improve and he becomes "the Boss." In chapters 31 to 33 Hank and King Arthur disguise themselves as commoners and are treated as such until Hank overreaches himself. In chapter 34 Hank becomes a slave again. In chapter 38 Hank is rescued and returned to his authority as "the Boss." The swift sequence of chapters 40 to 44 depict another turnabout in Hank's fortunes. All that he had created has come apart, and the church's interdict strips him of all his followers except Clarence and fifty-two boys. Despite his protestations that he is bringing civilization and democracy to England, he persists in a battle with an army that more truly than he represents the great majority of the English. In the final analysis, Hank wreaks a horrible slaughter in the causes of democracy (which, his protestations notwithstanding, never even got started during the process of Hank's metamorphosis into a despot) and progress being conferred on a people who did not want them. The holocaust of the Battle of the Sand-Belt was a definitive defeat for Hank and everything he stood for. Back in his own time at the end of the novel, Hank might technically be "free"—in a political sense—but he slips away once again into a final dream. Was Hank free? Clearly, he was *not* the master of his destiny. If anything, he was the plaything of powers beyond his control. In *A Connecticut Yankee* Twain suggests that hubris has consequences; it is no accident that the church strikes the blow that topples Hank. If it had not, then there would have been no bar to Hank's absolute despotism, an eventuality he himself entertains (in chapter 10).

As the church puts an end to Hank's dreams of "progress," therefore, so did it put an end to the probability that something worse than what already existed would be created. In making clear that Hank Morgan had literally no chance of success in his endeavor to master history, Twain went so far as to pursue his theme in motifs that dealt directly with chance and such of its synonyms as luck and fortune. Although Hank's lack of reflectiveness may be read as a serious shortcoming that causes him to misunderstand his situation, it can also be read as an effect of being silently manipulated. This point is dramatically suggested by events that occur in chapters 2 and 5. We have already called attention to Twain's use of coincidence as a "plain view" concealment of ideas and literary strategies he used to shape his fiction. Almost certainly the most dramatic examples of this technique in all of his literature occur in chapter 2 when Hank, in the dungeon, learns from Clarence that he is in King Arthur's court on June 19, 528. "But all of a sudden I stumbled on the very thing, just by luck. I knew that the only total eclipse of the sun in the first half of the sixth century occurred on the 21st of June, A.D. 528, O.S., and began at 3 minutes after 12 noon. I also knew that no total eclipse of the sun was due in what was to me the present year—i.e. 1879" (17).[37] All readers can quickly determine for themselves how unlikely it is that anyone would know the schedule of eclipses for the present year, and how even less likely it is that anyone would just happen to know that a total solar eclipse occurred at three minutes after noon on June 21, 528 O.S. Readers who do not pause at and reflect on this extraordinary claim further lay themselves open to the novel's hoax.

Notice, moreover, that the information occurred to Hank "all of a sudden" and "just by luck." We have already previously established that Twain did not believe in luck, chance, or accident, and that he used his readers' credence in these entities as cover to allow him to build cases for predestination. Twain's beliefs in this matter had not changed by 1889. Hank's admission as to the abrupt and unexpected way his highly specific information about eclipses came to him leads to the conclusion that the information was planted in him. That this was no stray occurrence is shown by the repeated, albeit less dramatic, use of the same technique in chapter 5 when Hank is told he is about to be burned at the stake: "It came into my mind, in the nick of time, how Columbus, or Cortez, or one of those people, played an eclipse as a saving trump once, on some savages, and I saw my chance" (40). Notice again the passive role of Hank ("it came into my mind"), the coincidence ("in the nick of time"), and the reference to chance. Again, Hank is being externally manipulated when he unreflectingly gives himself credit for knowledge it was virtually incredible for him to have. Even more basically, Hank never reflects on his own origin, that "by chance" he had been cast into the mold of a maker of armaments—"guns, revolvers, cannons, boilers, engines, all sorts of labor-saving machinery" ("A Word of Explanation" 4)—and that this fact determines what he will do in sixth-century England.

In retrospect, it can be seen that predestination under the cover of the misnomers of "chance" and "accident" is a major element in the novel's structure. In chapter 9 ("The Tournament") Hank complains, seemingly extravagantly, about a tired old joke Sir Dinadan told. "Just as he finished, the call boy came, so, haw-hawing *like a demon*, he went rattling and clanking out like a crate of loose castings, and I knew nothing more. It was some minutes before I came to, and then I opened my eyes just in time to see Sir Gareth fetch him an awful welt, and I *unconsciously* out with the prayer, 'I hope to gracious he's killed!' But by *ill luck* . . . Sir Sagramour caught my remark and thought I meant it for him" (77–78, emphases added). As a result, Sir Sagramour challenges Hank to a duel several years in the future. Thus a "chance" remark, unconsciously uttered, and meant for someone else, becomes the cause of the momentous chapter 39 ("The Yankee's Fight with the Knights"), during the course of which Hank uses pistols for the first time and believes he has doomed knight-errantry and again demolished Merlin's reputation. That chapter is the beginning of the end for hubristic Hank, but its cause was something trivial, an "accident."

Chapter 42 ("War!") and the death of Arthur are similarly driven by "accidents." During Hank's absence, Sir Launcelot could not resist making a "killing" on the stock market—another one of Hank's imports (and a form of gambling—that is, a dependence on chance) from his own century—and beggaring the other investors. Two of them happened to be Sir Agravaine and Sir Mordred, Arthur's nephews. Seeking revenge on Launcelot, they realized that Queen Guenever's amours with Launcelot gave them, "by luck" (412), an opening to Arthur, who until then had no idea of what was going on. Arthur laid a trap for Launcelot, who walked into it but killed thirteen of the fourteen witnesses (note the recurrence of the symbolic thirteen). Only Mordred escaped, but he split the kingdom into two parts, and his army opposed the king's. The two armies faced each other at Salisbury, both restrained by a common intention to arrange a peace treaty. But Arthur, lacking confidence in Mordred, gave orders that if a sword were raised during the peace negotiations, his forces should attack. Mordred gave a similar order. Then, "by chance" an adder bit a knight's heel, and the knight forgot the order and raised his sword to slash at the snake. As a consequence, the two armies clashed with tragic results. Just as the call-boy is likened to a demon above, a snake—the symbol of evil—suddenly appears and fulfills its biblical curse of biting the heel of a human. It is incredible to think that Twain was unaware of what he was doing by emplacing these "accidents" or that he would deny that they happened by "appointment."

One other related motif that runs through the novel might be mentioned: allusions to the card games euchre and poker.[38] Both games were very popular in the United States in the late nineteenth century, particularly in the West wherever gambling took place, and the allusions to the games are frequent and easy in Hank's mouth. Gambling, of course, usually involves chance—except when opponents are not equally matched, or when the game is fixed—so the frequent allusions to card games are all important connections to the novel's underlying theme of predestination. Hank turns away, for example, from speculating on how he might have gotten to sixth-century England "till its *appointed* day and hour should come" (2:17, emphasis added) with a resolution to be practical: "One thing at a time, is my motto—and just play that thing for all it is worth, even if it's only two pair and a jack" (2:17). In other words, he stays in the game even when dealt a poor or undistinguished hand, bluffing as much as is necessary. "Bluffing," of course, is a poker term, but it perfectly describes Hank's actions—and proclivities—throughout the novel.

As pointed out earlier, when faced with the imminence of being burned at the stake, he says, "It came into my mind, in the nick of time, how Columbus, or Cortez, or one of those people, played an eclipse as a saving trump once, on some savages, and I saw my chance." The use of the euchre term "saving trump" implies that Hank had a high card the opposition did not suspect him of having. When Merlin orders the torch to be set to the wood around Hank just as the eclipse was beginning, Hank bluffs the assembly with the threat of instant death by lightning and thunder. He is believed by Arthur, and freed. Although Hank does not realize it, at some level he is playing a card game throughout the novel. Initially, Hank appears to play with skill, but although card games are often regarded as games of chance, Twain—from both the standpoints of his countertheology and his experience as a former westerner who saw a lot of cardsharps practice their trade—did not believe in chance. Therefore, although Hank is allowed to take some "tricks" in this game, he is not going to be able to beat the dealer.

Because of his skills and his bluffing, Hank wins an appointment as "perpetual minister and executive to the king" with a one percent bonus on the increased revenues he planned to create (6:49). Vis-à-vis the king and his court, Hank becomes the dealer. The king in effect leaves the table at this point, and one of the first things Hank does is stack the deck against Merlin. The subsequent explosion of Merlin's tower all but destroys Merlin's reputation as a magician (and a competitor), and leaves Hank free to deal as he wishes.[39] This is just the first of a number of episodes in the novel where he shows himself to be unscrupulous as a dealer and a player. He is especially fond of having an ace up his sleeve, some surprise in the form of a gadget or a technological system or fallback position his sixth-century opponents could not imagine.

Hank's putative goal is to establish a "new deal" (13:114). This sounds good enough on an abstract level, but the details are devilish. The schools and factories Hank sets up,[40] the twentieth-century inventions such as the telephone and telegraph and weaponry that Hank introduces, and especially the surreptitious mining of his factories he prudently puts into place, are all done relatively quietly and may be understood as cards he puts into his hand as he prepares for the next big game of his career—against the church. Hank admits that "I was afraid of a united Church" (10:81), and he intends to take no chances on losing to it in a showdown.

In chapter 39, after "snaking" several knights out of their saddles with the "fateful coils" of his lariat, Hank is about to face the "right bower" of Sir Launcelot. (In euchre, the right bower is the strongest card in the deck.) Before this can happen, however, Merlin steals Hank's lariat (Merlin is also not scrupulous about playing fairly). This ups the stakes. Merlin thinks Hank is now weaponless, and forces the duel between Hank and Sir Sagramour to continue. When Sir Sagramour draws near with his sword ready to strike, Hank suddenly uses the ace in his sleeve, a revolver, and shoots Sagramour dead. Hank then "bluffs" by challenging any and all knights to attack him. ("At such a time it is sound judgment to put on a bold face and play your hand for a hundred times what it is worth; forty-nine times out of fifty nobody dares to 'call,' and you rake in the chips" [392].) Five hundred knights answer the challenge, and Hank fires eight more shots, killing a knight with each shot, then bluffs again by pointing both nearly empty revolvers at the charging mass. But cowed by the strange engines of death (whose effects, in Hank's mind, mean that "the march of civilization was begun"), the knights break and flee.

One last major allusion to cards occurs in the layout of the Battle of the Sand-Belt. There are twelve concentric circles around the cave; thirteen Gatling guns are emplaced to fire; and Hank's party consists of himself, Clarence, an "old woman," and fifty-two boys who had been specially raised by Hank and Clarence.[41] There are fifty-two cards in a deck, with four suits of thirteen each. There are also fifty-two weeks in a year, a symbolic (and ironic) allusion to time. It is difficult to believe that Twain's use of these specific numbers is arbitrary. As the showdown nears, Hank decides to go on the offensive. He uses card language when he expresses confidence at holding "a fair hand—two-thirds as good a hand as the enemy. Oh, yes, we'll rise up and strike; that's our game" (42:422–423). After the ensuing slaughter, Hank is put into a thirteen centuries' sleep by the old woman, who was Merlin in disguise. Laughing at his success, Merlin brushes up against a wire and dies with the laugh on his face. Reverting one last time to the language of cards, we can see that Merlin was a joker in the deck, and that although Hank had been allowed to win a few hands during the game, he was up against a dealer who not only was omniscient and omnipotent but who also dealt from a stacked deck. Considering *A Connecticut Yankee* from the motif of cards, therefore, it is possible to see the motif as one in a series of redundant and mutually supporting devices in the novel, all of which lead to the same end: the impossibility of human freedom. As Twain implies in this novel, the choices that are available to humans are all selected by the dealer, who ensures that our hands lead to a predestined end.

Each of these approaches discloses the same pattern in *A Connecticut Yankee*: the rise of a common man to a position of power, his succumbing to irresistible temptation that exposes his unintentional and insidious corruption, and his tragic fall. Readers are led to sympathize with Hank Morgan at first, then to be appalled at seeing the flourishing of the self-deceit and despotism intrinsic in his nature, and finally to return to some measure of sympathy with him at the end when he loses all, even the simple human blessings of wife, family, and love. *A Connecticut Yankee* thus follows, with some variations but immeasurably more depth and power, the pattern of *Roughing It*. Also implicit in both novels is the sense that although the humans in them are blameworthy, they are destined victims of a cruel and overmastering power that manipulates events almost imperceptibly to deny them freedom, fulfillment, and happiness. In the end, we are returned to the familiar conclusion: Twain indicts both God and humanity.

A Connecticut Yankee is a testimony to the persistent and growing power of Twain's oldest, deepest, and gloomiest convictions. As he described life, it was a shocking deception, a grim and mirthless hoax contrived of false hopes. A serious hoax told from the perspective of a well-intentioned but unreliable narrator who himself was a victim of life's deceptions, *A Con-*

necticut Yankee is surpassingly brilliant and successful, a powerfully moving artistic counterpart of the subject it depicts. In Twain's countertheological view, if humanity was damned, then this life was hell. Hell was not to be enjoyed nor, therefore, was this life; something was always destined to come along to spoil the illusions of freedom and happiness. These goals were never meant to be achieved by the great majority of human beings, and the hope for an impossibility is destined to failure and disillusion. By 1889 Twain had come to the innermost conclusion that no hope was justified, but one fear was: that something worse was always possible.

No. 44, The Mysterious Stranger

THE FALSE PROMISE OF THE MIND

And false prophets shall rise, and shall shew signs and wonders, to seduce,
if it were possible, even the elect. —Mark 13:22

Between 1897 and 1908, Mark Twain attempted at least four times to render a supernatural story based on the exploits of a "mysterious stranger" who pays a visit to unsuspecting youths and in one way or another undermines the pat religious thinking of their communities. The earliest "versions" of this tale, written in 1897 and 1898, dramatize without ambiguity Twain's affirmation of a harsh universe lorded over by an uncaring and malicious God. Twain's treatment of such themes in these initial Mysterious Stranger texts, though considerably less nuanced than in earlier works, is fundamentally consistent with the heretically Calvinist undercurrents in his writings dating back to the early 1860s. However, with the last of these so-called Mysterious Stranger manuscripts, *No. 44, The Mysterious Stranger* (composed between 1902 and 1908), Twain departs radically not just from the narrative strategy of his previous mysterious stranger stories but also, if only temporarily, from his reluctant acceptance of a counter-theological cosmos and its cruel sovereign.

Beginning with Bernard DeVoto's seminal study of the texts that comprise the Mysterious Stranger manuscripts in his *Mark Twain at Work* (1942), twentieth-century academic scholarship has tended to read the mysterious stranger stories in essentially two ways. First, critics have viewed the stories, oftentimes dismissively, as a record of Twain's persistent pessimism during the last fifteen years of his life—what DeVoto famously termed (and subsequent generations of critics have reiterated) Twain's "symbols of despair"—and his enduring conviction that the Calvinist interpretations of God, humanity, and the universe in which he had been indoctrinated as a child were manifest and true.[1] Even critics such as Susan Gillman who have argued for a more serious consideration of the writings of Twain's late period conclude that the Mysterious Stranger texts expose a pervasive psychic gloom in the last decade or so of Twain's life.[2] Second, much of Twain scholarship has regarded the various Mysterious Stranger stories—"The Chronicle of Young Satan" (composed between 1897 and 1900), "Schoolhouse Hill" (composed 1898), and *No. 44, the Mysterious Stranger*[3]—as expressions of a single work and have routinely drawn generalized conclusions and applied them to the Mysterious Stranger manuscripts as a whole. Taken together, it is easy to understand why commentators have been so willing to consider these various manuscripts as versions of a single work. Each of the "drafts" has in common with others at least some element of character, setting, and/or plot. In some cases Twain borrowed large sections of one text and worked it into another. And there is little doubt that Twain moved, for example, from the text of "The Chronicle of Young Satan" to that of "Schoolhouse Hill" with certain correspondences in mind. Still, Twain scholarship has yet to appreciate fully the degree to which these various "drafts" truly differ from each other in tone, import, and theme. In particular, *No. 44, The Mysterious Stranger*, considered separately from the others, yields insights into an underappreciated transformation in Twain's thinking at the turn of the century.

Sherwood Cummings's 1988 study, *Mark Twain and Science: Adventures of a Mind*, is one among numerous studies which over the years have demonstrated persuasively that Twain was, throughout his career, closely attuned to the intellectual trends of his day. Though enormously consequential to the development of his art, Twain's interest in contemporary science and philosophy, for the most part, according to Cummings and others, had the general effect of affirming and extending Twain's preexisting views. In the 1880s and 1890s, however, Twain encountered ideas that arguably altered his thinking more profoundly than anything had since his reading of Thomas Paine in the late 1850s. At the end of the nineteenth century these new ideas were grouped under the term "psychical research"; today we know this field as the science of psychology. So powerful was the effect of this emergent science on Twain's thinking that it eventually enabled him—albeit for a brief period of time—to displace his Calvinist-inspired countertheological vision. The individual arguably most responsible for providing this last best hope for Mark Twain was William James.

Few critics of Twain have explored the considerable influence that William James likely had on Twain and his writing in the first decade of the twentieth century.[4] Even those who have mentioned James in their analyses of Twain's life and work have tended to refer to James only in passing and usually without much substantive discussion of the ways in which James might have influenced Twain. A notable exception is Jason Gary Horn, whose insightful book *Mark Twain and William James: Crafting a Free Self* (1996) breaks new ground in calling attention to the depth of this important relationship. Citing biographical evidence, correspondence, and evidence from books by James that Twain purchased and read, Horn establishes a basis for Twain's understanding of the science of psychology, particularly as the field emerged in the last two decades of the nineteenth century. Specifically, Horn argues that Twain's reading of James's *The Principles of Psychology* (1890) in the early 1890s provided Twain with scientific corroboration for his most abiding convictions regarding the essential nature of the human psyche, particularly his "long-standing belief in a divided self" (7). Horn is generally correct in his broader thesis that both James and Twain recognized the potential ameliorative power of transcendence that results from the psychological process of recognizing and confronting one's own "interior" or subconscious self, but he perhaps goes too far in his suggestion that both writers conceptualized that resulting transcendent experience as a positive, self-affirming *religious* experience. There is no question that James embraced moments of religious awakening as the supreme expression of psychological health; however, Twain's conclusions about Jamesian insights into human psychology took him in a very different direction.

William James's views on religion have been well documented both through disclosure in his own writings as well as in the last hundred years of scholarship of his life and work. "Religion," James boldly declares, for example, in a letter to his brother Henry dating from the mid 1890s, "is the great interest of my life" (Perry 165). But more than just an intellectual pursuit, religion for James existed as a sincere personal conviction. In notes for the lectures that would eventually become the basis for *The Varieties of Religious Experience: A Study in Human Nature* (1902), James writes, "A man's religion is the deepest and wisest thing in his life. . . . Remember the whole point lies in really *believing* that through some point or part in you you coalesce and are identical with the Eternal" (Matthiessen 232).

As for characterizing James's particular theological beliefs, scholars agree that James provides something close to a self-portrait in *The Varieties of Religious Experience*, where he discusses the religious sensibility he terms "healthy-mindedness." According to James, the "healthy-minded" view of religion begins with a rejection of the accepted orthodox notion that good and evil necessarily exist as a fundamental cosmic dialectic. Evil, he argues in *Varieties*, "is emphatically irrational, and *not* to be pinned in, or preserved, or consecrated in any final system of truth. It is a pure abomination to the Lord, an alien unreality, a waste element, to be sloughed off and negated, and the very memory of it, if possible, wiped out and forgotten" (132–133).

But like Walt Whitman, whom he identified as the "supreme contemporary example" of "healthy-mindedness" (*Varieties* 84), James was far from simply being an Emersonian idealist. In other words, James, though fundamentally an optimist, anchored his theology in the practical world of experience and believed, as Whitman did, that a rejection of evil is not the same as a rejection of its positive existence. As F. O. Matthiessen explains, James "was saved from the superficial optimism attendant upon that attitude (as Whitman was also) by at least an occasional recollection of the fissures always lurking beneath the smooth melioristic surfaces, by a greater depth of spirit than that in which he habitually lived" (232). And as much as anything else, it was this eminently pragmatic religious perspective that motivated James's initial explorations into the human psyche through psychology.

There is little doubt, as Horn makes clear throughout his study, that the larger arc of James's theorizing about psychology, especially as expressed in *The Principles of Psychology* and *The Varieties of Religious Experience*, privileged curative efforts that moved the psychically ailing individual into a state of religious "healthy-mindedness" as a means for achievement of psychological integrity and health. James termed this process "religious reconciliation" (*Varieties* 164) and explained it as a kind of religious conversion that takes on the guise of a transcending mystical experience following the unifying of one's exterior and inner selves. In a chapter titled "The Divided Self" from *The Varieties of Religious Experience*, for example, James explains:

> I shall next ask you to consider more closely some of the peculiarities of the process of unification, when it occurs. It may come gradually, or it may occur

abruptly; it may come through altered feelings, or through altered powers of action; or it may come through new intellectual insights, or through experiences which we shall later have to designate as "mystical." However it comes, it brings a characteristic sort of relief; and never such relief as when it is cast into the religious mould. Happiness! happiness! Religion is only one of the ways in which men gain that gift. Easily, permanently, and successfully, it often transforms the most intolerable misery into the profoundest and most enduring happiness.

But to find religion is only one out of many ways of reaching unity; and the process of remedying inner incompleteness and reducing inner discord is a general psychological process, which may take place with any sort of mental material, and need not necessarily assume the religious form. . . . For example, the birth may be away from religion into incredulity. (175–176)

Even with his tacit qualifications throughout the second half of the passage that religious awareness is only one expression of the relief that follows psychological integration of the "selves," it is clear that, for James, psychological insight is articulated in the most ideal circumstances through a sort of profound religious awakening.

In his attempt to make a case for ideological parallels between James and Twain, Horn makes similar claims for Twain: "During the 1890s, Twain, too, had ushered his psychical interests to the foreground as he increasingly turned toward fictional explorations of the psyche and toward those religious experiences that would be more clearly articulated a few years later in James's *Varieties*" (14). As Horn sees it, Twain moved closer—in his fiction as well as in his personal beliefs—at the turn of the century toward an acceptance of James's brand of optimistic, pragmatic Christianity. But evidence from the evolutional development of the Mysterious Stranger manuscripts, as well as the text itself of *No. 44, The Mysterious Stranger* (not to mention numerous details from Twain's biography), suggests otherwise. In fact, rather than "moving toward those religious experiences" that James documents in *The Varieties of Religious Experience*, Twain moved in the direction away from positive religious thinking, perhaps taking to heart James's concession from *Varieties* that religious experience is only one of the ways that individuals might enter into a heightened consciousness. That is to say Twain recognized in James's insights into human psychology a variety of freedom of the individual will completely independent from religious mindedness—a way to escape from religion as opposed to a better understanding of it. And *No. 44, The Mysterious Stranger* provides support for the possibility that Twain saw in the science of psychology—at least temporarily—a potential vehicle for supplanting the heretical views that had influenced his personal and artistic vision since the mid-nineteenth century.

Mark Twain composed *No. 44, The Mysterious Stranger* in five stages between November 1902 and September 1908, with the greater portion of the manuscript (nearly 480 of its 587 pages) written in the nineteen months from January 1904 to July 1905. Linking *No. 44, The Mysterious Stranger* to the other narratives of the Mysterious Stranger manuscripts is a storyline involving the sudden appearance of a supernaturally gifted character in a small village. However, several distinctions exist between *No. 44, The Mysterious Stranger* and previous versions of the story.[5] First, the gifted protagonist of *No. 44, The Mysterious Stranger* is never identified as, suggested to be, or in any way associated with a divine being. Forty-Four is, as the title of the story suggests, a mysterious stranger. The Satan figures of the earlier texts, such as "The Chronicle of Young Satan" and "Schoolhouse Hill," are depicted as angels from heaven visiting Earth; Forty-Four, on the other hand, is a completely secularized portrait.

Second, overt religious ideology plays little more than an ancillary role in *No. 44, The Mysterious Stranger*. Earlier versions of the mysterious stranger stories depend almost exclusively on theological matter for narrative development. "The Chronicle of Young Satan," for example, which has been fairly characterized as among Twain's most heated attacks on conventional religious thinking, seems at times little more than a forum for Twain to assault the damned human race and its absurd conceptions of God and the universe in which human beings believe they live. By contrast, *No. 44, The Mysterious Stranger* focuses mainly on its protagonist's intellectual growth. Religion simply provides the story with a universal baseline of ignorance from which individuals such as August Feldner, Heinrich Stein, and Frau Adler are able to distance themselves through intellectual development. All three characters, for example, are shown to overcome a mental lethargy synonymous with religious faith, specifically through their acquisition and practice of literacy. Twain was so explicit in his intentions to create this contrast in *No. 44, The Mysterious Stranger* that in revising the opening chapter from earlier texts of the story, he added that Frau Adler's Bible lessons were "all written out" (4), which is just one among dozens of references to the subversive nature of literacy that focus attention in this draft on the crucial act of reading itself. Just as religion seems to shrink curiously into the background of *No. 44, The Mysterious Stranger*, so, too, does Twain virtually ignore treatment of what he called the Moral Sense, heretofore a hallmark concept in the development of the Mysterious Stranger texts and later a target of some of his most ferocious criticism of God.

This is all to say that at some point between when Twain set aside "The Chronicle of Young Satan" around 1900 and before he began the composition of *No. 44, The Mysterious Stranger* in 1902, he had made a decision to shift the narrative strategy of his Mysterious Stranger story from religious satire to something more focused on the psychic quest of his tale's central character. Insofar as August's exploits involve his discovery and exploration of the interior world of the mind, the very stuff of the new science of psychology itself, Twain's modifications to the Mysterious Stranger story after 1902 appear in large part due to his increasing curiosity about human psychology, in particular his reading of William James. Moreover, the fact that the Mysterious Stranger stories from their earliest conception in 1897 to *No. 44, The Mysterious Stranger* move steadily away from wholesale religious diatribe and into a more nuanced reflection on the nature of human consciousness absent theological connotation indicates that contrary to Horn's assertions, Twain pondered the emerging science of psychology at the turn of the century apart from any religious application—except, of course, as a means for displacing his Calvinist-inspired countertheology.

While most critics agree that *No. 44, The Mysterious Stranger* deals primarily with August Feldner's intellectual and spiritual education, few have noted the distinct process and the actual means by which August eventually achieves the fullness of enlightenment. For instance, August's cognitive transformation, considered as a whole, takes place over the course of the story in four discernible stages, each marking a specific as well as a significant sense of growth. Each of these stages, though layered in meaning, contains at some level ideas that are consistent with Jamesian psychology. Also important to understanding this process is a realization of the essential relationship between August and his teacher, Forty-Four. Although the latter's identity, history, and physical nature have long been considered by scholars to be thoroughly enigmatic, truly a "mysterious stranger," evidence within the text demonstrates that Forty-Four is neither precisely a stranger to August nor is his origin completely a mystery.

The first stage of August's intellectual journey entails the conception of his desire to learn, and occurs as he moves from the village of Eseldorf to Castle Rosenfeld. In the opening passages of the story, Twain describes Eseldorf and the rest of Austria as "asleep" (3). Setting a deceptively idyllic scene on the surface, Twain's depiction of the village is, at a deeper level, an indictment of its inhabitants' completely unenlightened state of existence. Characterized by an exaggerated sense of superstition and blind faith in religion, Eseldorf embodies a mentally oppressive atmosphere that inhibits any substantial development of the mind. Within the first few passages of the narrative August recalls his earlier days in the village:

> We were not overmuch pestered with schooling. Mainly we were trained to be good Catholics; to revere the Virgin, the Church and the saints above everything; to hold the Monarch in awful reverence. . . . Beyond these matters we were not required to know much; and in fact, not allowed to. The priests said that knowledge was not good for the common people. (4)

Eseldorf, as we have said, is yet another manifestation of Twain's fictional small-town setting. It is St. Petersburg, Camelot, Dawson's Landing, and Hadleyburg. But what is unique about the portrayal of Eseldorf is the way that Twain immediately and directly couches his attack on the village expressly in terms of religion. This serves a number of functions. First, as we have said, it defines religion as the source of ignorance from which August will develop. Arguably, the not-so-subtle larger implication here is that religious thinking is not just *a* source but *the* source of human ignorance. This point is especially significant given the trajectory of the narrative toward displacing religious ideology, human superstition, and a tendency toward human credulity with intellectual integrity as defined by modern psychology. Second, it casts religion and its principals either as wicked oppressors or, in the case of those religious-minded individuals who engender sympathy such as Father Peter and Frau Marx, as naïve victims. In this sense, then, Twain merely presents a version of his own religious attitudes in action. Eseldorf, like St. Petersburg, is a cosmos writ small, ruthlessly lorded over by Father Adolf, its own version of a malevolent father figure who strikes fear in the hearts of his followers, instills in them a sense of human worthlessness, and ultimately punishes all without compassion while holding himself above his "laws."

Third, and most important, the village of Eseldorf and its oppressive religious sensibility correspond to the inaugural stage in James's process of moving toward psychological "reconciliation." In *The Varieties of Religious Experience* James distinguishes between two general religious types. One, which we have discussed, is "healthy-mindedness." James counted himself among the "healthy-minded." The second type is what he termed "the sick soul." In Jamesian psychology, particularly as laid out in *The Varieties of Religious Experience*, "the sick soul" is characterized as an ailing individual in need of psychic healing due to being overburdened by "the consciousness of evil" (138) and who suffers from "religious melancholy" (149). Critics have suggested that Twain himself fit the description of James's sick soul.[6] Indeed, James points out that extremist branches of Protestant Christianity, merely by virtue of their harsh theological vision, fall into this particular category: "If the individual be of tender conscience and religiously quickened, the unhappiness will take the form of moral remorse and compunction, of feeling inwardly vile and wrong, and of standing in false relations to the author of one's being and appointer of one's fate. This is the religious melancholy and 'conviction of sin' that have played so large a part in the history of Protestant Christianity" (170–171). Even though August is Catholic (the story is set in 1490, before the Protestant Reformation), his religious sensibility serves to represent a generally despairing Christian perspective, as he and the villagers of Eseldorf clearly exhibit in common a sense of innate sinfulness and fear-laden piety consistent with Calvinism as well as Catholicism and other extreme expressions of Christianity. In essence, then, the villagers of Eseldorf, which includes August, suffer the symptoms of the Jamesian sick soul. Consider Frau Marx, for example, who in reaction to Father Adolf and his punishments is described as "frightened," "swoon[ing] with fear," and "perishing with despair" (6). August, as a suffering "sick-soul," enters the process of healing, as described by James, first through his recognition of an interior self and then eventually through a unification with that interior self.

The character of Frau Adler also serves as a vehicle for Twain's ironic treatment of education in the opening chapter. "She was a cunning woman," Twain writes, "and sought only those few who could read—flattering them by saying it showed their intelligence" (4). Attempting to remedy Eseldorf's plight of ignorance, Adler quietly begins to teach several villagers her lessons. Once the church learns of this, however, Father Adolf promptly instills a sense of panic and fear into the townsfolk through religious superstition, which puts an abrupt end to Adler's teaching. It is important, though, that these mostly sympathetic villagers receive their instruction specifically through the relatively newly acquired art of reading, for this establishes a direct relationship between the printed word and the intellect that will become an essential part of August's education away from religious thinking. Victor Doyno's study of Twain's creative process, *Writing* Huck Finn*: Mark Twain's Creative Process* (1991), argues that the notion of literacy is both a major concern and a theme throughout most of Twain's fiction. Similarly, Steven Mailloux suggests in his *Rhetorical Power* (1989) that the didactic fiction Twain grew up with and later satirized, such as Sunday school books, juvenile periodicals, and advice-to-youth books, created a crucial "rhetorical context" of literate education in which he wrote his fiction (128). Twain almost certainly drew in part from his youthful catechism in Hannibal when constructing his depiction of Eseldorf and Father Adolf's approach to pedagogy. In fact, a number of August's experiences are curiously similar to pivotal episodes in Twain's own life, strongly suggesting that with *No. 44, The Mysterious Stranger,* Twain may have been attempting to fictionalize aspects of his own mental and spiritual development. But in a larger sense the characterization in chapter 1 of Eseldorf as absolutely devoid of intellectual activity serves primarily as a baseline of ignorance from which August will eventually begin to drift away.

By moving from the village to Castle Rosenfeld, August not only escapes Eseldorf's oppressive atmosphere but is exposed to an environment conducive to the acquisition of knowledge through reading.[7] Within August's first year at the castle he becomes an apprentice in Stein's print shop (presumably necessitating on his part a heightened state of literacy and a higher level of intellectual dexterity) and develops respect for his mentor's devotion to study. Describing Stein, August notes: "He was a scholar, and a dreamer or a thinker, and loved learning and study, and would have submerged his mind all the days and nights in his books and been pleasantly and peacefully unconscious of his surroundings" (12). As the first intellectual August has ever met, Stein, with his ostensible dedication to mental improvement, provides stimulation for August to emerge from a state of psychic slumber associated with life in Eseldorf. At the same time, however, despite its positive effect on August, Stein's reading is not presented here in an altogether affirmative fashion. Stein is, after all, depicted as "pleasantly and peacefully unconscious" of the realities of the world around him (12). He might plausibly be described as escapist or self-deluding. In this sense, then, Stein is not unlike other characters in Twain's works, including Huck Finn, Jim, Hank Morgan, and others who by sheer inability to comprehend the truth of their existence indulge a life that is false, a delusion—they submit to the dream, the cosmic hoax. Nevertheless, given the direct relationship between reading and learning established in the first few chapters and the fact that August, like Huck, had never before been "overmuch pestered with schooling," the introduction of Forty-Four into the story occurs precisely when August, longing to follow Stein's example, is experiencing a profound desire to learn. It would seem extremely coincidental, however (not to mention slightly contrived), if Forty-Four, who assumes the role of August's educator, should simply arrive in deus ex machina–fashion just as August is ready to begin this journey to intellectual enlightenment. But his arrival is not coincidental. Indeed, substantial textual evidence indicates that Forty-Four's sudden appearance at Castle Rosenfeld is neither accidental nor an implausible act of destiny.

Although Forty-Four appears to be of an unknown, supernatural origin, as most scholars have suggested, several clues within the text support another possible interpretation. Arguing that "critics have taken Mark Twain's separation of the mysterious stranger and the story's first person much too literally," Robert Lowery (109) persuasively contends that Forty-Four is merely August's metaphorical perception of himself. Others, including William Gibson and John Tuckey, have recognized that Forty-Four and August essentially coalesce and become unified in the story's final chapter; yet most commentators, including Sholom Kahn, have not entertained the notion that August and Forty-Four could actually be one and the same from the very beginning. Thus far scholars have overlooked the crucial fact that the names "August" and "Forty-Four" support the idea of a wholly intimate, alter-ego relationship between the two characters. In addition to being a Germanic surname, August is the eighth month of the year, commonly represented as "8" in a date sequence. Forty-Four, of course, is numerically expressed as "44," whose digits when added together equal 8. The two characters are also curiously close in age, for August informs the reader that he is "16" years old (16), and that Forty-Four is "apparently sixteen or seventeen years old" (17). Further, much of the "mystery" surrounding Forty-Four's sudden appearance at Stein's print shop begins to make more sense if one considers his role as the personification of August's intellect: Twain introduces Forty-Four into the novel precisely at the moment when August first becomes aware of his intellectual nature and his desire to learn. August, in other words, begins moving at this moment toward the recognition that he is comprised of two selves, which Twain expresses allegorically in the naming of the novel's mysterious stranger—August, "8," is actually two selves, symbolically represented by Forty-Four's presence in the narrative as well as by his curious name, "4 and 4."[8]

This interpretation of August's and Forty-Four's names and relationship to each other is further corroborated by Jamesian theories of psychology. In both *The Principles of Psychology* and *The Varieties of Religious Experience* James argues that all individuals are comprised of two selves. James himself defines the nature of the two selves in a number of different ways, but in the end he settles generally on the notion that we are all constituted by a physical self and a spiritual self. The physical self, as James sees it, is essentially that part of ourselves that is corporeal, social, outward, and conscious—the "Empirical Me" (*Principles* 291). The spiritual self, on the other hand, consists, James notes, of "a man's inner or subjective being, his psychic faculties or dispositions, taken concretely" (*Principles* 296). In *The Varieties of Religious Experience* James further distinguishes the two selves, referring to them, respectively, as the "shallower or lower sphere" and the "profounder sphere" (97) or "higher nature" (100). Whether taken to mean the dialectic of the body and mind, the outward and inward, or the physical and the spiritual, James's theory of the divided self corresponds neatly to Forty-Four's tutorial about the nature of the "Workaday-Self" and "Dream-Self" in chapter 18 of *No. 44, The Mysterious Stranger*:

> "The way of it is this," he said. "You know of course that you are not one person, but two. One is your Workaday-Self, and 'tends to business, the other is your Dream-Self and has no responsibilities, and cares only for romance and excursions and adventure. . . . It has far more imagination than has the Workaday-Self. . . . But you understand, they have no substance, they are only spirits. The Workaday-Self has a harder lot and a duller time; it can't get away from the flesh, and is clogged and hindered by it; and also by the low grade of its imagination." (97)

First, consider the ways that Twain's "Workaday-Self" and James's physical self resemble each other: both are defined by their bodily natures, the visible part of our being; both are characterized by temporal limitation, concerned primarily with the rational and mundane; and both are considered the subordinate part of the self. Second, Twain's "Dream-Self" and James's spiritual self are similarly alike: both are regarded as the inward, the spiritual part of our being; both are oriented to functions of the mind; and both are considered to be hierarchically superior to the physical portion of the individual.

Additionally, the relationship of August and Forty-Four itself echoes the key distinctions between the Jamesian selves insofar as August and Forty-Four exist as parts of a single identity, another—arguably, the central—example of the Workaday-Self/Dream-Self motif within *No. 44, The Mysterious Stranger*: August, the physical self, is consistently portrayed as lesser, limited, and mortal; Forty-Four, the spiritual self, is just as consistently shown to be superior, boundless, and mystical. And the larger action of the novel leads directly from August's recognition that he consists of two selves to his and Forty-Four's unification in the final chapter, all of which is fundamentally consistent with the central tenets of Jamesian psychology. Look closely, for example, at James's explanation of the individual's recognition that we are comprised of a physical and spiritual self at the beginning of the process toward psychological unification and how it resembles August's situation and intellectual status as Forty-Four is introduced into the narrative: "But whether we take it abstractly or concretely, our considering the spiritual self at all is a reflective process, is the result of our abandoning the outward-looking point of view, and of our having become able to think of subjectivity as such, *to think ourselves as thinkers*" (*Principles* 296). When Forty-Four appears, August, owing to Stein's example, has just begun to think of himself as an intellectual creature. As this event initiates August's psychic quest in *No. 44, The Mysterious Stranger*, Forty-Four's arrival would seem to mark August's first steps toward intuiting that he, too, is comprised of a physical and a spiritual self, or as Twain puts it, a "Workaday-Self" and a "Dream-Self." August is beginning to think of himself subjectively at Castle Rosenfeld—and Forty-Four materializes. August, in other words, has crossed the threshold into a contemplation of himself in concrete as well as abstract terms, a prerequisite for inaugurating the process of Jamesian unification and psychic transcendence. And while the full thematic significance of Twain's seemingly peculiar choice of names for the novel's central characters will emerge only after the Duplicates episode, the profoundly fundamental connection between August and Forty-Four is, nevertheless, underscored and echoed very early in the narrative.

With the suggestive symbolism of August's and Forty-Four's names and the timely appearance of Forty-Four, *No. 44, The Mysterious Stranger* seems at least slightly reminiscent of Edgar Allan Poe's "William Wilson," in which the first-person narrator recognizes too late the metaphorical alter-ego of himself as a conscience-stricken, autonomous, but weaker individual.[9] Here, too, it could be claimed that a gradual process of education takes place throughout the tale. Scholarly supposition of Twain's admiration of Poe's work is well documented, and Poe's stories with "double motifs," as Alan Gribben has argued, particularly appealed to Twain, himself "a tireless chronicler of twins, disguises, exchanged roles, and contrasting personalities" ("Spiritual Derelicts" 19). That Forty-Four functions as an apotheosis of August's intellect is not only quite plausible but also is consistent with further evidence within the text, including the novella's final episode. Just as Forty-Four's appearance in the story marks the inception of August's desire to educate himself, so *No. 44, The Mysterious Stranger* begins to reveal itself to be a compelling mixture of secular bildungsroman and psychic allegory. The elements of bildungsroman are unmistakable (that is, August's gradual maturing and his cognitive advancement); with the introduction of characters who either explicitly or implicitly minister to August's development while metaphorically representing certain abstract concepts, the novel at times takes on allegorical dimensions.

As the story moves forward, August grows intellectually and approaches the second stage of his self-education, the conquering of his fear of popular opinion. Now that August has actually "freed" his mind from the limitations of illiteracy, underscored by the fact that Forty-Four is initially referred to as "Jail-bird" (21) (as in ex-convict), he begins to experience a heightened sense of awareness that lifts him above the herd mentality of the print-shop crew. But it is not enough, Twain makes clear, for August at this point in his development simply to "have submerged his mind all the days and nights in his books and been pleasantly and peacefully unconscious of his surroundings" as Stein longs to do. Twain seems to be making the point that with each stage in August's growth, it is necessary for him to continue to progress beyond his last big breakthrough, that while the acquisition of literacy and the emergence of an intellectual curiosity are indeed great accomplishments, in and of themselves they mean little if not regarded as steps along the way to higher development. Yet August remains tormented by a painfully sensitive self-consciousness and a fear of publicly acknowledging Forty-Four: "Privately my heart bled for the boy, and I wanted to be his friend, and longed to tell him so, but I had not the courage, for I was made as most people are made, and was afraid to follow my own instincts when they ran counter to other people's. The best of us would rather be popular than right" (26). Consequently, August, unable to forsake the security of the status quo, is forced to slink about the castle and meet with Forty-Four only at night and in complete secrecy.

The second stage of August's self-enlightenment is marked, like the first, by the appearance of a visitor to Castle Rosenfeld. Personifying the mental posture of indifference that August must adopt to continue his intellective journey, Doangivadam (whose name can, of course, be pronounced "don't give a damn" and is an example of the novel's undercurrent of allegory) quite literally enables August and Forty-Four to divorce themselves both physically and ideologically from the rest of the print-shop crew. The Doangivadam episode immediately invites comparison with Thomas Carlyle's famous chapters from *Sartor Resartus* (1831), "The Everlasting No," "The Center of Indifference," and "The Everlasting Yea," which document the conversion of the character Teufelsdröckh from a state of rejection to affirmation but only after moving through a period of indifference or detachment from the world around him. Significantly, James cites Carlyle and his Teufelsdröckh in both *The Principles of Psychology* and *The Varieties of Religious Experience* as he makes the case that in the process of psychic unification of the two selves, one must necessarily enter into a period of indifference. Whether Twain relied on James or his own copy of *Sartor Resartus*,[10] it seems that he, too, may have had Teufelsdröckh in mind as he conceived of August's transformation in the middle chapters of *No. 44, The Mysterious Stranger*.

While August's overall sense of timidity and fear only slowly melts away, Doangivadam's presence immediately inspires Forty-Four to stand up to the herd and indict them as the wrongdoers. The fact that Forty-Four in effect represents August's intellect possibly accounts for the period of delay between their respective reactions. Though in his mind August desires to stand up to the print-shop crew at once, his overriding awareness of human vulnerability holds him back. In addition, Doangivadam, whose words of advice are more than once referred to as "wisdom" (70), is praised as a "very learned" man (50), suggesting the adversarial relationship between true knowledge and popular opinion. And importantly, it is just as necessary for August to carry forward the gains he has made in this second stage of his development as it was for him to move beyond the gains made in the first stage with Stein, for later in the narrative Twain demonstrates through Doangivadam's drunkenness and his advice to August in chapter 25 to deal with adversity by drinking heavily (which is, of course, just another variety of "not giving a damn") that while Doangivadam's lesson of indifference serves August well at an early point in his development, it would become debilitating if adopted as a governing personal philosophy.

In a broader movement within the story, August's increasing awareness is paralleled by his steadily declining obedience to religion. Although Twain weaves the subplot of Father Adolf's exploits into the primary story line mainly to satirize religion and the clergy, it also serves to effect a change in August. Critics like Kahn argue that these digressions have "no apparent purpose" (119), but they do, in fact, function as a sort of backdrop against which the reader is able to gauge August's declining belief in the authority of the church after leaving Eseldorf. Almost unnoticeably, August evolves from an individual who profoundly believes in the power of the Sisters of the Perpetual Adoration to one who carelessly forgets to pray for Forty-Four's lost soul. It is also significant that Forty-Four, in the role of August's intellect, harasses Father Adolf and the magician in similar fashion, thereby linking religion to magic, illusion, and deception.

Further, Twain's criticisms of religion and the story's more spiteful characters, though acrimonious at times, are more frequently presented in masterfully controlled episodes of vintage Twainian humor, especially in light of Twain's treatment of similar issues in "The Chronicle of Young Satan." The differences in tone between these works are largely the result of Twain's apparent recovery of his comic voice in *No. 44, The Mysterious Stranger* to satirize various institutions and individuals. Michael Kiskis, in fact, has argued that between the mid 1890s and 1910, Twain only gradually came back to humor as a primary tool in his work after recuperating from the dual tragedies of his bankruptcy in 1894 and the death of his daughter Susy in 1896 ("Coming Back to Humor"). Indeed, while the infamous episode from "The Chronicle of Young Satan" in which a cold and indifferent "mysterious stranger" named Young Satan creates and then unfeelingly annihilates his miniature race of human beings typifies Twain's acerbic tone throughout that story, Twain couches much of the criticism in *No. 44, The Mysterious Stranger* in scenes and episodes rich with irony and humor that convey a much less bitter narrative mood.

Throughout chapter 10, for example, as August explains the history of the Sisters of the Perpetual Adoration and Father Peter recounts several miraculous appearances of Christ throughout medieval Europe in order to raise contributions for repairs to the chapel, Twain satirizes religious superstition and criticizes church materialism subtly but, most importantly, without the vitriol typical of "The Chronicle of Young Satan." This narrative shift ultimately suggests that by the time he commenced the story of August Feldner's intellectual journey in 1902, Twain had already begun to move away from the straightforward invectives of the late 1890s and early 1900s and to some degree had essentially returned to the crafting of intricate tales that critique indirectly through the development of character and plot. *No. 44, The Mysterious Stranger* is filled, additionally, with dozens of memorable humorous character sketches, the choicest of which is August's portrait of Moses Haas in chapter 7:

> Moses was setting type, pulling down his guide for every line, weaving right and left, bobbing over his case with every type he picked up, fetching the box-partition a wipe with it as he brought it away, making two false motions before he put it in the stick and a third one with a click on his rule, justifying like a rail fence, spacing like an old witch's teeth—hair-spaces and m-quads turn about—just a living allegory of falseness and pretence from his green silk eye-shade down to his lifting and sinking heels, making show and bustle enough for 3,000 an hour, yet never good for 600 on a fat take and double-leaded at that. It was inscrutable that God would endure a comp like that, and lightning so cheap. (37)

The vernacular jargon, overstated similes, outrageous descriptions, and unforgettable punch line all work together in this passage to communicate both an attitude of measured disapproval and vivid characterization that distinguishes the work as a whole. In this late novel, Twain's comic voice returns at times to its mature best.

Considering *No. 44, The Mysterious Stranger* from beginning to end, it can be seen that it steadily becomes more fantastical and dreamlike, less concerned with peripheral characters and setting, and more intensely focused on August and Forty-Four. In a sense, then, the story is very much the portrayal of August's reflective journey inward, with each stage of his progression toward enlightenment paralleling the constricting focus of the novella. Proceeding with his intellectual evolution, August moves beyond any concern for popular opinion and enters the third stage of his journey toward enlightenment, which, like the first and second stages, is marked by the appearance of new characters in the story.

Symbolic of his profound introspective reflection, the love triangle episode involving August, his Duplicate, and Marget Regen represents August's unflinching recognition of human nature. Through his participation in the love triangle incident, August learns firsthand that coexisting within all individuals yet remaining distinct and separated from one another are both the limitations of the human condition and, paradoxically, the very means by which people might transcend their earthly foibles. The episode, in effect, mirrors the very psychological journey August undertakes over the course of the larger narrative as he comes to grips with both Forty-Four's spiritual nature and his own relationship to the story's mysterious stranger. The important distinction with this sequence of chapters, however, is that August learns about the differences between the flesh-bound mortal and the enlightened spirit by actually experiencing those states firsthand as opposed to relying on Forty-Four's tutelage. Indeed, Forty-Four's momentary departure from the story clears the stage for August to interact with his Duplicate, Emil Schwarz, without aid or guidance as he comes to understand the complexities of human consciousness as both mortal and spirit and from the dual perspectives of actor and observer. This reading of the episode not only accounts for Forty-Four's curious and sudden disappearance from the narrative but is also consistent with turn-of-the-century progressive education reforms that championed "learning by doing" pedagogies, which Twain both endorsed and publicly supported in the last decade of his life.

By 1894 progressive education reform had become part of mainstream conversation in the United States.[11] That year Francis W. Parker, associate and intellectual forerunner of John Dewey, published *Talks on Pedagogics: An Outline of the Theory of Concentration* (1894). Parker's book, according to biographer Jack K. Campbell, "was instantly successful" (135). Publications such as the influential literary magazine the *Critic* featured articles on *Talks on Pedagogics*, while professional organizations, including the National Education Association, debated its ideas. What Parker argues for in the book is a new educational model emphasizing a "learning by doing" philosophy. His was one among several challenges by educational theorists in the late nineteenth century to the timeworn but largely conventional pedagogical practice of passive student learning through abstract lecture and rote memorization. According to Joop Berding, Parker's philosophy, and subsequently Dewey's, drew fundamentally from the three major educational reform movements of his day.[12] The first movement grew out of the work of Friedrich Froebel, father of the kindergarten philosophy who advocated early childhood learning through play and work. The second, known as the child study movement, developed as a result of an enormously influential psychological study conducted by G. Stanley Hall in the 1890s. The child study movement essentially argued that the educational development of adolescents is closely related to the stages of psychological development and that for each stage there are certain appropriate learning activities. The third reform movement, the Herbartian, consisted primarily of advocates of educational thinker Georg Friedrich Herbart and promoted the theory of apperception, the idea that adolescent learning takes place when classroom lessons carve new impressions in the mind that somehow connect with past personal experience. Although Parker and Dewey expressed dissatisfaction with certain elements of each of these three educational reform movements, both men were staunch allies in their larger goal of developing modern pedagogical methodologies informed by nineteenth-century scientific breakthroughs in the areas of child development and human understanding.

Soon after Parker's death in 1902, Dewey relocated from the University of Chicago to Columbia University in New York and emerged as the most prominent advocate of the "learning by doing" philosophy of education. In the first two decades of the twentieth century, Dewey's pedagogical theories influenced not only classrooms around the country but also other venues that proponents of progressive education reform attempted to utilize in the promotion of their cause. The Children's Theater of the Jewish Educational Alliance, located on the Lower East Side of New York City, for example, directed by Alice Herts and whose board of directors included Mark Twain in 1907 and 1908, viewed itself as principally serving an educational mission while affording young people access to the world of dramatic theater. Herts's book *The Children's Educational Theater* (1901)

reveals the influence of Dewey's educational theories on her work as director of the Children's Theater. In a chapter titled "The Dramatic Instinct
of the Young Child, and Its Satisfaction" Herts provides the following excerpt from an essay by fellow Children's Theater director Percival Chubb
of New York Society's Ethical Culture School:

> Our recent pedagogy has not been insensible of the great losses suffered by
> the child through the change in our civilization from one of rural type to one
> of urban type; but it has had its eye chiefly on the so-called manual activities
> of the child—that side of the old life of the child on the farm or in the small
> semi-rural town, to which Professor Dewey and his disciples have drawn our
> attention. They have insisted upon the practical recognition of the principle
> of self-activity and the fundamental motor-nature of the child. The child
> learns by doing, by trying, and we must give back to him in new forms the old
> opportunity for instructive activity which he had by doing things about the
> home and the farm. (78)

Herts's inclusion of the passage in *The Children's Educational Theater* points
not just to her familiarity with Dewey and his pedagogical ideas but also,
presumably, to her endorsement and application of them at her own theater. Herts, then, provides a plausible point of contact between Twain and
Dewey's educational theories at about the same time that Twain would have
been composing the latter chapters of *No. 44, The Mysterious Stranger*.

Louis J. Budd contends in *Our Mark Twain: The Making of His Public
Personality* (1983) that the Children's Theater of the Jewish Educational
Alliance was a cause to which Twain did more than simply lend his name.
Twain, in fact, spent long afternoons at the theater in 1907 and 1908 doing
routine office work. In a letter written in September 1908 to Amelia Hookway, whose Howland School Theater in Chicago had just performed *The
Prince and the Pauper*, Twain discloses the degree to which he, like Herts,
had been convinced—whether directly or indirectly—of Dewey's philosophy of "learning by doing" while associated with the Children's Theater:

> I have been reading the eloquent account in the Record-Herald and am plea-
> surably stirred, to my deepest deeps. The reading brings vividly back to me
> my pet and pride: The Children's Theater of the East side, New York. And
> it supports and re-affirms what I have so often and strenuously said in public
> that a children's theatre is easily the most valuable adjunct that any educa-
> tional institution for the young can have, and that no otherwise good school
> is complete without it.

It is much the most effective teacher of morals and promoter of good conduct that the ingenuity of man has yet devised, for the reason that its lessons
are not taught wearily by book and by dreary homily, but by the visible and
enthusing action; and they go straight to the heart which is the rightest of
right places for them. Book morals often get no further than the intellect, if
they even get that far on their spectral and shadowy passage: but when they
travel from a Children's Theatre they do not stop permanently at that halfway
house, but go on home. . . . Our young folks do everything that is needed
by the theatre, with their own hands; scene-designing, scene-painting, gas
fitting, electric work, costume-designing—costume making, everything all
things indeed. (Tuckey, *Little Satan* 72–73)

Twain's celebration of theater as an "effective teacher" and his disparage-
ment of lessons taught "wearily by book and dreary homily" reflect the
same sentiment as turn-of-the-century efforts to replace old-school, pas-
sive-student learning models with the fundamentals of Parker's and Dewey's "learning by doing" educational strategies. It is likely, therefore, that
Twain could have had these pedagogical theories in mind as he composed
the chapters that involve the love triangle incident in 1907 and 1908.

An enormously significant episode, the love triangle incident occupies
nearly 25 percent of the total text of *No. 44, The Mysterious Stranger*. It has
been one of the most confusing parts of the story largely because of the fact
that August, depending on the perspective of other peripheral characters
involved in the episode, appears to be a different person. To Marget and
Emil, he is August; to Marget's Dream-Self, Lisbet, he is Martin von Giesbach. In addition, there is the bewildering correlation between August,
Martin, and Emil. Which character (or characters) is the Dream-Self?
Which is the Duplicate? What is the difference between the Dream-Self
and Duplicate? But despite the seemingly chaotic nature of the love triangle
incident at the surface, the episode advances Twain's theme of August's intellectual development steadily and efficiently. For instance, as the episode
commences late in the story in chapter 23, August reveals that he is now
"barely seventeen" (117). The fact that he is a year older than he was at the
beginning of the novel not only subtly reaffirms August's growth (physical
as well as intellectual) but also places August at an age where the sexual
activity that he discusses and pursues over the next several chapters would
be perceived as more acceptable.[13] Critics have long recognized Twain's
enduring Victorian anxieties regarding the subject of adolescent initiation

into sexual awareness, and his careful and explicit reference to August having recently turned seventeen—thus arguably crossing the threshold into young adulthood—seems to be in part generated by those concerns.

The events of the love triangle incident begin after Forty-Four has disappeared from the castle, leaving August alone with his recently acquired ability to make himself invisible to others. As August experiments with this special power, he repeatedly uses it to place himself near Marget Regen, Stein's niece and the object of August's affection throughout the story. But more than simply roaming undetected in these scenes, August, much to his surprise, realizes suddenly that his invisibility brings with it the attributes associated with a spiritual state of being. After kissing Marget in chapter 23, August notes:

> Her body trembled with each kiss received and repaid, and by the power and volume of the emotions that surged through me I realized the sensations I knew in my fleshly estate were cold and weak by contrast with those which a spirit feels.
>
> I was invisible, impalpable, substanceless, I was transparent as the air, and yet I seemed to support the girl's weight and bear it up. No, it was more than seeming, it was an actuality. This was new; I had not been aware that my spirit possessed this force. (120)

Though August originally wants only to get nearer to Marget by becoming invisible, the experience ultimately leads to his beginning to fathom all that Forty-Four had attempted to teach him about the differences between spirit and flesh, the Dream-Self and the Workaday-Self—indeed, the very natures of Forty-Four and August themselves. It is only upon his actually assuming for himself a spiritual condition, that of the Dream-Self *firsthand*, that August begins to grasp the distinctions between the two disparate states of being that Forty-Four has been attempting to teach him throughout the narrative, particularly as they relate to the differences of perception and feeling. Put in the context of Jamesian psychology, August has at last begun to appreciate fundamentally the nature of the "divided self," a major step toward psychic healing and transcendence.

Immediately upon August's realization here that he is experiencing the world as a spirit, he learns that he has actually been kissing not Marget but Marget's Dream-Self, Lisbet. Lisbet, in turn, recognizes August not as August but as August's Dream-Self, named Martin.[14] All too happy to take advantage of Lisbet's confusion, August simply pretends to be Martin and continues to explore the nuances of the spiritual state as he carries on with his Dream-Self lover. But more than just a mere comedy of errors, Lisbet's mistaking of August for Martin and August's playing along throughout this scene work thematically to reinforce the idea that August is now functioning in the narrative as a spirit and Dream-Self. As a result, Twain is able to dramatize August's symbolic evolution over the course of the love triangle incident from dull workaday mortal to enlightened spirit to signify August's gradual understanding of the different states of human existence.

Twain advances the motif of August's evolution upward through the states of human existence by bringing August into contact with Emil, August's Duplicate. August, who earlier in the narrative is portrayed as equal or perhaps inferior to Emil, is now cast as Emil's superior both in terms of awareness and abilities. August, for example, appears to run circles around Emil as August abuses the now seemingly pitiable Duplicate at the end of chapter 23. August, angry and jealous that Emil might be in love with his beloved, lashes out at him:

> I could not endure it. I flew at him and with all of my spirit-strength I fetched him an open-handed slat on the jaw that sent him lumbering and spinning and floundering over and over along the same floor till the wall stopped him. He was greatly surprised. He got up rubbing his bruises and looking admiringly about him for a minute or two, then went limping away, saying—
> "I wonder what the hell *that* was!" (123)

Again, Twain's depiction here is significant in that it emphasizes August's recent mental and physical ascension over the apparently bewildered Emil—so bewildered, in fact, that Emil in this episode resembles August as he was portrayed earlier in the novel. August in this and subsequent scenes involving Emil, therefore, is in one sense afforded the extraordinary opportunity to see himself from the point of view of an outsider. Both literally and figuratively, Emil is a personification of August. He is a Duplicate, which Twain defines in chapter 18 as a "Dream-Self" that has been pulled out of the "Original" and endowed with "fictitious flesh and bone" (97). In this episode, however, Emil also serves as a symbolic flesh-and-bone stand-in for what August was before the love triangle incident, which in turn effectively allows August to see himself and reality temporarily from Forty-Four's advanced spiritual perspective.

As the episode continues, August makes an attempt in chapter 24 to untangle for the reader the clutter of identities introduced in the previous chapter:

> By ferreting out of my memory certain scraps and shreds of information garnered from 44's talks I presently untangled the matter, and arrived at an explanation—which was this: the presence of my flesh-and-blood personality was not a circumstance of any interest to Marget Regen, but my presence as a spirit acted upon her hypnotically—as 44 termed it—and plunged her into a somnambulic sleep. This removed her Day-Self from command and from consciousness, and gave command to her Dream-Self for the time being. Her Dream-Self was a quite definite and independent personality, and for reasons of its own it had chosen to name itself Elisabeth von Arnim. It was entirely unacquainted with Marget Regen, did not even know she existed, and had no knowledge of her affairs, her feelings, her opinions, her history, nor of any other matter concerning her. (124)

Aside from helping the reader make sense of the growing cast of characters, this passage is also significant in the way that it might be read to correlate to the relationship between August and Forty-Four. Marget and Lisbet, despite being parts of the same identity, are strangers to each other in much the same way that August perceives Forty-Four to be a stranger, even though they, too, as we have argued, are parts of a single person. The placement of this passage in the novel makes sense if we allow the love triangle incident at one level to be read as Twain's further revelation of the true nature of the relationship between August and Forty-Four. Just as important, perhaps, and paralleling August's growing awareness of the true nature of his reality, the reader's steadily increasing awareness occurs simultaneously with August's as he moves through this important episode.

Twain begins to nudge the love triangle incident toward climax near the opening of chapter 24 as August introduces the concept of the third "self," the Soul:

> There was another thing which I had learned from 44, and that was this: each human being contains not merely two independent entities, but three— the Waking-Self, the Dream-Self, and the Soul. The last is immortal, and the others are functioned by the brain and the nerves, and are physical and mortal. (124)

As August goes on to explain, the Soul constitutes the essential self. It is that which remains after the Workaday-Self and the Dream-Self dissolve away. The Soul, in other words, is the integration and unification of the constituent parts of the individual within the self. When one considers the love triangle incident triumvirate of Emil (the Workaday-Self); August, as he pretends to be Martin (the Dream-Self); and August, who now reveals that "when I was invisible the whole of my make-up was gone . . . my soul—my immortal spirit—alone remained" (125), it becomes clear that Twain further advances August into something like the role of a Soul here in chapter 24, thus completing August's firsthand symbolic ascent through all states of human existence. Twain's descriptions of the immortal Soul in *No. 44, The Mysterious Stranger* suggest a thorough intellectual awareness, an absolute integration of body, mind, and spirit that parallels the eventual unification of August and Forty-Four in the final chapter. More important, Twain's concept of the "third self" here in chapter 24 echoes key elements of James's theories of psychic unification.

In *The Principles of Psychology* James argues that the component parts of the individual—the physical self and the spiritual self—need to be regarded ultimately in the context of their eventual synthesis, a state he terms "the Soul" (342).[15] The Soul functions precisely in Jamesian psychology as it does in *No. 44, The Mysterious Stranger*, for James and Twain both envision the Soul as the immortal transcendent state of being resulting from psychic unification of the two selves. August's temporary assumption of the climactic state of the Soul is, again, principally symbolic in that it reflects his comprehension of that state of being. His actual transcendence, foreshadowed here, takes place in the final chapter only after he and Forty-Four, his authentic Dream-Self, coalesce into a fully synthesized entity. August's comprehension of the role of the Soul completes the symbolic journey of comprehension he undertakes in the love triangle incident.

Forty-Four abruptly returns to the castle in chapter 26 just after August appears to have sorted out the states of human existence in the love triangle incident. Curiously, however, Forty-Four reappears in blackface, singing nineteenth-century American minstrel standards.[16] Scholars have struggled to make sense of this and other seemingly inexplicable narrative digressions, particularly those of the middle and late chapters of *No. 44, The Mysterious Stranger*, which provide the narrative with so much of its fanciful or—in the minds of many—farcical feel. It is understandable why some critics have simply written off these elements of the novel, viewing them either as the products of Twain's momentary whim or (less likely) the result of his inability to sustain a focus for the story. Nevertheless, many of the so-called narrative eccentricities are in fact consistent with the deeper currents of the novel. On the one hand, they correspond to certain specific elements within Jamesian psychology. On the other hand, and even more crucially, it is precisely within some of these more outlandish episodes that signs of discernible shifts begin to emerge in Twain's thinking about the new science of psychology. So consequential are these shifts, in fact, that it is our contention that midway through the writing of *No. 44, The Mysterious Stranger*, Twain realized that he was unable to maintain his earlier sense of faith in the science of psychology to purge the Calvinist-inspired sensibility that partly motivated him as he began the writing of the novel. Indeed, the novel's more bizarre scenes and episodes are key to a full appreciation of Twain's failure to escape from, and his eventual return to, his heretical religious thinking during the period between 1902 and 1908.

Forty-Four's impressive abilities, which range from his apparently inherent knowledge of Greek and Latin to his arsenal of "magical" powers, obviously defy the laws of literary verisimilitude. Yet Forty-Four's gifted nature is easy enough to explain if we remember that he is a metaphorical representation of August's intellect. What we see, then, in Forty-Four's characterization is to some degree an expression of August's powers of imagination. Forty-Four's ability to create, to vanish, to travel through space and time all demonstrate Twain's faith in the nearly unlimited potential of the mind. At the same time, there are numerous thematic explanations for several key incidents in *No. 44, The Mysterious Stranger* that showcase Forty-Four's preternatural capabilities. For example, as is the case with other plot elements early in the novel, Forty-Four's knowledge of Greek and Latin serves to emphasize the crucial role that literacy plays as a pathway to the individual's profound enlightenment. Soon after Forty-Four appears at the castle, Stein inquires as to his skills. Among other deficiencies, Forty-Four claims that he has not "studied" Latin or Greek (34). A few pages later, the evil Katzenyammer, looking to embarrass Forty-Four in front of Stein, believes he has caught Forty-Four in a lie when the mysterious stranger indicates he has knowledge of foreign languages from his past experiences as a printer's apprentice, but Forty-Four provides a rationale: "'Oh, no,' said the youth, earnestly, 'it is quite different. He asked me if I had *studied* it—meaning in a school or with a teacher, as I judged. Of course I said no, for I had only picked it up—from books—by myself'" (39). The emphasis of Forty-Four's response here draws attention to the fact that he has educated himself through reading. Like Frau Adler and Stein (and to some degree even August), Forty-Four is distinguished among the characters of the novel by his achieving a certain degree of mental self-improvement through literacy. And like the others whom Twain sets apart based on their ability and desire to read, Forty-Four comes off immediately as a sympathetic character. Additionally, insofar as Forty-Four represents August's intellect in the narrative, the revelation of his autodidacticism here is yet another expression of August's demonstrated mode of enlightenment. As it turns out, Forty-Four's "special powers" with language are plausible as well as consistent with central motifs in *No. 44, The Mysterious Stranger*.

Forty-Four's travel through space and time, which includes his accurate prediction of the future as well as August's exposure to those forthcoming events, might also be accounted for using this kind of thematic approach. Remembering that William James explains the process of psychic unification and transcendence of the soul in terms borrowed from mystical experiences helps make Forty-Four's and August's travel through space and time seem less peculiar. In *The Varieties of Religious Experience* James explains that his broader theories of "religious reconciliation" have their sources in the general concepts of mysticism: "One may say truly, I think, that personal religious experience has its root and centre in mystical states of consciousness; so for us, who in these lectures are treating personal experience as the exclusive subject of our study, such consciousness ought to form the vital chapter from which the others get their light" (379). The conception of mysticism James employs as an analogy for understanding his notions of psychic healing here and throughout *The Varieties of Religious Experience* is a fairly conventional understanding of the mystical experience: generally speaking, the process begins with the soul undergoing some form of purification process, which leads to spiritual transcendence and illumination, and ultimately results in a perfect comprehension of, and/or unification with, the divine. James argues that (within his system) as the individuals approach the healing point of psychic unification between their physical self and their spiritual self, they will undergo something akin to a mystical transcendence, which includes numerous experiences that correspond to those that August and Forty-Four undergo in *No. 44, The Mysterious Stranger*: "The kinds of truth communicable in mystical ways, whether they be sensible or supersensible, are various. Some relate to this world,—

visions of the future, reading of hearts, the sudden understanding of texts, knowledge of distant events, for example" (410). James's identification of "visions of the future, reading of hearts, the sudden understanding of texts, [and] knowledge of distant events" as consistent with the latter stages of psychic unification of the selves to some extent resembles numerous events and episodes involving August and Forty-Four. Forty-Four's "visions of the future"—including his banquet of corn pone, fried chicken, and coffee in chapter 22; his knowledge of minstrel songs in chapter 26; and his retrieval of a Boston newspaper from 1905 in chapter 30, to name a few—can all be partly explained as expressions of the "mystical ways" of "religious reconciliation" or the psychic healing that attends unification of the selves.

Ultimately, however, there was for Twain a fatal paradox embedded in his characterization of Forty-Four lying in wait for him from the very beginning. Although Forty-Four's curious powers can be read as Twain's fictional expression and endorsement of Jamesian psychological processes, they also represent what would become the very undoing of Twain's hope for psychology as a means for finally displacing his heretical countertheology. Twain embarked on the writing of *No. 44, The Mysterious Stranger*, as he often did with other texts over the course of his career, as a way of putting to the test ideas in which he was deeply and genuinely engrossed. Evidence within *No. 44, The Mysterious Stranger*, as well as biographical and historical information, strongly suggests that Twain was intrigued by the promise of the new science of psychology to ameliorate one's "training" and transcend the Calvinist vision of the cosmos that had circumscribed his consciousness from an early age. However, as Twain worked through the assertions of Jamesian psychology in the fictional laboratory of *No. 44, The Mysterious Stranger*, particularly as they related to the unlimited powers of the Dream-Self in his characterization of Forty-Four, it must have gradually occurred to him that the promises of Jamesian psychology had simply returned him to the foundational truisms of Calvinism. Like Oedipus, who ran from his fate only to meet it head-on, Twain's exploration of these philosophical and scientific countermeasures to his childhood religious indoctrination led him right back to the central tenets of his countertheology: that all is predestined and that freedom is an illusion.

Forty-Four's knowledge of nineteenth-century American cuisine, songs, and historical events in the middle and late chapters of *No. 44, The Mysterious Stranger* can all be accounted for to some degree if read as expressions of Jamesian psychological transcendence. At the same time, Forty-Four's travels to the future, whether considered expressions of psychic healing or not, most certainly would also have struck Twain as corroboration of the foundational tenets of Calvinism, namely the predestined nature of the cosmos. In other words, if James's theories of psychology posit that the future is knowable, does it not follow that the future has already been determined? If the future has already been determined, then Jamesian psychology, at least for Twain, has not truly offered an alternative way of understanding human nature and the universe in which it exists. At the very least, Twain ultimately would have questioned how James's claims for a freedom of the will and his acceptance of a foreordained future could have been compatible. (Moreover, would not a knowable future necessarily imply an intelligent source for that order?) In the end, it is very likely that, for Twain, all the new science of psychology really afforded was a clearer revelation of the cosmic hoax to which he had always subscribed. This perception must have occurred to Twain as he brought August through the final stages of his development in *No. 44, The Mysterious Stranger*, and, therefore, what began as hopeful venture for Twain, the exploration of a possible ideological antidote to his countertheology, eventually returned him back to the very place he had begun intellectually in 1902.

William Dean Howells's story "A Difficult Case" (1900) provides evidence of Twain's habit of putting ideas to the test in just the way described above. "A Difficult Case" is the tale of the confrontation of Clarence Ewbert, a young optimistic minister, with Ransom Hilbrook, an elderly religious skeptic. Ewbert and Hilbrook are initially drawn to each other in a series of conversations that culminate in a debate over questions of the afterlife. Hilbrook, who early on lost both his wife and their only son, has lived a bitter life and remains doubtful that the hereafter is likely to turn out to be any better than one's earthly experience. Ewbert sets out to persuade the old man. Both men are well-read and familiar with the literature of metaphysics, so Ewbert attempts to convince Hilbrook by using philosophy and logic. Despite his cynicism, Hilbrook longs to embrace a more affirming vision of the afterlife and is temporarily persuaded by Ewbert that there is reason for hope. However, weeks later, after he has reflected on the linchpin of Ewbert's argument more thoroughly, Hilbrook ultimately concludes: "There ain't anything *in* that. I got to thinking it over, when you was gone, and the whole thing went to pieces. That idea don't prove anything at all, and all that we worked out of it had to go with it" (211). Elsewhere Lawrence Berkove has argued that Howells based Hilbrook on Twain, a fact that was widely recognized, even by Twain himself, at the time of the story's publication.[17] What Howells's story reveals through its portrayal of Hilbrook is not just Twain's more pessimistic tendencies regarding questions of God and the afterlife but also, more importantly, Twain's desire to pursue in good faith philosophical antidotes to his heretical thinking. In the end, however, like Hilbrook, Twain found himself unconvinced that his heretical view of the cosmos was wrong. Indeed, much of the so-called inconsistent tone of *No. 44, The Mysterious Stranger* appears to make more sense if read in light of the fact that Twain's realization that James's psychology failed to live up to its implied promise of deliverance occurred to him only incrementally as he wrote the text between 1902 and 1908.

Returning to the broader issue of August's step-by-step intellectual development in the novel, after Emil is "set free" by Forty-Four near the end of chapter 29, August enters the fourth and final stage of his self-education, which, like the others, is marked by the entrance of new characters into the plot. Summoning the "Assembly of the Dead," Forty-Four introduces August to a metaphorical representation of his accumulated knowledge. In what Kahn terms a "random mingling of biblical and pagan, historical and Darwinian, elements" (183), this history pageant marks August's assimilation of a complete and unabridged education. John Tuckey speculates that Twain's letter to Amelia Hookway quoted above, praising her Children's Theater program in Chicago, could perhaps have been "written on the same day" (*Mark Twain and Little Satan* 72) he composed the pageant episode for *No. 44, The Mysterious Stranger*. Indeed, Twain remarks in that September 1908 letter about live theatrical productions: "No other teacher is for a moment comparable to it: no other can make the dead heroes of the world rise up and shake the dust of the ages from their bones and live and move and breathe and speak and be real to the looker and listener . . . and no other can paint a history-lesson in colors that will stay, and stay, and never fade" (*Mark Twain and Little Satan* 72–73). Given Twain's acknowledged admiration of the history pageant as an educational forum, its appearance in *No. 44, The Mysterious Stranger* precisely as August achieves complete enlightenment affirms the presence of a central motif of education running throughout the story. Afterward, August reports that "by the grace of Forty-Four's magic I could understand them" (184), confirming that August, dependent on Forty-Four as a physical representation of his intellect, has attained full illumination about even the illustrious dead.

In the final chapter of *No. 44, The Mysterious Stranger* August achieves complete enlightenment, as Forty-Four reveals that he is merely a creature of August's imagination. At its most basic level, the novel is indeed the story of August Feldner's journey from the darkness of blind faith in religion to the light of rational integration. After the miracle of the printed word is opened to him in Stein's print shop, and with the help of Forty-Four's guidance, August gradually overcomes his fear of popular opinion, divests himself of religious superstition, and explores notions of human consciousness. However, despite the hopeful theme of enlightenment running throughout the story, August in the end is left frightened and appalled by what he has come to learn about the human condition and the universe in which it exists. August's education has fundamentally awakened him from the dulling placidity of his dreamlike existence in Eseldorf into the nightmarish reality that humankind endures not under the supervision of a compassionate and caring divine being, but abandoned in a hellish cosmos, all of which Forty-Four discloses to him unequivocally in the novella's infamous final passage:

> "It is true, that which I have revealed to you: there is no God, no universe, no human race, no earthly life, no heaven, no hell. It is all a Dream, a grotesque and foolish dream. Nothing exists but You. And You are but a Thought—a vagrant Thought, a useless Thought, a homeless Thought, wandering forlorn among the empty eternities!"
>
> He vanished, and left me appalled; for I knew, and realized, that all he had said was true. (187)[18]

Three points need to be made about this passage as it relates to the broader implications of Twain's conclusion to the novel. First, it must be acknowledged again that because the last chapter was written relatively early in the novel's composition, there may seem to be a number of inconsistencies between it and the rest of *No. 44, The Mysterious Stranger*. Moreover, because Twain never authorized the book's publication, it remains a matter of scholarly conjecture whether the ending fits the fundamental logic of the narrative. That said, we believe the ending can be seen to fit. In fact, while certain layers of the plot closest to the surface in the final chapter may appear incompatible with the trajectory of the rest of the novel, we argue that at its deepest level, the closing scene reveals a coherent vision consistent with *No. 44, The Mysterious Stranger*'s major themes.

The second point to be made about the conclusion is that its tone is undeniably despairing. While critics such as Robert Lowery have tended to read the final chapter more optimistically,[19] the repetition and application of descriptions such as "grotesque," "foolish," "vagrant," "useless," "homeless," and "appalled" to characterize August throughout the closing scene are inescapably bleak. Again, though written out of sequence several years before Twain brought the manuscript to a point where the novel might be considered "completed," the final chapter of *No. 44, The Mysterious Stranger* reflects the thinking of an author who in the end appears unable to have shaken his Calvinist perspective. Consider, for instance, the vehemence with which Forty-Four attacks fundamentalist theology:

> Strange, indeed, that you should not have suspected that your universe and its contents were only dreams, visions, fictions! Strange because they are so frankly and hysterically insane—like all dreams: a God who could make good children as easily as bad, yet preferred to make bad ones; who could have made every one of them happy, yet never made a single happy one; who made them prize their bitter life, yet stingingly cut it short; who gave his angels eternal happiness unearned, yet required his other children to earn it; who gave his angels painless lives, yet cursed his other children with biting miseries and maladies of mind and body; who mouths justice, and invented hell—mouths mercy, and invented hell—mouths Golden Rules, and forgiveness multiplied by seventy times seven, and invented hell. (187)

Although Forty-Four's diatribe is couched as a dismissal of such beliefs, its vitriol and passion betray Twain's lingering attachment to its ideas. The speech is yet another example of Twain's use of the "diverted target." The frenzied tenor of the attack, the specificity of the charges, and the anger underlying it all suggest that rather than reflecting Forty-Four's humorless dismay about humankind's religious constructs, the passage betrays both Twain's enduring rage with the God at the center of his countertheological vision as well as Twain's deep-seated frustration at his inability to have fully divested himself of the core tenets of that vision via the science of psychology. And, of course, the couching of his personal anxieties in this manner additionally affords Twain a measure of plausible deniability with his more sensitive readers.

The third and perhaps most important point that needs to be made about the final chapter is that there is potentially more to Twain's reference to August as a "Thought" than has been generally allowed by critics. Historically, scholars have read Forty-Four's revelation that August is nothing but a "Thought" and his insistence that "nothing exists save empty space and you!" (186) largely in the context of philosophical solipsism. However, there are problems with this perhaps too literal interpretation of the closing scene. Forty-Four, for example, tells August at the beginning of the chapter that the "future life," the glimpses of the future that he provided for August earlier in the novel, "was a vision—it had no existence" (186). On this point Forty-Four is simply—and demonstrably—wrong, perhaps even misleading. The truth of the matter is that the future as depicted in the novel, and as revealed by Forty-Four, is real and does have "existence" because each of the "predictions" he makes from the fifteenth century eventually does come true. In other words, Twain's twentieth-century contemporaries, or we as twenty-first-century readers, know that the songs Forty-Four sings, the exotic food he serves, and the notable events he describes actually did come to pass—they remain today, as they were at the time of the novel's composition, verifiable facts of history. Moreover, the overarching premise of the novel, that August narrates the story from old age directly to an implied audience, establishes that August necessarily believes that there are other people in existence besides him. These facts, therefore, begin to call into question Forty-Four's reliability as a mouthpiece for Twain's views in this final chapter in ways that are reminiscent of Hank Morgan throughout *A Connecticut Yankee in King Arthur's Court* (1889). Like Stein, Doangivadam, and Emil before him, Forty-Four has played a crucial role in August's development, but he, too, eventually outlasts his usefulness. As a metaphorical representation of August's intellect, Forty-Four here dramatizes the ways in which the human mind is capable of deluding the individual (if one's ideas are not tested against anything outside oneself). For these reasons, the argument that August has simply embraced solipsism as *No. 44, The Mysterious Stranger* draws to a close fails to account for and accord with other important elements of the novel.[20]

A more satisfactory way of understanding the ending of *No. 44, The Mysterious Stranger* is afforded first by considering *The Principles of Psychology* and then by returning once more to Twain's matrix of countertheology. Interestingly enough, James, in *The Principles of Psychology*, also employs the term "Thought" and defines it as the phenomenal expression of one's immortal and essential being. James explains further as he discusses the concept of Thought in the context of its relationship to the Soul:

> Thought also has being,—at least all believers in the Soul believe so—and if there be no other Being in which it "inheres," it ought itself to be a "substance." If *this* kind of simplicity and substantiality were all that is predicated of the Soul, then it might appear that we had been talking of the soul all along, without knowing it, when we treated the present Thought as an agent, an owner, and the like. But the Thought is a perishing and not immortal or incorruptible thing. Its successors may continuously succeed to it, resemble it, and appropriate it, but they *are* not it, whereas the Soul-Substance is supposed to be a fixed unchanging thing. By the Soul is always meant something *behind* the present Thought, another kind of substance, existing on a non-phenomenal plane. (345)

What James describes here is very similar to what one sees at the deepest thematic layers of the last chapter of *No. 44, The Mysterious Stranger*. As James would have it, "Thought" is an "agent," a mortal articulation, of the "fixed unchanging" Soul. Put another way, James asserts that an individual's authentic and comprehensive sense of identity resides in one's Soul, and "Thought" is the term he uses to describe a small, fractional expression of that total and unified self in a given moment of time. Thus when Forty-Four divulges that August is nothing more than a "Thought" and is free to "dream other dreams" (186), he is effectively telling August, who has been trapped his entire life in a single limited conception of himself as a corrupt child of God in a cruel cosmos, that he has always had the power to comprehend himself and his world in alternative ways. With every successive conception of himself and the universe that August might pass through, he expresses a new "Thought" and another articulation of his Soul. It is in this sense that Forty-Four's revelation to August that the universe and its contents have no real substance ought to be ultimately understood.

Forty-Four's revelation here in the final chapter of the novel is not far removed conceptually from traditional Judeo-Christian notions of the world as insubstantial, created out of nothing, and sustained by the breath of God. Even so, supposition of the insubstantiality of the universe as expressed in the context of conventional Judeo-Christian cosmology (and, as we have seen, in Jamesian psychology) is an inherently affirmative conception. That God formed and maintains the universe is a foundational article of Christian faith traditionally regarded as a sign of God's generosity and love. What, then, of the hopeless tone of Twain's conclusion to *No. 44, The Mysterious Stranger*? August's despair in the final chapter is the result of his awakening from the dreamlike consciousness in Eseldorf into the frightening realization that he and the universe are ultimately without substance. August's reaction at the end of the novel is that of an individual for whom the "reality" is worse than the dream because of the inherent instability implied in Forty-Four's revelation. In other words, August's negative reaction here is to the fact that there is ultimately no stability to reality in the way that the "false consciousness" of his life in Eseldorf seemed to provide.

We have argued above and elsewhere that the central motif in *No. 44, The Mysterious Stranger*, the notion of reality as a dream or "false consciousness," is fundamental to Twain's canon. *A Connecticut Yankee*, for example, is entirely structured on Twain's notion that life is little more than an illusion: none of the humans in the novel are quite conscious of the true nature of their existence. All live and struggle in a dream. Some move from one dream to another, but they remain deceived about their state.[21] But unlike Hank Morgan, who, as we have argued, is fatally insensitive to the implications of living in a dream, August, like the narrator of *Roughing It* (1872), is exceptional in Twain's canon insofar as he is ultimately aroused from his delusion through Forty-Four's tutelage and as a result becomes aware, tragically, of what Twain believed at that time was the true essential nature of human existence and the universe. And echoing at least in part the vast complexities at the heart of the Edenic myth, specifically the eating of the fruit of the Tree of the Knowledge of Good and Evil in which Adam and Eve, too, seek knowledge and as a result of their enlightenment are "awakened" to the terrifying reality of a life vastly different than the one they knew as unaware creatures in paradise, *No. 44, The Mysterious Stranger* exposes the fundamental ironies of knowledge and its unforeseen incumbent complications.

As such, Forty-Four's revelations in the closing chapter put August into the position God had faced when he addressed the *tohu* and *vohu*, the nullity and void of uncreation, and spoke orderly creation into existence. August finds himself, led on by Forty-Four's final diatribe, confronting the task of creating existence out of nothing, just as God had done. Except chagrined by the awesome and humbling project, August is appalled by the challenge, for, mortal and fallible, he glimpses his inadequacy to be a creator. He is serious and responsible, unlike the flighty Forty-Four, who has brought him to the frontier of the difference between humans and God and dared August to do what he himself had backed away from: to become a creator and deal with the consequences of his imagination. *No. 44, The Mysterious Stranger* might thus be viewed as Mark Twain's book of Job, in which humanity in the person of August is daunted both by the overwhelming magnitude of the infinite requirements of transforming nothingness by imagination into being and also of sustaining and regulating it with immortality, along with the fearsome knowledge of good and evil.

In the end, Mark Twain's turn-of-the-century ventures into the science of psychology were not as much a dead end as a loop that eventually led him back to the main trail of his Calvinist countertheology. All is predestined after all, but while the less perceptive may end up in the outer circles of hell, like the little girl with poppies in her hair in *A Connecticut Yankee*, the more perceptive, like August—and Twain himself—penetrate to the deeper circles, there to experience despair and a longing for the less bleak illusions of benighted humanity.

The Last Letters from Earth

BETWEEN DESPAIR AND COMPASSION

I will be gracious to whom I will be gracious, and will show mercy on whom I will show mercy. —Exodus 33:19

In December 1899 *Harper's Magazine* printed "The Man That Corrupted Hadleyburg," one of Mark Twain's most acclaimed stories. Ten years later, in December 1909, Twain worked for the last time on an unfinished manuscript he titled "Letters from the Earth," which would remain unpublished in his own lifetime.[1] Scholarship of the last sixty-five years has generally regarded the period between the appearance of "The Man That Corrupted Hadleyburg" and the setting aside of "Letters from the Earth" as Twain's darkest, in which he descended into despair, suffered bouts of crippling depression, and, according to some, perhaps even teetered on the brink of insanity itself.[2] At least on its face, then, this period in Twain's career would seem to have provided optimal conditions for the full artistic disclosure of his heretical countertheological beliefs. And in some ways it did. However, despite the fact that evidence from the events and writings of the last ten years of Twain's life leaves us with a disturbingly cheerless portrait, this period is also one in which he experienced moments of unprecedented creativity and appears to have regained a capacity for humor that seemingly had all but disappeared from his writing just years earlier. Moreover, during this highly controversial decade, Twain's notions of God, humankind, the cosmos, and—perhaps most crucially—who or what was to blame for the human condition underwent enormous transformation.

Since the early 1970s critical discussions of Twain's final decade as a writer have inevitably begun, for better or worse, by dealing in some way with the thesis of Hamlin Hill's *Mark Twain: God's Fool* (1973). Hill's well-known portrait of Twain as a bitter, irrational, and lonely old man is certainly compelling given the sheer volume of evidence, biographical and otherwise, Hill marshals in making his case. Subsequent scholarship, including most notably Laura Skandera Trombley's research dealing with the Ashcroft-Lyon affair and what she terms Twain's "annus horribilis" of 1908-1909,[3] has corroborated and expanded certain elements of Hill's original analysis. At the same time, however, other critics have observed more balance in Twain's temperament and work in his last decade as an artist. William Macnaughton's *Mark Twain's Last Years as a Writer* (1979), probably the most direct scholarly response to Hill's book, views the last decade of Twain's life not as a time of artistic failure but rather as years in which he produced "high quality" works "not markedly inferior to the writing that he produced in any other period during his career" (241-242). Michael Kiskis's analysis of Twain's turn-of-the-century autobiographical dictations similarly reveals the marked degree to which humor reemerged as a crucial element of his writing in the last years of life.[4]

Tom Quirk, in his *Mark Twain and Human Nature* (2007), offers perhaps the most succinct rejoinder to Hill: "Twain's last years may have been hellish, but there remained available to him some avenues of temporary happiness, and one of them was to ponder the nature of his fellow human beings" (241-242). Quirk focuses specifically on Twain's reflections on human nature as a source of "temporary happiness" during the last decade of his life. We concur somewhat on this point and would add that while the fundamental tenets of Twain's countertheology remained intact as he experimented with narrative form between 1899 and 1909, Twain shifted considerably in his theories to account for the source of human suffering and expressed a deepening compassion for the human race as he pondered it. There is substantial evidence, in fact, that Twain came to sympathize with humankind in those last ten years in ways that he had not earlier.

Twain variously—and sometimes simultaneously—found humanity to be funny, ridiculous, vicious, disgusting, and damned, but seldom sensible and never stable. It supplied him with endless opportunities to express humor, pity, anger, and despair. Twain found its maker sublime, mysterious, sinister, terrible, and hateful. He believed that God created everything good and could have kept it so; instead God allowed—or directed—the first couple to sin once and then visited an awful and ongoing punishment upon them, all their descendants, and all the world forever, which Twain found not only strange but profoundly unjust. "Lord, how we are made—

how strangely we are made!" says Mary Richards in "The Man That Corrupted Hadleyburg" (137). That short and simple comment, particularly when taken pejoratively, is as good a capsule summary of Twain's core philosophy as anything he ever wrote. And it applies to the maker as well as to the human race.

Readers and critics alike have tended to view "The Man That Corrupted Hadleyburg" as an emblem—perhaps even the supreme expression—of the pessimism that characterizes the later writings of Twain's career. An interesting feature of this consensus, however, is that there have been essentially two diametrically opposed ways of arriving at this general interpretation of the story. The first views "Hadleyburg" as an articulation of Twain's late determinism. Taking cues from Bernard DeVoto's analysis in *Mark Twain at Work*, where he writes that the story reveals "man's complete helplessness in the grip of the inexorable forces of the universe" (115), scholars from Gladys Bellamy to Tom Quirk have argued that the citizens of Hadleyburg demonstrate the degree to which Mark Twain had concluded "that human conduct is regulated by outside influences and training" (Quirk, *Mark Twain and Human Nature* 236–237). "Hadleyburg," according to this line of inquiry, written in the vein of literary naturalism, presents the fall of the nineteen leading citizens as both predictable and inevitable given the fact that human nature, as depicted in the story, is governed deterministically by self-interest, greed, and hypocrisy. The stranger, apparently exceedingly knowledgeable in matters of the human condition, "devises almost laboratory conditions for the testing of human behavior," argues Bellamy (308), and sets in motion a chain of events to which the citizens of Hadleyburg react uniformly and inexorably.

A second trend in Twain criticism, taking a different view of the story, considers "The Man That Corrupted Hadleyburg" to be first and foremost an exposé of the ugliness that fundamentally defines human nature. Self-interest, greed, and hypocrisy are indeed the hallmark characteristics of human behavior, but critics like Everett Emerson, Susan K. Harris, and Cynthia Ozick see the Richardses and others as victims of nothing more than the selfish choices that they make.[5] The characters of the story, in other words, have agency in their collective demise. Every one of the nineteen families succumbs to the temptation by consciously deciding to claim a reward that each one knows is not theirs. Thus the tale highlights the corruption that lies beneath the surface of Hadleyburg's leading citizens—and, by implication, all of us. Like St. Petersburg, Dawson's Landing, Eseldorf, and many of Twain's other fictional small-town settings, Hadleyburg, according to this line of reasoning, serves as a metaphor for universal human depravity.

While both readings possess merit, the fact that Twain scholarship views the story as an expression of philosophical determinism *and* of the role of free will in human depravity suggests that neither interpretation provides a fully satisfactory appraisal of the story. We believe that "The Man That Corrupted Hadleyburg" is perhaps best understood in the context of Twain's countertheology, which also offers the benefit of effectively resolving the dilemma presented by these two opposed readings. To begin, the mysterious stranger of the story seems to be no ordinary mortal. He had an incredible amount of money at his disposal; he wandered for a year at a time; he was bitter, malicious, and vengeful; his knowledge of the town was infernally intimate; and when he finally thought up his plan to corrupt (a Calvinist term) the entire town, "it lit up his whole head with an evil joy." The stranger, therefore, has more than a touch to him of Satan, the tempter, and the illustration of him that originally appeared in *Harper's* emphasized his devilish looks: pointed chin, ears, and eyebrows; deep and glowing eyes; and an evil grin. As for its part, Hadleyburg is a rigidly and narrowly righteous town—smug, sanctimonious, coldly indifferent to strangers, and only superficially honest, a fact that its own citizens are apparently aware of: Mary Richards's first reaction, for example, after the stranger leaves the sack of coins, is to lock her doors. But more than anything, Hadleyburg is proud of itself. The narrator, in fact, mentions Hadleyburg's sense of pride no fewer than three times in the story's opening paragraph. Pride goes before the fall, runs the proverb, and Christianity regards pride as the first of the seven deadly sins. In this respect, Hadleyburg is indeed set for a fall.

With the tempter motif and the depiction of the fall of the town due to its wicked behavior, the dramatic structure of "The Man That Corrupted Hadleyburg" appears at least slightly reminiscent of the biblical story of the fall from Eden, a myth that Twain returned to over and over again in the last two decades of his life. In addition to these larger structural elements, consider that, as in the Genesis story, the tempter in "Hadleyburg" also first approaches a woman who is alone. Mary Richards is initially afraid of the mysterious stranger, but eventually, we are told, "her curiosity was roused and she went straight for the sack" (Berkove, *Short Stories* 208).

After the stranger departs, Mary Richards presents Stephenson's sack to her husband, who immediately succumbs to temptation, just as Adam succumbed after Eve presented the apple to him. As if to underscore the point, Twain repeats the scenario with the very next married couple he introduces to the reader. Mrs. Cox, wife of the editor-proprietor of the town newspaper, sways her husband to give in to his desire for riches by suggesting aloud that they might keep knowledge of the sack a secret and quietly split the money with the Richardses.

And as in Twain's numerous other retellings of the Edenic myth, Hadleyburg's fall is portrayed as inevitable. In the words of Edward Richards, "We—we couldn't help it, Mary. It—well, it was ordered. *All* things are" (249). Although earlier in the story Mary Richards scoffs at the idea that everything is "ordered," even she comes to accept this as the only possible way of accounting for their fate: "Ordered! Oh everything's *ordered*, when a person has to find some way out when he has been stupid. Just the same, it was *ordered* that the money should come to us in this special way, and it was you that must take it on yourself to go meddling with the designs of Providence—and who gave you the right" (217). Insofar as Twain posits the idea that the events of the story are "ordered" and a function of "the designs of Providence" (mention of which is often a hint of seriousness in Twain's writing), neither the Richardses nor any of the other nineteen leading citizens, though appearing to make choices in the story, actually have much real say in the way that things play themselves out. They are as they were made: hopelessly human. In this sense, then, their actions are indeed beyond their control—but not because they are victims of a deterministic cosmos, as numerous scholars have argued in the past.[6] If anything, the story demonstrates that "training," generally considered a cornerstone of philosophical determinism, is itself a hoax. In their foolish attempt to override their fundamentally sinful natures through extensive conditioning, the citizens of Hadleyburg actually highlight the failure of training to account satisfactorily for human behavior. And never mind that Hadleyburg does an obviously poor job of teaching honesty to its young. It simply does not matter. Human nature, at least in Twain's view, is fixed and corrupt, a fact borne out repeatedly by the actions of the citizens of Hadleyburg from beginning to end. Furthermore, no amount of training—good or bad—could have altered the "order" of things for the citizens of Hadleyburg. To believe that they could escape their destinies as self-interested human beings through training, to alter the designs of Providence in other words, is itself an act of pride, a delusion on the part of the citizens of Hadleyburg.

Hadleyburg is indeed a corrupt town right from the beginning, and there is as much irony embedded in the story's title as there is in its conclusion. When the narrator sardonically claims in the final paragraph that Hadleyburg "is an honest town once more," Twain conspicuously draws the reader's attention both to the fact that it never really was an "honest" town and that it is certainly not one now (171). The town leaders, who all mendaciously claimed to have offered the advice "go and reform" when they believed lying would make them rich, never even considered in their condescending pride the need to take the advice they claimed to have given. The shallowness of the town's vaunted honesty is exposed when it changes its name after its embarrassment, as if that would alter its basic character or even was an honest action.

Thus the portrait of human nature Twain presents in "Hadleyburg" is devastating and severe. But it is not without precedent. The spleen with which Twain delivers his indictment of the human race here might be described as unusually intense, but his fundamental irritation with humanity is detectable as far back as the satires and burlesques he wrote at the beginning of his career. "The Story of the Bad Little Boy That Bore a Charmed Life" (1865) and "Story of the Good Little Boy Who Did Not Prosper" (1870), for example, parody the soupy morality promoted in the simplistically religious tales of Sunday school tracts, and thus the theology behind the instruction, but religious satire is only part of Twain's purpose here—and perhaps not even Twain's primary aim. Gladys Bellamy argues, for instance, that the real target of the two stories is "the perversity of the human race" (111), which view is borne out by the moral depravity exhibited at the core of both works. Theft, deceit, cruelty, and murder predominate in the action of these tales. Jim, the "universally respected" protagonist of "The Story of the Bad Little Boy," for example, progresses from stealing apples and abusing animals as a boy to "all manner of cheating" and murder as an adult (23). In contrast, in both tales Twain dismisses good behavior as either a fantasy of religious teaching or outright inimical to basic human nature. Edgar M. Branch likewise contends that the view of the fundamentally corrupt makeup of humankind drives both tales and links them thematically to the cynical vision of later narratives such as *The Tragedy of Pudd'nhead Wilson* (1894).[7]

"The Second Advent," written in 1881, similarly attacks human nature in ways that anticipate "The Man That Corrupted Hadleyburg." In "The Second Advent" the town of Black Jack, Arkansas, is revealed to be deeply hypocritical.[8] Just as the citizens of Hadleyburg at the end of the story in effect abandon their Christianity out of pride and self-interest, so in "The Second Advent" do the people of Black Jack find that the interposition of the deity in their affairs causes such havoc that they in effect reject Jesus and legally restrict Christianity to a nominal form. The people of Black Jack also demonstrate that they, too, are extremely cruel. By the conclusion of the story, the town, described by Twain now as "the maddened populace" (322), puts an end to the second Advent by hunting down and crucifying "the Savior" and eleven of his twelve disciples. As a way of punctuating his condemnation of the townspeople, Twain reveals in the closing sentences of the story that the Judas-like twelfth follower was not only spared but rewarded by the citizens of Black Jack for his betrayal of the others with thirty pieces of silver.

In a much broader sense, "The Second Advent," through this central storyline, again asserts that foundational idea in Twain's canon: human nature is fixed and does not change. The fact that nearly two thousand years later the citizens of Black Jack behave in precisely the same fashion to events obviously similar to those such as the virgin birth, the visitation of the three wise men, and Christ's ministry, as recounted in the New Testament, demonstrates that human behavior at its most fundamental level is dreadfully constant. The assertion that history repeats itself with regard to human nature is, as we have argued, among the most significant implications of the Grangerford-Shepherdson episode of *Adventures of Huckleberry Finn* (1885) as well as *the* controlling metaphor of *A Connecticut Yankee in King Arthur's Court* (1889).[9] And that the people of Black Jack act the way they do in the story, despite their knowledge of the Bible's condemnation of the people who rejected Christ during the "original" Advent and Passion, only serves to showcase the hypocrisy and conceit that lie at the heart of Twain's vision of humanity.

Twain, at different points in his career, invoked the idea of a modern nativity as a way of expressing his disgust with human nature. As late as 1906 Twain continued to reflect on the likely reaction of contemporary Christians to the scenario at the center of "The Second Advent." In a notebook entry dated June 20, 1906, for example, he writes, "The Immaculate

Conception could not be repeated successfully in New York in our day.[10] It would produce laughter, not reverence and adoration."[11] The following year Twain also commented in the margins of his copy of Rufus K. Noyes's *Views of Religion* (1906) that "if it should turn out that a Chicago virgin has given birth to God Almighty, would Chicago believe it?[12] Even on the testimony of shepherds and cowboys?"[13] Twain's assertion in these musings as well as in "The Second Advent" is not only that the human race is foolish and morally disappointing but also that human nature is fixed, literally unchanged in the nearly nineteen hundred years since the time of Christ's birth. There is humor in "The Second Advent," but it is a grim humor. For Twain, most of the preachments about the goodness of God and the human race were adult equivalents of the Sunday school tracts that he satirized a decade earlier.

Although "The Man That Corrupted Hadleyburg" concludes without the violence of "The Second Advent," Twain's attitude toward the inhabitants of Black Jack and Hadleyburg is consistent. The final twist of "The Man That Corrupted Hadleyburg," the ironic juxtaposing of the town's earlier and later mottoes, tells it all. The first one, quoting from the Lord's Prayer, boasts of how devout it is. The latter, however, effectively denies its Lord by rewording the humble prayer into a dare. Nothing was learned; nothing was taken to heart; nothing changed. Hadleyburg was corrupt at heart when the stranger arrived, and all he did was make the town reveal its true character. The story is intricately devised, and all elements work together to present a very bleak view of human nature. As such, "The Man That Corrupted Hadleyburg" represents something of a high-water mark for Twain's antipathy for humankind.

Although Twain continued to express this kind of hostility in his later work, after the publication of "The Man That Corrupted Hadleyburg" he began to portray humanity with greater compassion while placing the blame for human flaws on God with ever increasing intensity. Indeed, one notes the frequency with which Twain repeats in work after work from his last decade the notion that human beings "are as they were made," leaving open the implication that the ultimate responsibility for humanity's foibles lies outside their control, but with their maker. For Twain, this shift in his view of human nature represented a significant modification within his countertheological vision, and one that continued to develop during his remaining years.

Written in 1898, at about the same time as "The Man That Corrupted Hadleyburg," "The Great Dark" shares a number of characteristics with the better acclaimed tale. "The Great Dark" is an incomplete story, lacking a conclusion and containing some minor inconsistencies. We include it in our discussion, however, because although unfinished, it is one of the most powerful stories Twain ever undertook to write and constitutes an important part of his literary record. Scholarship has linked this story, like "The Man That Corrupted Hadleyburg," to events in Twain's life and has identified some autobiographical elements in it. In a letter to William Dean Howells, dated August 16, 1898, Twain expressed his intention to make the first half or three-quarters of the story comic (*Twain-Howells Letters*, 676). This intention notwithstanding, and while there are humorous passages throughout, the story as a whole is far from comic. In notes he left about the story, Twain outlined his conclusion. After ten or fifteen years of aimless wandering in unremitting darkness, the ship on the drop of water that is its world comes into the reflected beam of light under the microscope. The "great dark" gives way to a hot, white glare that dries up the sea. A previous meeting of the ship with another lost vessel had resulted in the children of both the captain and the protagonist, Edwards, being abducted as prisoners. Once the water evaporates, Edwards and the captain take a grueling trip over the dry seabed to that ship, only to find all aboard dead and their children's bodies mummified by the heat. The captain is maddened by grief. Meanwhile, back on their own ship, crew members get drunk and begin killing one another. Others, including Edwards's wife and other daughter, die of stress and sorrow. The story was supposed to end with Edwards awakening from his dream, at home with his family, but whom he now regards as dreams—"reality" having been transformed into a matter of alternative dreams.

The most frightening part of the story, however, deals with the Superintendent of Dreams, another "mysterious stranger" figure. When Edwards orders him, early in the voyages, to end the dream immediately, the superintendent replies, "The dream? *Are you quite sure it is a dream?*" As we explained in our chapter on *A Connecticut Yankee*, the issue of dream versus reality is, in Twain's works, more than a matter of psychological perception. Here as in his 1889 novel, Twain contemplates the proposition that existence and linear history are hoaxes, that the same unchanging events are continuously being replayed in different temporal dimensions, and that existence is illusory, a matter of slipping from one of these dream dimensions into another.

Twain was fascinated by the telescope, as "Captain Stormfield's Visit to Heaven" (1909/1995) shows, and by the microscope, as "The Great Dark" makes clear. He was predictably drawn to the thought that just as humans can look down upon tiny organisms invisible to the naked eye that are huge and terrifying in their own dimension, so might we and everything of our world seem equally minute and inconsequential to larger and more sapient beings. In fact, Twain speculated at one time that only God truly exists as an independent and infinite being, and that everything else, from microscopic organisms to human beings to astronomical systems, are merely particles in his arteries, of which he is unaware and to which he is largely indifferent.[14]

A letter Twain wrote to Olivia Langdon on January 8, 1870, clearly shows that his skepticism of the centrality of humankind and our planet was on his mind at a very early stage in his career:

> I have been reading some new arguments to prove that the world is very old, & that the six days of creation were six immensely long periods. For instance, according to Genesis, the *stars* were made when the world was, yet this writer mentions the significant fact that there are stars within reach of our telescopes whose light requires 50,000 years to traverse the wastes of space & come to our earth. And so, if we made a tour through space ourselves, might we not, in some remote era of the future, meet & ~~shake han~~ greet the ~~lag~~ first lagging rays of stars that started on their weary visit to us a million years ago?—rays that are outcast & homeless, now, their parent stars crumbled to nothingness & swept from the firmament five hundred thousand years after these journeying rays departed—stars whose people lived their little lives, & laughed & wept, hoped & feared, sinned & perished, bewildering ages since these vagrant twinklings went wandering through the solemn solitudes of space?
>
> How insignificant we are, with our pigmy little world!—an atom glinting with uncounted myriads of other atom worlds in a broad shaft of light streaming from God's countenance—& yet prating complacently ~~about~~ of our speck as the Great World, & regarding the other specks as pretty trifles made to guide our schooners by & inspire the reveries of "puppy" lovers. Did Christ live 33 years in each of the millions & millions of worlds that hold their majestic courses above our heads? ~~Ou~~ Or was *our* small ~~glov~~ globe the favored one of all? Does one apple in a vast orchard think as much of itself as we do?—or one leaf in the forest,—or one grain of sand upon the sea shore? Do

the pismires argue upon vexed questions of ~~theology~~ pismire theology,—&
do they climb a molehill & look abroad over the grand universe of an acre of
ground & say "Great is God, who created all things for Us?"

I do not see how astronomers can help feeling exquisitely insignificant,
for every new page of the Book of the Heavens they open reveals more &
more that the world we are so proud of is to the universe of careering globes
~~is~~ as is one mosquito to the winged & hoofed flocks & ~~hea~~ herds that darken
the air & populate the plains & forests of all the earth. ~~Verily, What is Man,
that he should be considered of God?~~ If you killed the mosquito, would it be
missed? Verily, what is ~~m~~Man, that he should be considered of God?

One of these astronomers has been taking photographs of tongues of
flame 17,000 miles high that ~~shot~~ shoot aloft from the surface of the sun, &
waver, & sink, & rise again—all in two or three minutes,—& sometimes in
one minute swinging a banner of flame from left to right a distance of 5,000
miles—an inconceivable velocity! Think of the hurricanes that sweep the
sun, to do such miracles as this! And other tongues of flame stream upward,
~~arch &~~ bend & hang down again, forming a crimson arch 28,000 miles in
height, through which our poor globe might be bowled as one bowls ~~an apple~~
a football between a boy's legs. (*Letters* 4:12–13)

Contemplating such evidence of the inconceivable immensity of the universe
eventually undermined Twain's intention to become a Christian believing
in a personal God and stayed in his thoughts for the rest of his life, as his
representations of the enormity of the universe in his later works bear out.

Twain's unfinished novel "3,000 Years among the Microbes" (1905) is
a later fictional expression of this idea. The very notion of infinity implied
to Twain that finite humankind and its world and solar system are of relatively trivial importance. "The Great Dark" gloomily extends this point by
allegorically picturing a ship that is a symbol of the world, but a nightmare
world, the plaything of a superior but malicious being, a world that does
not know where it is going and, for the most part, proceeds in the dark.
This world, moreover, moves like a planet in an orbit around a sun of intense light and heat—really the focused beam of a microscope—which is,
ironically, worse than the darkness itself and would be fatal if experienced
directly. The manipulator of the microscope does not care about the tiny
beings that inhabit the ship or the drop of water it floats on. From the perspective of this story, the captain's statement in his last speech that the ship
"is in the hands of God" could be literally true, God being the manipulator
of the microscope. But that fact does not imply a benevolent, personal, and

caring God, and Twain does not find it any source of comfort. And this is in large part the point of the story.

In contrast to "The Man That Corrupted Hadleyburg," the human beings in "The Great Dark" are not the object of Twain's criticism. At worst, for example, Edwards is presented as perhaps slightly foolish for mistaking his reality for a dream and vice-versa. The true target of condemnation in "The Great Dark" are the "realities" created by the all-powerful, indifferent manipulator of the microscope—and, of course, the manipulator himself for creating these "realities." And because Twain's implied image of God in this story is so harsh, human beings by comparison come off not only as helpless victims but also as deserving of sympathy. The citizens of Hadleyburg might be subject to forces out of their control inasmuch as their ends as corrupt beings have been foreordained, but their conduct in the story itself elicits none of the pity Twain appears to reserve for the Edwardses and others in "The Great Dark." That Twain could compose "The Great Dark" and "The Man That Corrupted Hadleyburg" at nearly the same time, stories that represent two very different attitudes toward humankind, reflects not confusion on Twain's part but good-faith tension in the writer's mind regarding human nature itself. "The Man That Corrupted Hadleyburg" represents, in large part, the climax of Twain's early attitude toward humanity, one that is focused almost exclusively on the simple fact that human beings are generally deplorable creatures. It is important, however, to recognize that while this is predominantly the view of humanity that governs Twain's writing from the first sketches through the late 1890s, it dwells lightly on the *causes* of human wickedness; it is concerned mainly with the *effects* of the human condition. "The Great Dark," however, reflects a view of human nature that Twain came to embrace increasingly in the final ten years of his life. In this latter conception of the human condition, Twain begins to explore not just what people are but how they got that way. The result of Twain's concern in his late writings about causation in matters of the human condition indicates a newfound sympathy for the human race.

The composition history of the Mysterious Stranger manuscripts discussed in the previous chapter corroborates the assertion that Twain's attitudes toward humankind altered noticeably in the last years leading up to the turn of the century.[15] The first draft of "The Chronicle of Young Satan," the earliest version of Twain's so-called Mysterious Stranger story, was written between October 1897 and January 1898. In terms of tone, the original version of "The Chronicle of Young Satan" shares much with "The Man That Corrupted Hadleyburg" as it focuses primarily on attacking human vanity both through Satan's numerous frank conversations about human nature with the young boys of the story and through the town's generally contemptible behavior, particularly that of its most vicious citizen, the priest Father Adolf. In November 1898, however, when Twain began to write "Schoolhouse Hill," the tone of the Mysterious Stranger manuscripts shifts dramatically. Whereas the initial draft of "The Chronicle of Young Satan" is marked throughout by a tone of contempt, "Schoolhouse Hill," by contrast, is relatively lighthearted and even comical at times. The portrayal of Satan in "The Chronicle of Young Satan" is that of a cold, uncaring individual who exhibits almost no compassion for humankind. On the other hand, Twain depicts the Satan figure of "Schoolhouse Hill" not only as an affable individual who acts graciously toward the villagers (except the sinister Bascom family) but also as someone who is genuinely interested in—and evidently concerned for—the human race. The overall mood of the Mysterious Stranger manuscripts from this point in late 1898 through the writing of *No. 44, The Mysterious Stranger* (composed between 1902 and 1908) essentially maintains much of the sympathetic tone of "Schoolhouse Hill," focusing on themes of education, knowledge, and enlightenment.

Perhaps nothing Twain wrote in the first decade of the twentieth century serves as better illustration of his improved attitude toward human nature than the collection of texts based on the biblical first family.[16] "Extracts from Adam's Diary" (originally written in 1892 but heavily revised in 1905), "Autobiography of Eve" (written 1901), and "Eve's Diary" (1905) present the first representatives of the human race as foolish, stubborn, and self-interested. However, the source of Adam's and Eve's flaws is not the variety of human pride that condemns characters from Twain's earlier works, but their predestined childlike naïveté. Twain presents Adam and Eve as children—children who have been abandoned to an unjust fate and whose actions follow a preestablished course to ruin. The implied villain of these texts remained consistent, of course: an uncaring, unjust, and thoroughly cruel God who created the human race seemingly only to make it suffer, a race whose only offense appears to be that it behaves in ways that accord with the manner in which it was made.

"The Autobiography of Eve" opens on the eighth day of creation, with Eve, in the privacy of her diary, asking three seemingly simple questions: "Who am I? What am I? Where am I?" (Baetzhold and McCullough 42). On the surface, Eve's questions reflect a basic sense of childlike confusion about herself and the world around her. She is, after all, only a few days old and understandably disoriented. More deeply, however, Eve's queries also represent the questions that will come to occupy the minds of philosophers throughout human history. In her supreme innocence Eve effectively asks, but not in so many words, "what is the meaning of life?" But whether taken superficially or more philosophically, Eve's questions are a clear sign to the reader that she has been left by her creator—literally and figuratively—to fend for herself, a point she makes explicitly later in the narrative:

> Interests were abundant; for we were children, and ignorant; ignorant be-
> yond the conception of the present day. We knew *nothing*—nothing what-
> ever. We were starting at the very bottom of things—at the very beginning; we
> had to learn the a b c of things. To-day the child of four knows things which
> we were still ignorant of at thirty. For we were children without nurses and
> without instructors. There was no one to tell us anything. (54)

Twain simultaneously accomplishes two objectives in this passage. First, he generates a great deal of compassion for Eve specifically and humankind generally by portraying his protagonist as curious and helpless, but apparently not angry at the fundamental unfairness of her treatment. There is a detectable amount of "tenderness," as Howard Baetzhold and Joseph Mc-Cullough aptly put it,[17] in Twain's portrayal of Adam and Eve throughout his Edenic writings, and the tone of this particular scene is indicative of the humorous and kindhearted tone Twain employs in these later texts based on the story of the Fall.

Second, the passage delivers devastating implied criticism of Eve's maker. The list of questions begged by Eve's self-portrait is long: What kind of god would create beings so vulnerable? Why create beings only to forsake them? Why not assist them? Why set them up for an inevitable fall? Why so cruel? Although God is only mentioned in passing as "The Voice" in the Edenic texts, Twain ascribes to him responsibility for human nature, flaws and all, through Eve's repeated observation throughout the Adam and Eve diaries that she and Adam are hardly to blame for their condition as human beings. As Eve explores the sources of her affection for Adam in "Eve's Diary," she observes: "It is not on account of his brightness that I love him—no, it is not that. He is not to blame for his brightness, such as it is, for he did not make himself; he is as God made him, and that is sufficient" (31). Superficially, Eve's remark only directly attributes Adam's intelligence (or lack thereof) to God's design; however, Twain's point in passages such as this is to place responsibility for everything human where it logically belongs—with the maker.

But for their part, Adam and Eve introduce love into the world and create a paradise for themselves despite God's injustices. This serves as the strongest argument for accelerating Twain's willingness to forgive the human race in his last years. Indeed, the quality of affection the two share is largely unprecedented in Twain's writings prior to this point. Forty years after the expulsion from Eden, for example, Eve writes in her diary:

> It is my prayer, it is my longing, that we may pass together—a longing which shall never perish from the earth, but shall have place in the heart of every woman that loves, until the end of time; and it shall be called by my name.
>
> But if one of us must go first, it is my prayer that it shall be I; for he is strong, I am weak, I am not so necessary to him as he is to me—life without him would not be life; how could I endure it? This prayer is also immortal, and will not cease from being offered up while my race continues. I am the first wife; and in the last wife I shall be repeated. (33)

Humility, self-sacrifice, and loving concern for others define the vision of human nature expressed here. Not only does Eve care deeply for Adam, she also asserts that her capacity for love, far from being unique, is intrinsic to humanity and will be replicated in lovers for ages to come. Thus human nature is fixed in Eve's view; however, note that it is a markedly different portrait of human behavior from Twain's cynical pronouncements on humankind in works like "Hadleyburg" written just a few years earlier. And Twain's Adam and Eve, like Milton's, because of their love for each other, would rather be together though expelled from Eden than remain in Eden separately, as evidenced by Adam's famous last line in "Eve's Diary": "Wheresoever she was, *there* was Eden" (33).[18]

What Is Man? (1906) is the culmination of Twain's decades-long attraction to determinism, the idea that free will does not exist, that whatever we are, whatever we do, and whatever we become are the predictable outcome of external influences upon us. It is similar to predestination in its effect.

It eliminates choice and volition as causative elements in human thought and action and thereby treats the human being as a machine. Determinism, however, is different from predestination in its etiology. It is fundamentally scientific in its conception and without consideration of ultimate cause, or purpose, insists on a mechanistic accounting for all behavior and mental activity. Predestination, on the other hand, ascribes the total and purposeful control of the universe and all that is in it to an omniscient, omnipotent, and, according to the Bible, benevolent creator. It therefore, unlike determinism, assigns meaning and value to existence; nothing is random or accidental; everything is part of a plan, in many respects inscrutable to humans, that reflects the will of the creator.

Determinism is decidedly a concept with which Twain grappled both personally and artistically throughout the last three or four decades of his life. Evidence of his sincere interest in the idea exists in his letters, speeches, essays, and fiction. To put an even finer point on it, Quirk explains in *Mark Twain and Human Nature* that "in the ongoing debate between naturalists and environmentalists during this era, Twain was on the side of the environmentalists, lopsidedly so perhaps" (219). We do not disagree, biographically speaking. But ontologically, determinism was never Twain's deepest or most abiding conviction. Even in those texts where he consciously endeavors to foreground the idea of training, Twain, whether consciously or not, seems to undermine its very plausibility with plots and characters that make stronger arguments for the fixed nature of "essential" human identity and for a preestablished design immune to alteration by human hands. Regardless of how intellectually committed Twain was to notions of environmental determinism, his default position as an artist in matters of human nature was governed, so his best fiction suggests, first and foremost by a profoundly ingrained acceptance of a foreordained order to the cosmos. Determinism attracted Twain for many of the same reasons that the science of psychology did. But in the end, neither was able to permanently override his countertheological sensibility. Twain's Calvinist-inspired view of the cosmos simply explained more and better than any other philosophical system that he entertained, and evidence of Calvinism's accuracy appeared manifest everywhere he looked.

There is no question that Twain took determinism seriously, devoted much careful thought to it, and even situated explicitly deterministic passages within his literature. It is potentially far more formidable than any other digressions from his countertheology; nevertheless, in the final analysis determinism falls far short of providing a satisfactory basis for understanding Twain. It is not ubiquitous in Twain's fiction; it sometimes competes with but it never amounts to a rejection or complete replacement of his countertheology; and it is neither a theological nor a philosophical culmination of his thoughts about a personal state of beliefs. As the evidence shows, while he was writing *What Is Man?* and after it as well as before it, Twain kept on thinking and writing about theological issues and characters drawn from religion. In terms of relevance to the larger corpus of his literature, therefore, as well as to evidence of consistency, the influence of Calvinism on Twain's artistic vision is far more pervasive. It is possible, moreover, that in his struggle for truth or for relief from pain, Twain for a time allowed both determinism and his countertheology to compete for dominance in his mind, now emphasizing one position and now emphasizing the other. If so, while he was consciously and willfully deterministic, at his deeper, creative level he remained committed, whether consciously or not, to the tenets of his countertheology.

The Prince and the Pauper (1881), for example, is generally considered to be Twain's earliest novel-length experiment with the influence of training on the individual. Edward Tudor's transformation from uncaring prince to empathetic ruler occurs gradually over the course of the narrative as he is exposed firsthand to the cruelties of the royal law for which his father, the king, is responsible. The good-natured Tom Canty is likewise altered by his experience, but he moves in the opposite direction into someone who would eventually publicly deny his own mother. Tom's bad training is reversed by novel's end, but what of Edward's "good" training? As Quirk explains, it apparently took hold more permanently: "Twain may have inferred the 'mildness' of Edward's character from a certain leniency of the king's laws during his brief reign, or he may have assented to David Hume's characterization of the young monarch in his *History of England* as possessing 'mildness of disposition, application to study and business, a capacity to learn and judge, and an attachment to equity and justice'" (*Mark Twain and Human Nature* 117).

Determinism clearly supplies the ideological frame for much of the action of *The Prince and the Pauper*, but less certain is the degree to which Twain remains dedicated in the novel to the proposition that training operates as the primary influence on human nature. Edward goes from bad to good and Tom goes from good to bad because of their respective experiences throughout the narrative. All of this, the plot makes clear, is due to training. However, at the end of the novel Tom reverts to being good again—though not because he is "trained" a third time, but rather because his heart smites him after he denies his mother while pretending to be the prince. Tom's final transformation, which must have originated from within, appears to have taken place *despite* the training he receives during his time at Westminster. What, therefore, is Twain's assertion regarding training, if training is so easily reversible and overridden by innate forces that operate independent of environmental influence? And what of the broader implication that the only training that endures is the training that conditions the individual to behave nobly? The young protagonists of *The Prince and the Pauper* seem as much governed by a sense of conscience or innate virtue as they are by environmental forces. In fact, the portrayal of Edward and Tom anticipates in significant ways Twain's presentation of Huck in *Adventures of Huckleberry Finn* (1885), which Twain worked on during periods both before and after he wrote and published *The Prince and the Pauper*. Huck, like Edward and Tom, is an anomaly of independence of mind and character. And despite the bad training he receives in St. Petersburg, resulting in what Twain years later would famously describe as Huck's "deformed conscience," Huck is ultimately motivated to action by innate virtue—his "sound heart," as Twain put it—which overrides the racist cultural training of St. Petersburg when he decides that he will go to hell and aid Jim in his quest for freedom. In the final analysis Edward and Tom also come off as fundamentally good boys whose inherent senses of decency are temporarily short-circuited by the corrupting environment at Westminster. Does anyone really believe, for example, that Tom Canty would have turned out to be anything but kind and sympathetic as an adult if he had not undergone the switch with Prince Edward? It seems unlikely. Our point here is not to deny that evidence exists in *The Prince and the Pauper* of Twain's interest in determinism, but rather to call attention to the fact that it is but one of several shaping forces on the characters and events of the novel—and not even the most consequential.

The Tragedy of Pudd'nhead Wilson (1894) is another text routinely cited as evidence of Twain's commitment to the proposition that "training is everything." Reflecting this view, Sherwood Cummings asserts, for example:

Everyone growing up and living there is trained to think and behave as either master or a slave. Roxy's self-imposed training in becoming a slave to her son and in making her son feel like a master is, though conscious at first, an epitome of the unconscious training the town's inhabitants are always undergoing. So rigorous is that training and so contrary the roles that anyone forced to shift from one to another at maturity would suffer a profound psychic upheaval. (189)

Valet de Chambers, the son of the slave Roxy who was only one-sixteenth black, and Tom Driscoll, the son of Percy Driscoll, one of Dawson Landing's leading citizens, both undergo the kind of psychic upheaval that Cummings describes after it is revealed to them that Roxy had switched them in their cradles. Neither, in fact, is really ever able to recover from their training into the new identities they received after being switched as infants. And if that were all there were to the novel, then perhaps it would be the case that training is all there is, as David Wilson's memorable maxim asserts in chapter 5. But training is not the most important force governing Dawson's Landing.

We have referred earlier in our analysis to Twain's "fingerprints," unique and distinctive signs of his deepest values. Nowhere, however, is the term more literally appropriate than in its application to *Pudd'nhead Wilson*. The novel culminates, of course, with David Wilson winning a court case by dramatically introducing fingerprint evidence to prove conclusively that Chambers and Tom are not who they appear to be. A great deal of useful scholarship has been devoted to identifying Twain's purposes in this novel; overlooked, however, has been one of the book's most powerful and dramatic uses of fingerprints as explicit signs of the fixed nature of one's essential identity. Although "training" seems to dictate characters' experiences throughout much of the novel, it is the true identities of Chambers and Tom that ultimately determine their destinies in the book's closing chapters. Dawson's Landing, although it may not be fully cognizant of the fact, recognizes the higher authority of identity *despite* training when it restores the real Tom as Percy Driscoll's heir and later sells the real Chambers down the river precisely because of Wilson's fingerprint revelations in court. There is no question that training causes terrific damage to both individuals: the real Tom, for example, suffers from the effects of illiteracy as well as psychological alienation from both the white and black communities of Dawson's Landing, and the real Chambers's suffering in slavery would presumably be intensified because of the fact that he had lived so much of his life believing he was a free white man. But training is certainly not everything here. True or essential identity, as represented physically by one's fingerprints, apparently matters more.

Further, that both Chambers and Tom are stamped from birth (as indeed all humans are) with unique and absolute marks of identity signifies, literally and metaphorically, that their destinies were determined from birth. In the language of poker, their futures had been laid out in the hands they were dealt. One was to be a slave, another free. Using the evidence of fingerprints as positively determinative, Wilson proves which boy was which and rectifies Roxy's deception. The most bitter irony of the novel is that Roxy's pronounced motivation for the switch—protecting her own son from being sold down the river—comes to pass in spite of her attempts to subvert Chambers's and Tom's foreordained identities (established and fixed by their fingerprints) as slave and freeman, respectively. Both boys are in fact restored to those destinies. The same is true, of course, in *The Prince and the Pauper.* Edward and Tom are returned to their destinies— which are likewise established and fixed, in this case by history itself—as heir to the throne and commoner, respectively, despite their temporary escapes into false identities. Accordingly, training appears to function in both *The Prince and the Pauper* and *Pudd'nhead Wilson,* as it does in "The Man That Corrupted Hadleyburg," as a red herring, a hoax in the sense that "training" facilitates a delusion or a false impression of the self, temporarily masking the authentic identity that is inevitably exposed. Even though Edward Tudor, Tom Canty, Valet de Chambers, Tom Driscoll, and Mary and Edward Richards undergo periods of training that seem to alter who they really are, each character is restored to his or her authentic self, as defined by Twain's narrators, by the story's end.[19]

"Letters from the Earth" has been rightly characterized as Mark Twain's final word on the nature of the cosmos, God, and the damned human race.[20] Set aside unfinished just a few months before his death in April 1910, the manuscript of "Letters from the Earth" truly provides a last glimpse into Twain's thinking on those topics that occupied his mind at its deepest levels throughout his career. But unlike most critics who, like Hamlin Hill, have read "Letters from the Earth" as an indictment of "the vanity of human behavior and the absurdity of historical theology" (*Mark*

Twain: God's Fool 248), we believe that the sentiment of the narrative is better explained by Twain's altered attitude toward human nature in such later texts as "The Great Dark," the Adam and Eve diaries, and *No. 44, The Mysterious Stranger*, which present the human race comparatively sympathetically. The ending of *No. 44, The Mysterious Stranger*, in particular, is extremely similar to "Letters from the Earth" and provides an excellent comparison for analysis.

In one last attack upon his old enemy, the God of the Bible, Twain summed up his accumulated animosity. Forty-Four's diatribe in the famous final chapter of *No. 44, The Mysterious Stranger* is, as we have argued, largely an attack on God couched in a seeming critique of human foolishness. The same can be said of Satan's descriptions of human beings in "Letters from the Earth." Both instances are examples of Twain's use of the techniques of the "diverted target." Although Satan routinely begins his reports, especially those dealing with human conceptions of God, by pointing to human folly, his criticisms of human beings, when examined closely, are usually brief and limited to relatively mild comments such as "Man is a marvelous curiosity" and "Man is without doubt the most interesting fool there is" (Baetzhold and McCullough 221, 245)—hardly examples of Twain's rage toward humanity, as Hill and others would have it. Again, human beings are only superficially the subject of Satan's letters. The real target of "Letters from the Earth" is God—and not just the God of human invention or God as Twain would have preferred him to be, but God as Twain actually believed him to be. Satan's insistence that his descriptions of God are merely ridiculous inventions of the human imagination is a dramatic device that provides Twain a degree of both artistic detachment and plausible deniability that he needs to pull off his assault on the worshipped creator.

Letter VII is an excellent illustration of Twain's technique throughout "Letters from the Earth." The episode begins humorously with an account of how the fly survived the Flood. Satan's letter quickly turns to the subject of disease, which he identifies as an invention of God, "a trap, set for an innocent victim" (238). The tone then shifts and becomes forbidding as Satan elaborates for several paragraphs on the cruelty of disease, eventually calling it "the Creator's Grand Army" (238) that wages constant warfare on humanity. The descriptions in the first half of Letter VII present a malicious God, one who is hardly the invention of the human imagination, as Satan claims throughout "Letters from the Earth," but whose cruelty is demonstrable. Disease exists, after all, as a function of viruses and bacteria, which turn-of-the-century medicine—a subject that interested Twain greatly—was then making apparent. Insofar as God is the source of all creation, it follows, so Twain argues, that he is responsible for yet another (invisible) stratum of potential human suffering.

After informing Michael and Gabriel about the nature of disease, Satan follows up with a description of humankind's attitude toward "the Creator":

> With these facts before you will you now try to guess man's chiefest pet name for this ferocious Commander-in-Chief? I will save you the trouble—but you must not laugh. It is Our Father in Heaven!
>
> It is curious—the way the human mind works. The Christian begins with this straight proposition, this definite proposition, this inflexible and uncompromising proposition: *God is all-knowing, and all-powerful.*
>
> This being the case, nothing can happen without his knowing beforehand that it is going to happen; nothing happens without his permission; nothing can happen that he chooses to prevent.
>
> That is definite enough, isn't it? It makes the Creator distinctly responsible for everything that happens, doesn't it?
>
> The Christian concedes it in that italicized sentence. Concedes it with feeling, with enthusiasm.
>
> Then, having thus made the Creator responsible for all those pains and diseases and miseries above enumerated, and which he could have prevented, the gifted Christian blandly calls him Our Father!
>
> It is as I tell you. He equips the Creator with every trait that goes to the making of a fiend, and then arrives at the conclusion that a fiend and a father are the same thing! Yet he would deny that a malevolent lunatic and a Sunday school superintendent are essentially the same. What do you think of the human mind? I mean, in case you think there is a human mind. (239)

First, it is important to note that the passage here is framed by criticisms of humankind that are relatively innocuous—Satan's comments at the beginning and end of the excerpt here amount to little more than slaps at human reasoning and gullibility. Second, Satan insists that the description of God he provides is a creation of Christian theology, which allows for an implied distinction between it and a report of the "real" deity. But this distinction is largely false and points to Twain's "diverted target" technique throughout "Letters from the Earth" of masking his attack on God by appearing to criticize human theology as the source of the terrible portrait, rather than the figure of the portrait itself. Third, Satan's description of God here and throughout "Letters from Earth" amounts to an assertion that the cjreator is responsible for everything that happens, which is, of course, another way of repeating the central theme of other later writings like the Adam and Eve diaries that human beings are as they were made. Everything in the passage above, for example, builds to and falls away from this single point. Finally, consider the way in which the portrait of God here comports with Twain's countertheological God: cruel, cold, and unjust—a "fiend," as Satan puts it. That Twain appears to dismiss the characterization through Satan as an invention of the human mind does little to mitigate this fact. Moreover, there is just too much passion in Satan's report—and Forty-Four's in the final chapter of *No. 44, The Mysterious Stranger*, for that matter—for the tone of the narrative to be a complete function of Satan's detached disbelief. The more plausible explanation is that the tone of "Letters from the Earth" derives from Twain's anger at a malicious deity.

Twain's attack on God in "Letters from the Earth" reaches its peak in a familiar place, the idea that God could have chosen to make humankind happy but did not. As Satan continues his critique of humanity's foolishness near the middle of the narrative, he notes:

> For instance, he concedes that God made man. Made him without man's desire or privity.
>
> This seems to plainly and indisputably make God, and God alone, responsible for man's acts. But man denies this.
>
> He concedes that God has made angels perfect, without blemish, and immune from pain and death, and that he could have been similarly kind to man if he wanted to, but denies that he was under any moral obligation to do it. (245)

The central idea here represents what Twain considered to be the principal injustice of God's design: why did God make human beings so flawed when it would have been just as easy to make them good? Significantly enough, Forty-Four asks the very same question during his diatribe in the final chapter of *No. 44, The Mysterious Stranger*. This suggests that rather than having left such conceptions of the deity behind earlier in his life, issues of God's malice toward humanity continued to preoccupy Twain's mind well into the final decade of his life.

As a by-product of his attack on an unfair God, Twain manages to generate considerable sympathy for humanity in "Letters from the Earth," much as he does in such late texts as "The Great Dark" and the Adam and Eve diaries. There are, to be sure, numerous examples in "Letters from the Earth" of Satan's condemnation of humanity's failings, particularly with regard to white racism and Western imperialism. But far more space is devoted to cataloging God's cruelty toward human beings. In the middle of his recounting of the story of Adam and Eve, for example, Satan observes:

> The best minds will tell you that when a man has begotten a child he is morally bound to tenderly care for it, protect it from hurt, shield it from disease, clothe it, feed it, bear with its waywardness, lay no hand upon it save in kindness and for its own good, and never in any case inflict upon it a wanton cruelty. God's treatment of his earthly children, every day and every night, is the exact opposite of all that, yet those best minds warmly justify these crimes, condone them, excuse them, and indignantly refuse to regard them as crimes at all, when *he* commits them. Your country and mine is an interesting one, but there is nothing there that is half so interesting as the human mind. (231)

Satan goes on to point out the injustice of God's treatment of Adam and Eve, his "children," as Satan refers to them throughout the passage, reminding readers that Adam and Eve were not equipped with the Moral Sense (which, strictly speaking, is functionally moot in a predestined cosmos anyway) before they committed their "crime" so they could not have known the difference between right and wrong, good and evil. The argument here is, of course, a familiar one in Twain's late writings. Taken as a whole, Satan's accounting of God's malice toward humanity in "Letters from the Earth" is thorough and ranges from the "construction" of human physiology (and the differing sexual temperaments of men and women throughout their lives), to the creation of awful diseases like hookworm and African sleeping sickness, to the invention of hell and the punishment of eternal damnation. In each of these examples, as well as many more throughout "Letters from the Earth," human beings, whom Satan reminds us "did not create themselves" (231), are presented, both directly and indirectly, as victims of a ruthless God, a characterization that is consistent with many of the writings from the last decade of Twain's career.

We have not purposed to reveal the "Truth" about God and humans, but merely to describe the countertheology—the theology Twain struggled with—that is at the heart of Twain's best fiction. It explains his artistry in his best works, and it links Twain's early work to his high period and from there to his late work in a straight line. In the end, it needs to be stated that we do not see Twain deriving any pleasure at all from his countertheological views. Here is a man who passionately would have preferred to believe in sentimental justice: wrongs being righted, virtue being rewarded and vice being punished, suffering being brought to an end and happiness taking its place, the natural goodness of the common man and woman, prayers of the righteous being answered, and the reformation of hypocrites and evildoers. But instead he set out to describe reality as he saw it in practice and not as he wished to see it—and what he saw was terribly painful for him, all the more so because he was doubly disillusioned: by the reality and by the need to strip away illusion and expose the hoax in order to see the truth. Like Jonathan Swift, who hated the Irish, the English, landlords, merchants, and other classes of humankind but loved Tom, Dick, and Harry as individuals and stood up for the downtrodden and sought to alleviate suffering by charitable endeavors at the same time that he was deriding cities, regions, nations, and the human species for their bigotry, moral pusillanimity, hypocrisy, and cruelty, Twain similarly was continuously stirred to action and the supplying of relief to victims of oppression and injustice brought to his attention even as he poured scorn on the human race's mistaken notions. Twain was capable of creating lovable characters: Huck, Jim, children (including Tom Sawyer before he joined in adult behavior), Joan of Arc, Aunt Rachel, and other admirable individuals in much of his fiction. A real misanthrope would not have included so many and such outstanding exceptions or made them so appealing to his readers, or composed "Eve's Diary" and "Extracts from Adam's Diary." A dyed-in-the-wool atheist would not have written "Captain Stormfield's Visit to Heaven" or the sublime opening pages of "Letters from the Earth."

It is important, perhaps, for us to emphasize one last time that we have not endeavored to paint Twain completely in somber hues. Our single purpose has been to establish a viable and useful interpretive approach to a difficult but superlative author. Although we have concentrated on documenting the existence and importance of a serious thematic dimension of his art and thought that may be disturbing to many, it is only because we think it necessary to an understanding of Twain that has not hitherto been systematically addressed. As for the motives behind his themes, we have nowhere suggested that cheap iconoclasm was among them. Even when—

and perhaps especially when—his surfaces are humorous, Twain himself shows no evidence of taking comfort in attacking his targets or advancing his themes or writing with a pen truly warmed up in hell.

Twain may be described as an American Prometheus who, at great personal cost, devoted himself to the task of bringing light to humankind. Both in his literature and in his heart was a deep and sincere yearning to be free. Nor was Twain the only American author of his time to be so skeptical of God and his goodness. Melville, Hawthorne, Dickinson, Bierce, and Crane, among others, expressed serious doubts about the nature and extent of human freedom. What ultimately makes Twain an inspiring instead of a depressing author is his fundamental humanitarianism, the obverse side of his countertheology. He was, in part, a product of the American values of life, liberty, and the pursuit of happiness, and, concomitantly, the American hatred of slavery, cruelty, and injustice—even if the opposed tyrant proves to be a malevolent deity.

Chapter 1. Twain's Countertheology

1 See Stanley Brodwin, "Wandering between Two Gods: Theological Realism in *Connecticut Yankee*," "The Theology of Mark Twain: Banished Adam and the Bible," "Mark Twain's Theology: The Gods of a Brevet Presbyterian," and "Blackness and the Adamic Myth in Mark Twain's *Pudd'nhead Wilson*"; and James D. Wilson, "Religious and Esthetic Vision in Mark Twain's Early Career" and "History as Palimpsest: The Layers of Time in *Life on the Mississippi*."

2 William Phipps, *Mark Twain's Religion* (2003); and Harold K. Bush, *Mark Twain and the Spiritual Crisis of the Gilded Age* (2006).

3 Joe Fulton, *The Reverend Mark Twain: Theological Burlesque, Form, and Content* (2006). His earlier book, *Mark Twain in the Margins: The Quarry Farm Marginalia and the Composition of* A Connecticut Yankee in King Arthur's Court (2000), is a formidable application of Twain's marginalia in Lecky's historical analyses of European religion to the topic of the composition of *A Connecticut Yankee*. But the implication that because Twain was impressed enough by passages in Lecky's books to underline and annotate them necessarily means that he assimilated the marked passages into his personal beliefs is called into question by the ironic observation that he wrote on the inside back cover of his personal copy of volume 2 of Lecky's *History of European Morals*: "If I have understood this book aright, it proves two things beyond shadow or question: 1. That Christianity is the very invention of Hell itself; 2. & that Christianity is the (most) precious and elevating and ennobling boon ever vouchsafed to the world" (first reported by Davis, 14, no. 6:4; subsequently used by Baetzhold [*John Bull* 138]; since verified in private correspondence from Kevin Mac Donnell, of Austin, Texas, the book's present owner, to Berkove. Mac Donnell further noted that Twain's markings and annotations indicate successive readings

of the book over the years, and he suggests that the comment probably dates to the late 1870s or early 1880s). In other words, the book was equally persuasive on contradictory perspectives on its main theme. That left Twain free to form his own conclusions. It is our position that Lecky's books without doubt influenced Twain's fiction, but that the influences were such as could be subordinated to his preexisting and prevailing countertheology.

4 From "[Three Statements of the Eighties]" in Twain, *What Is Man?* 56–57.

5 A posthumous first publication of Mark Twain's *The Mysterious Stranger* in 1916 confused and misled readers and scholars for nearly half a century. In 1963 John S. Tuckey discovered that Twain's editors had perpetrated a fraud when they attempted to pass off the 1916 publication as Twain's work. Since the late 1960s critics have regarded *No. 44, The Mysterious Stranger* as the most reliable version of Twain's Mysterious Stranger novel. The controversy resulting from Tuckey's research about the distortions and fabrications in that 1916 edition is described and debated most recently in *Centenary Reflections on Mark Twain's "No. 44, The Mysterious Stranger,"* ed. Joseph Csicsila and Chad Rohman (Columbia: U of Missouri P, 2009).

6 For a general background of Presbyterian theology in the antebellum South and how it tended to be traditionalist, see Morton Smith, "The Southern Tradition."

7 For the strong and long-lasting influence on Twain of his reading of Tom Paine's iconoclastic deism, see Sherwood Cummings, *Mark Twain and Science: Adventures of a Mind.*

8 Twain to Howells, January 7, 1884, *Twain-Howells Letters* 2:461.

9 Howard G. Baetzhold and Joseph B. McCullough have restored this work with passages excised from the original manuscript. Their version is much longer and more substantial than the familiar abbreviated form, "Extracts from Captain Stormfield's Visit to Heaven." For the full text and an informative commentary on it, see their *The Bible According to Mark Twain* (1995).

10 The great majority of entries in *The Bible According to Mark Twain* deal with God as revealed in the Old Testament.

11 The text of Paine's edition of the *Notebook* is unreliable. We want to express our gratitude to Robert Hirst, general editor of the MTP, for his assistance here and elsewhere in correcting our quotations against the manuscript originals in their original holograph notebook (NB 37) and typed transcription page (TS 49).

12 Inasmuch as Twain, even as late in life as 1906, when he wrote "Eve's Diary," in which Eve finds evidence in Eden that God is planning for the Fall, commits to the view that all was predestined from eternity, he takes the minority and more extreme supralapsarian position within Calvinism; that is, the belief that God predestined from *before* creation the fall of humanity and who would be saved, as opposed to the infralapsarian position, the belief that God predestined these things after the Fall. For more on the differences between the two positions, see Hodge 2:316–321.

13 For example, his oft-quoted remark about the dying man who could not make up his mind which place to go to—both had their advantages: "heaven for climate, hell for company" (*Notebooks and Journals*, 538). Or his comment about Satan: "We may not pay him reverence, for that would be indiscreet, but we can at least respect his talents. A person who has for untold centuries maintained the imposing position of spiritual head of four-fifths of the human race, and political head of the whole of it, must be granted the possession of executive abilities of the loftiest order" (Budd, "Concerning the Jews," *Collected Tales* 2:355).

14 It is difficult to be certain of the exact nature of the impact on young Sam of the religious environment in Hannibal. Some early accounts, those of William Dean Howells and Vernon Parrington in particular, unqualifiedly characterized Hannibal as a "Calvinistic village," that is, a stronghold of orthodoxy. James D. Wilson represents what was generally accepted at the time of his writing when he observed: "[Twain's] early training in the Hannibal Presbyterian church and the support and example of his parents had left him a conscience keen to humanitarian concerns and personal moral responsibility, and a knowledge of, if not belief in, the basic tenets of Protestant faith" ("Religious and Esthetic Vision" 156). On the other hand, Alexander Jones's useful essay, "Heterodox Thought in Mark Twain's Hannibal," shows that there was a significant variety of religious thought in Hannibal to which Sam would have been exposed as a boy: in church hymnals, in the town at large, and even in his family. Terrell Dempsey reinforces this view but has uncovered new evidence about Twain's mother and sister which moves the balance point back toward the original notion. In sum, what is emerging is the position that even though Hannibal was not monolithically extreme in its Calvinism, and young Sam was certainly aware of differences of opinion about religion, the dominant influence on him was nevertheless that of traditional Calvinism.

15 Howells to Twain, October 9, 1899, *Twain-Howells Letters* 2:707.

16 Brodwin, "Mark Twain's Theology."

17 We are especially indebted to Brodwin for his being a "lion in the path," frequently ahead of us as a formidable but inspiring challenge in emphasizing a theological approach to Twain's literature. Although we diverge from a number of his analyses and conclusions, and also those of Fulton, another perceptive scholar who disagrees with Brodwin on different grounds, and proceed independently with our own views, we have several times adapted insights of his to our purposes. In this case, we have appropriated his useful term "countertheology," though we redefine it.

18 In the twentieth and twenty-first centuries many originally Calvinistic churches departed from, or modified, classical Calvinist stands. In summarizing the religion that Twain was taught and assimilated, we have used for verification the following respected texts which have largely expounded traditional Calvinism: the 1789 American version of *The Westminster Confession of Faith*; Ben A. Warburton, *Calvinism: Its History and Basic Principles, Its Fruits and Its Future, and Its Practical Application to Life* (1955); Leo P. Hirrel, *Children of Wrath: New School Calvinism and Antebellum Reform* (1998); Loraine Boettner, *The Reformed Doctrine of Predestination* (1973); Charles Hodge, *Systematic Theology* (1946); and Benjamin B. Warfield, *Selected Shorter Writings of Benjamin B. Warfield* (1970). It is clear, especially from the writings of the eminent theologians Hodge and Warfield, that Calvinism is far from being a simple and monolithic religion but has different—and occasionally oppositional—wings and interpretations. All agree, however, despite some degrees of emphasis and interpretation, on what is called the "Five Points of Calvinism," which have been arranged into the mnemonic acronym T-U-L-I-P: T, total depravity of fallen humankind; U, unconditional election of individual souls to their destinies; L, limited atonement of Christ only for those who believe in and submit to him; I, irresistible grace to those whom God elects; and P, perseverance of the saints in life paths that justify their election. In listing nine Calvinistic derivatives that Twain arrived at and that overlap but exceed the Five Points and admittedly contradict them by emphasizing the negative, we are presenting what Twain selected, retained, and adapted from his exposure to Calvinism, rather than a systematic paraphrase of orthodox Calvinistic theology, which is beyond the scope of this book and is tangential to its focus on Twain. It is not pretended that the elements in this countertheology are all "accurate" or "balanced" representations of Calvinism. However, Twain's friend, clergyman Joe Twichell, wrote him at one point, "Really you are getting quite orthodox, on the doctrine of Total Human depravity anyway." Twichell to SLC, September 5, 1901, CU-MARK. Our thanks to Robert Hirst for his help in locating this letter.

19 The idea that God is roused to wrath by humanity's sins is, of course, ex-

plicit and so often referred to in the Bible that every Bible religion refers to it. Calvinism, however, in a tradition that went back in America at least as far as Jonathan Edwards's sermon, "Sinners in the Hands of an Angry God" (1741), gave especial emphasis to the sinfulness of humanity and to the ongoing wrath of God.

20 Few religious doctrines raised Twain's ire and contempt more than that which affirmed the sinfulness and just damnation of unbaptized infants. As Fulton points out, Twain's opposition to it was fervent and practically life-long ("Theological Travels" 51–52); nevertheless, it was Calvinist doctrine like this on adults as well as children that influenced the formation of his counter-theology.

21 Biography establishes that Twain probably regarded some few extraordinary individuals—for example, Joan of Arc; his wife, Olivia; his daughter, Susy; and his friends Joe Twichell and William Dean Howells—as being so virtuous as to merit heaven. The thought, therefore, that according to Calvinism their deeds counted for nothing would have aggravated Twain's existing resentment of Calvinism's God.

22 In one of his creedal statements (October 2, 1906—significantly soon after the publication of *What Is Man?*), Twain affirms predestination in a way that seems an attempt to bridge to determinism by supplying its mechanistic conception with a first cause:

> I positively believe that the first circumstance that ever happened in this world was the parent of every circumstance that has happened in this world since; that God ordered that first circumstance and has never ordered another one from that day to this. Plainly, then, I am not able to conceive of such a thing as the thing we call an *accident*—that is to say, an event without a cause. Each event has its own place in the eternal chain of circumstances, and whether it be big or little it will infallibly cause the *next* event, whether the next event be the breaking of a child's toy or the destruction of a throne. (DeVoto, *Mark Twain in Eruption* 386)

The view of God in this statement partly conforms to the deistic notion of a nonintervening First Cause, and Twain occasionally recurs to it throughout his career as the way he would want to view God. But deism also regarded God as benevolent, and Twain most typically did not. Only in his calmly philosophical moods did he seem to prefer the deistic-type God—and usually in a context that implied wishful thinking; when he addressed life's realities of unfairness, pain, suffering, evil, violence, cruelty, malice, and war, his anger blazed afresh and was always directed toward the God of Calvinism.

23 Twain's objection to this position was long-standing. Between June 10 and 24, 1896, when imagining a God that he would create, he wrote: "He would recognize in Himself the Author & Inventor of Sin, & Author & Inventor of the vehicle & appliances for its commission; & would place the whole responsibility where it would of right belong: upon Himself, the only Sinner" (*Notebook* 301). Again we thank Robert Hirst for correcting Paine's text against the original in NB 38, TS 68–69.

24 One of the ludicrous incidents in Jim Blaine's rambling narrative of the "old ram" in *Roughing It* illustrates Twain's scorn of the notion of special providence. According to Blaine, an Irishman carrying a hod full of bricks fell on his Uncle Lem from a third story. The Irishman's life was saved by his falling on Uncle Lem, though it broke Lem's back in two places. Blaine is convinced that "there ain't no such thing as an accident"; in other words, Uncle Lem had served a special providence of preserving the Irish laborer (53:366). Beneath Blaine's strained logic and his imperfect understanding of what a "special providence" entailed is Twain's skepticism of the phenomenon. In the short story "The Second Advent" (*Fables of Man* 1881/1972) Twain describes a number of special providences that answer some petitioners' prayers but wreak havoc on the rest of the region. A paragraph from Twain's creedal statement from the 1880s quoted above also expresses his disbelief in special providences.

25 See her "Mark Twain's *Annus Horribilis*." Forrest Robinson additionally supports the position that Twain's last years were almost unbearably terrible when he attests to "a virtual mountain of direct testimony to the aging writer's contempt for human nature, hatred of God, anguished self-loathing, and impatient longing for the oblivion of the grave" ("Dreaming" 450).

26 A list of nineteenth-century American authors with Calvinist backgrounds would include Ralph Waldo Emerson, Henry David Thoreau, Nathaniel Hawthorne, Herman Melville, Emily Dickinson, Harriet Beecher Stowe, George Washington Cable, Harold Frederic, and Ambrose Bierce. Calvinism seems to have left a lasting impression on most of them. Bierce appears to have been an exception, although even he recalled enough to compose a one-liner that wittily summed up double damnation: "We were born so, and can't help it; and wouldn't if we could" ("Town Crier").

27 In a memoir written after Twain's death, Joe Goodman, his friend and former editor of Virginia City's *Territorial Enterprise*, recalled that at night after work Twain "would cast off the sportive guise he wore in the presence of the crowd" and would frequently discuss with Goodman "literary, scientific, or philosophical questions in an entirely abstract and impersonal way" (Berkove,

Insider Stories 2:1032). Even more specifically, Howells recollected times when he and Twain were by themselves, and Twain "would reason high—

'Of Providence, foreknowledge, will and fate,
Fixed fate, free will, foreknowledge absolute,'" (10).

28 Such as fate or fortune. Twain, however, never accepted Calvinism's claim to be able to reconcile freedom of the will with predestination. In 1902—after reading Jonathan Edwards's explanation of the process in his *Freedom of Will* (1754)—Twain wrote Twichell that the work was an "insane debauch" and was lit by "the glare of a resplendent intellect gone mad" (Paine, *Biography* 1156–1157).

29 In its self-conscious emphasis upon direct divine control of everything, Calvinism is particularly sensitive and hostile to any imputation that control can be ascribed to alternate causes. Nineteenth- and early-twentieth-century theologians of a traditional inclination made it clear that Calvinism recognizes, understands, and strongly opposes the threat to its doctrine of predestination posed by fatalism and foreordination and such mechanistic accounts for events as determinism. See especially Hodge 1:545–549 and Warfield 1:393–396.

30 Warfield defends predestination on the ground that it is of the essence of God that he control his creation: he made it and is responsible for everything in it (1:103–109). We do not intend to put words in Twain's mouth to respond to this argument, but we can observe that if Twain's objection to God is that God is not good because, being responsible for evil, he appears to employ it for the suppression and suffering of humanity, this view of the matter would explain the frequency of the scenarios in Twain's fictions of a controlling force that is omniscient and omnipotent, but not benevolent.

31 "Life was a fever-dream made up of joys embittered by sorrows, pleasure poisoned by pain; a dream that was a nightmare—confusion of spasmodic and fleeting delights, ecstasies, exultations, happinesses, interspersed with long-drawn miseries, griefs, perils, horrors, disappointments, defeats, humiliations, and despairs—the heaviest curse devisable by divine ingenuity" ("Letters from the Earth" 44).

32 Twain's recollection of a speech he gave on February 19, 1883.

Chapter 2. *Roughing It*

1 For a fuller discussion of this idea and also what other, specific influences played on Twain during his Nevada years, see Lawrence Berkove, "Nevada Influences on Mark Twain."

2 Quoted from Oscar Lewis's introduction to Dan De Quille's *The Big Bonanza*, xviii–xix.

3 In "'Seeing the Elephant': Some Perspectives on Mark Twain's *Roughing It*," Forrest Robinson credits Henry Nash Smith with an early notice of this phenomenon, but observes that Franklin Rogers subsequently limited it to only the first half of the book. Robinson himself pushes it farther, applying it to the whole work, and thus partly anticipates our reading of the book in this respect. In the same essay his reading of the Conrad Wiegand episode in appendix C of the book analyzes it for the serious issues it opens up.

4 From the first, *Roughing It* as autobiography has been taken with a grain of salt. In *My Mark Twain*, Howells recognized its "grotesque exaggeration" (113), and in his *Biography*, Paine flatly conceded that the book "was not accurate history, even of the author's own adventures" (454–455). Scholarship since then has confirmed this view and corrected many specific details.

5 For a full discussion of this topic, see Lawrence Berkove, "The Trickster God in *Roughing It*."

6 Percy G. Adams, in *Travel Literature and the Evolution of the Novel*, describes the ingenue, a relatively naïve protagonist, as a "necessary character in both fiction and travels" (276). Although Adams has little to say about Twain specifically, we are indebted to him for many insights about the close relationship of travel writing and novels, not the least of which is his observation how often, both historically and in modern times, "the travel book and the novel become one form" (284). Clearly, as regards *Roughing It*, we are in agreement with him.

7 Adams points out that travel literature has an ancient tradition of using prevaricating narrators, some of them (such as Thomas More in *Utopia*) first-person narrators. See especially chapter 3, "The Truth-Lie Dichotomy." But Twain had more immediate, homegrown antecedents. To name just a few of the more obvious: J. Ross Browne, a very popular author from the 1840s to the 1860s and one whom Twain read and with whom he was personally friendly, wrote several travel novels that used protagonists who narrated fictitious autobiography. Dan De Quille, Twain's Comstock colleague and roommate, put himself into fictional situations in the travel letters that were later collected as *Washoe Rambles*. Before him, Augustus Baldwin Longstreet did the same in the collected stories of *Georgia Scenes* (1835). Before them—and Twain probably suspected this—Benjamin Franklin partly fictionalized his *Autobiography*.

8 All parenthetical page references are to the text of the 1993 MTP edition of *Roughing It*. Where chapters are not identified in the text, they are cited in the parentheses as the number before the colon.

9 "Lay not up for yourselves treasures upon earth, where moth and rust doth corrupt, and where thieves break through and steal: But lay up for yourselves treasures in heaven, where neither moth nor rust doth corrupt, and where thieves do not break through and steal: For where your treasure is, there will your heart be also" (Matthew 6:19–21).

10 Gregg Camfield, in *Sentimental Twain: Samuel Clemens in the Maze of Moral Philosophy*, recognizes the coexistence of two contradictory voices in the book, identifies them as those of romantic fancy and of experience, and concludes that their function is to generate "the incongruity that constitutes much of the book's humor" (97). This is true as far as humor is concerned, but we are endeavoring to probe the deeper level of seriousness in the book and Twain's purpose to involve, trick, then ultimately undeceive the reader.

11 Jeffrey Melton perceptively observes that the narrator's enthusiasms, particularly in regards to nature, tend to be short-lived and end in disappointment (103–104).

12 This statement antedates Twain's firsthand knowledge of Mont Blanc and the Matterhorn that was acquired on the walking tour of the mountainous areas of Europe in 1878–1879 of which he wrote a fictionalized account in *A Tramp Abroad* (1880).

13 Le Sage's classic French picaresque novel, *The Adventures of Gil Blas de Santillana* (1735), is underestimated as an influence on Twain. Its translation was very popular in America in the nineteenth century, and it was a favorite of Twain's. Its loose and episodic form might well be a model not only for *Roughing It* but also for *Huckleberry Finn*. See also Alan Gribben's *Mark Twain's Library* (407) for its collection of Twain's references to *Gil Blas*.

14 The reference to a three-month "pleasure trip" is, on an autobiographical level, an instance of authorial manipulation of readers by withholding and distorting important information. Clemens was almost certainly fleeing the Civil War by going to Nevada. To call that a "pleasure trip" is disingenuous. But like much of the American population, North as well as South, he believed that the hostilities would not last more than three months.

15 For the appearances of Calvinism in *Huckleberry Finn* and *A Connecticut Yankee*, see the following respective chapters that discuss these novels.

16 The book abounds in such examples. For instance, the narrator is taken advantage of in the "genuine" Mexican plug incident in chapter 24; stockholders in a mine are deceived by a phony assessment in chapter 35; and chapter 44 is largely devoted to hoaxes ranging from salting worthless mines with slugs of sil-

ver cut from silver dollars to making accessories of journalists (including Twain) who, bribed by presents of "feet" in prospective mines, "followed the custom of the country, used strong adjectives and frothed at the mouth as if a very marvel in silver discoveries had transpired" (287) and thus lured the credulous.

17 The original of this portrait is most likely Jim Gillis, of Jackass Hill, California, the probable godfather of "The Notorious Jumping Frog of Calaveras County." An 1891 article by Dan De Quille on Gillis describes him as being very successful in his trade as a pocket miner: "He now has eight mines running in California and every one paying." This is further evidence that Twain was not bound to literal accuracy in *Roughing It*, but subordinated fact to his fictional purposes. See Lawrence Berkove, "Dan De Quille's 'Jim Gillis: The Thoreau of the Sierras.'"

18 As will be seen in the chapter on *Huckleberry Finn*, a similar sequence of events beginning with seeming freedom but leading to the loss of it will be repeated in the later book in amplified and more subtle form when Huck and Jim think they had escaped from St. Petersburg.

19 The endnotes of the 1993 edition of *Roughing It* make clear that the matter of the blind lead was somewhat more complicated than Twain indicated, and that Twain "invented some details." See the notes on 642–648, especially notes for 259, 268, and 269.

20 Clemens was fascinated by the possibility that there might be some validity to fortune-telling. *Huckleberry Finn* and *A Connecticut Yankee*, as well as *Roughing It*, make use of omens and superstitions that are borne out by subsequent events, and even late in his life Clemens visited a fortune-teller, albeit with skepticism. Daniel Hoffman deals extensively with fortune-telling in *Huckleberry Finn* in his essay "Black Magic—and White."

21 See Twain's discussion of temperament, in Letter VIII of "Letters from the Earth," as a law of God that is in opposition to the Bible's commandments.

22 In his discussion of "Everlasting Sunday," R. Kent Rasmussen observes that Twain "associated Sundays with stillness and inactivity," and that "throughout his writings, he generally uses 'everlasting' in a negative sense" (132). Rasmussen might have gone even further and noted that Sunday and Sabbath almost always have negative connotations in Twain's works.

23 Chapter 74 is strikingly adumbrated by the narrator's experience at Lake Tahoe in chapter 23. At first, he and his friend find the loveliness "fascinating, bewitching, entrancing" (152), where even talking would have "interrupted the Sabbath stillness and marred the dreams the luxurious rest and indolence

brought" (153). After their campfire carelessly gets out of control, however, the resulting forest fire devastates the area until "as far as the eye could reach the lofty mountain-fronts were webbed as it were with a tangled net-work of red lava streams. Away across the water the crags and domes were lit with a ruddy flare, and the firmament above was a reflected hell!" The implication of humans ruining an Eden is almost inescapable in this passage. Maybe "almost" is not needed, for the narrator soon admits "We were homeless wanderers again" (156).

24 We are indebted for this observation to our student Michelle Dulong, who advanced it in a paper on *Roughing It*.

25 We are obliged to our student Mark Brinker for suggesting the germ of this interpretation. It is worthwhile to contrast Twain's treatment of Buncombe with Shakespeare's treatment of Malvolio in the problem play *Twelfth Night*. Malvolio is afforded ample opportunity to reveal himself as a good candidate for a comedown; Buncombe is given almost none. At the end, when the hoax that humiliates Malvolio runs its full course and he storms out, Olivia says sympathetically, "He hath been most notoriously abused," and the Duke in agreement immediately orders "Pursue him, and entreat him to a peace" (V, i, 389–399). Shakespeare's goal is thus to create a just order by rectifying a cruel wrong; Twain's humor in this instance is either simply cruel toward a man who attempted only to stop a travesty of justice, or is aimed at exposing the system itself, or both.

26 Although *Roughing It* does not contain information on this point, Clemens regarded the biblical Joseph as a liar, a hypocrite, and a slaver. The narrator's description of the story of Joseph and his brethren as "beautiful," therefore, is yet another example of Twain's use of an opportunity to risk religious heresy when he had an expectation that his readers would be uncritical of a biblical narrative. The choice of this story is very probably a private joke Twain is enjoying at the expense of his audience. See Lawrence Berkove, "Mark Twain's Hostility to Joseph."

27 *Boswell's Life of Johnson*, ii, 374.

Chapter 3. *The Adventures of Tom Sawyer*

1 See Hamlin Hill, "The Composition and Structure of *The Adventures of Tom Sawyer*"; Judith Fetterley, "The Sanctioned Rebel"; Tom H. Towers, "'I Never Thought We Might Want to Come Back': Strategies of Transcendence in *Tom Sawyer*"; and Forrest G. Robinson, "Social Play and Bad Faith in *The Adventures of Tom Sawyer*."

2 See Henry Nash Smith, *Mark Twain: The Development of a Writer.*

3 Henry Nash Smith's groundbreaking essay "Mark Twain's Images of Hannibal: From St. Petersburg to Eseldorf," published in 1958, is a notable example of scholarship dealing with the setting of St. Petersburg and other towns like it in Twain's writings. Whereas Smith argues that Twain's recollections of Hannibal grew "considerably more complex" (3) over the course of his career, transforming from an idealized village early on to something more unseemly in the later writings, we see much more consistency in Twain's generally critical attitude toward these settings.

4 The reign of Nicholas I between 1825 and 1855 was regarded internationally as a singularly autocratic period in Russian (and European) history. The *London Times*, for example, wrote on March 7, 1855, five days after the death of Nicholas I: "Throughout Europe the death of the Emperor Nicholas has been followed by an immediate rise in the value of all public securities, and by a feeling of increased confidence and hope. The world stood more in awe of him than we in this country could conceive possible, and there is hardly a citizen of any continental state who does not breathe more freely since that incarnate despotism has ceased to wield the power of Russia." Although his successor, Nicholas II, who ruled until 1881, enacted liberal reforms such as the emancipation of the serfs in 1861, he, too, added considerably to Russia's infamy with the brutal suppression of the Polish rebellion of 1863–1864 known as the "January Insurrection" and other oppressive policies both at home and abroad. See, for example, Nicholas Valentine Riasanovsky, *Nicholas I and Official Nationality in Russia, 1825–1855* (Berkeley: U of California P, 1959).

5 See, for example, Bernard DeVoto, *Mark Twain at Work*; Walter Blair, *Mark Twain and Huck Finn*; Frank Baldanza, *Mark Twain: An Introduction and Interpretation*; and Kent Rasmussen, *Mark Twain A to Z*, 414.

6 As John Tuckey has pointed out, Twain nowhere in print ever precisely employed the phrase the "damned human race." It actually derives from chapter 19 of William Dean Howells's *My Mark Twain* (1910) in which Howells recalls hearing Twain use the phrase. See Tuckey's "Mark Twain's Later Dialogue," 532. Whether or not Twain actually used the phrase (and it seems likely that he did), it is fully consonant with his feelings on the matter.

7 All parenthetical page references are to the text of the 1982 Mark Twain Library paperback edition of *The Adventures of Tom Sawyer.*

8 The scriptural source for "spare the rod and spoil the child" is Proverbs 13:24; "man that is born of woman is of few days and full of trouble," as noted,

appears in Job 14:1 and is similar to Jacob's reply to Pharaoh in Genesis 47:9 that "few and evil have the days of the years of my life been."

9 In the opening chapter of his *Autobiography* Twain indicates that Aunt Polly was modeled after his mother, Jane Clemens (121). In recent years, Terrell Dempsey and Philip Fanning have pointed out that Jane Lampton Clemens exhibited behaviors that do not accord with Twain's favorable portraits of his mother. Dempsey, for example, details an instance in which Jane Clemens summoned her husband home to beat a slave for impudence (87), and Fanning reports her forbidding members of the family for an entire year to write to a young Sam Clemens for departing from home in 1852 and leaving his brother Orion's newspaper business in the lurch (29–30).

10 Twain briefly describes Joe Douglas, the model for Injun Joe, in his 1897 sketch "Villagers 1840–3." For a discussion of the mythical implications of the character of Injun Joe, see Robert Tracy's "Myth and Reality in *The Adventures of Tom Sawyer.*"

11 Twain's hostile attitude toward Native Americans as expressed both in his work and in his private and public pronouncements in the early and middle decades of his writing career has been well documented. Twain's depiction of Native Americans was in large part his response to the twin experiences of reading the "false" accounts of Indian characters such as James Fenimore Cooper's Chingachgook in romantic literature and his firsthand disillusioning experiences with some Native peoples in the West. That said, as James C. McNutt points out in "Mark Twain and the American Indian," Twain gradually became quite sympathetic toward and even admiring of Indians in the final decades of his life. For additional commentary on Twain's literary depictions of Native Americans see, for example, Kerry Driscoll, "'Only Heedlessly a Savage': Mark Twain's 'Indian' Identity," "'Man Factories' and the 'White Indians' of Camelot: Rereading the Native Subtext of *A Connecticut Yankee in King Arthur's Court,*" and "The Fluid Identity of 'Petrified Man.'"

12 It should be remembered that the citizens of St. Petersburg indicate that they are willing to behave brutally not only toward Injun Joe in *Tom Sawyer* but also toward Pap Finn in *Huckleberry Finn.* In chapter 11 of *Huckleberry Finn* Judith Loftus, speaking of Pap, tells Huck that St. Petersburg "wanted to lynch him, but he was gone." Ironically, this comes just before Loftus reveals that Pap was seen leaving town with "some mighty hard looking strangers." These strangers are, presumably, the same individuals who kill Pap. Twain's point here, as in the case of Injun Joe in *Tom Sawyer*, is clear: there is no difference between "civilized" people of St. Petersburg and the more conspicuously violent

characters—except, of course, for the mere appearance of respectability of the citizens of St. Petersburg. Doc Robinson is an excellent case in point. Though one would think him a prime example of the "civilized" stratum of the town's society, he is involved in grave robbing, both a crime and a sin; has tempted with money a fellow citizen to aid him; and, of course, has corrupted his students by getting them started in grave robbing. He thus fulfills Calvinism's view of humanity as being so evil by nature that even "good deeds" (if grave robbing can be so justified by its intent to serve an ultimately moral purpose) are so tainted by humankind's evil nature as to be damnably evil in the final analysis.

13 According to Gribben's *Mark Twain's Library*, Twain owned and read Buntline's work.

14 In chapter 25 Tom and Huck show up at the haunted house "at the appointed time" (180), which from information earlier in the episode is said to be midnight. The time at which Tom and Becky's adventure in MacDougal's Cave begins is never explicitly identified, but evidence suggests that the bulk of the action described in chapter 31 likely takes place late in the evening near midnight. In chapter 29 the picnickers return on the ferry just before ten o'clock. As Huck watches the ferry pass from the wharf, the narrator notes: "The night was growing cloudy and dark. Ten o'clock came, and the noise of vehicles ceased, scattered lights began to wink out, all straggling foot passengers disappeared, the village betook itself to slumbers and left the small watcher alone with the silence and the ghosts" (206). Huck then encounters Injun Joe a few hours later, whereupon he overhears the threat to the Widow Douglas. This is the point at which his "participation" in the MacDougal's Cave adventure begins. In chapter 31 the narrator returns to Tom and Becky who are actually in the cave. After a long period of wandering through the cave, they begin to panic because they realize they might be lost. Though the time at which this realization sets in is never identified (after all, how would Tom and Becky know what time it is deep in a dark cave anyway), it is plausible that it is late in the evening, likely close to midnight.

Chapter 4. *Adventures of Huckleberry Finn*

1 It is nowhere stated directly as such in the novel, but the reason that Huck and Jim did not simply cross the Mississippi River to Illinois, which was technically a free state, was that although the majority of Illinoisans were antislavery, many of the residents of the western and southern parts of the state were proslavery and would have turned Jim in. This is strongly implied in chapter 11 when

Judith Loftus tells the disguised Huck that if his father gets money, he will hunt for Jim all over the state, and that her husband and a friend are hunting for Jim right now (69–70).

2 This is essentially the argument advanced by Leo Marx's famous and still influential essay "Mr. Eliot, Mr. Trilling, and *Huckleberry Finn*," in which Twain is criticized for having lost his nerve in the last ten chapters after having used the relationship between Jim and Huck to develop powerful themes of equality and freedom up to that point.

3 Thomas Carlyle, in *Sartor Resartus* (1833–1834), proposed the metaphorical "philosophy of clothes," which quickly became an enormously popular and influential idea in the nineteenth century. It held that there comes a time in one's life when one's "clothes" become too constricting. It is necessary then to strip off those clothes, stand naked for a time, and then put on new clothes that fit. Twain was strongly influenced by Carlyle, and evidence of his ideas can be found in *The Prince and the Pauper*, *Huckleberry Finn*, and *No. 44, The Mysterious Stranger*, as well as *A Connecticut Yankee*. See also Baetzhold's entry on Carlyle in the *Mark Twain Encyclopedia* (126–128).

4 Quoted by Blair, *Mark Twain and Huck Finn*, 337.

5 All future page references will be to *Adventures of Huckleberry Finn* (Berkeley: U of California P, 2003). Where chapters are not identified in the text, they are cited in the parentheses as the number before the colon.

6 The depth of Twain's aversion to romanticism can be gathered from his habit of pointedly linking even in his fiction the names of romantic writers with death. In chapters 12 and 13 of *Huckleberry Finn*, for example, the wrecked steamboat *Walter Scott* is the location of three violent deaths. In chapter 31 an allusion is made to a possibly fatal accident aboard another steamboat, the *Lally Rook* ("Lalla Rookh" was the name of a once popular poem by the romantic writer Thomas Moore). Early in the incomplete and unpublished sequel to *Huckleberry Finn*, "Huck Finn and Tom Sawyer among the Indians" (probably written between 1881 and 1888), Tom Sawyer heaps extravagant praise upon the Indians. Later, after hostile Indians kill or capture the rest of their party, Huck asks a grief-stricken Tom where he had learned about Indian nobility and is told, simply, "Cooper's novels" (75–76). We are indebted to the Rare Book Room of the Detroit Public Library, where it is housed, for permission to examine the manuscript of the incomplete sequel and to quote from it.

7 It has long been noticed that the names Grangerford and Shepherdson suggest, respectively, two archetypical categories of historically competitive occu-

pations: farmers and graziers. The names additionally suggest at least two more levels of literary interpretation: the allegorical, in which the deadly feuding of neighbors leads to the Civil War; and the mythical, in the possible allusion to Cain and Abel ("And Abel was a keeper of sheep, but Cain was a tiller of the ground" [Genesis 4:2]). Twain's countertheology readily applies to this latter level in its reminder that the murder of Abel by Cain was the first example in human history of what sadly turned out to be a fixed inclination of human nature toward bloodshed. The hope, therefore, that through elopement Sophia Grangerford and Harney Shepherdson transcend the pattern of endless revenge of murder with more murder must be tempered by the realization that although they may have escaped the deadly feud of their families, the couple cannot escape predestined human nature.

8 Eric Solomon has listed six of these impersonations as "major deceptions" or "dissimulations" (173-174). Our preference for "impersonation" is more than a semantic quibble; we think "deception" is a misleading term. In his introduction to *Huckleberry Finn*, Henry Nash Smith comes closer to our meaning when he describes Huck's invented identities as "thumbnail autobiographies" (xix). We have chosen to emphasize not the fact that Huck lies, whether voluntarily or under compulsion, but the fact that Huck selects, or is given, whole characters to act out. As will be shown below, once Huck begins to impersonate one of his fictitious identities, he literally must live, think, and respond as that person would. In *Form and Fable in American Fiction*, Daniel Hoffman partially anticipates our position when he observes that Huck is obliged to play some roles and assumes others voluntarily, but that his "powers of transformation are not . . . illimitably protean. There are some selves which he cannot wear save at his peril" (346).

9 It is generally assumed that the two men hunting for escaped slaves buy off their consciences for not helping a smallpox victim by kindly floating a board to Huck with two twenty-dollar gold coins on it and advising him to seek help at a town twenty miles downstream. But their further advice to lie about the nature of his supposed father's illness and let the townspeople find out on their own about the smallpox suggests another motive, a malicious intent to spread smallpox to the inhabitants of that rival town. This alternate motive is consistent with the generally negative picture of human nature in this novel and with the Calvinist position (which Twain retains in his countertheology) that so corrupt is human nature that even what appear to be good deeds are tainted by evil motives. An earlier example of this occurs in chapter 9, when Jim dissuades Huck from looking at the face of the dead man in the floating wreck of a house because it was "too gashly" (61). The murdered man is actually Huck's father. As Spencer

Brown observed, what seems like a kind intention on Jim's part has an inverse reading—that Jim's motive in deflecting Huck from learning of the death of his father is to keep Huck from abandoning Jim once he realizes that there is now no reason why he should fear returning to St. Petersburg (45–46). Brown attributes Jim's deception to the corrupting influence of slavery, but Twain's countertheology assigns it an additional and deeper cause: the Calvinist position on the corruption of human nature that applies to all human beings, free whites as well as black slaves.

10 This tenth impersonation begins as a means to protect Jim from the suspicion of the Duke and Dauphin that Jim was an escaped slave. Huck opens with a question that shows that Twain knew exactly what the implication was of continuing with the raft voyage: "Goodness sakes, would a runaway nigger run *south!*" (20:166).

11 It is possible that Twain is comparing Huck by allusion to the Cynic philosopher Diogenes, who was famous for having courted natural simplicity by living in a tub and eschewing material possessions.

12 Hoffman, *Form and Fable*, 350. In his observation that Huck needs Jim in order to know who he really is, we are again indebted to Hoffman for an idea that has stimulated us to carry it further.

13 The Phelps farm episode is more complicated than it looks. First, it is an incredible coincidence that of all places where Huck and Jim's journey might have ended, it is a farm owned by a relative of Tom Sawyer. Even more incredibly coincidental is Tom's visit to the farm while Huck and Jim are on it. As has been previously pointed out, Calvinism does not allow for coincidence or chance; nor did Twain. Coincidence was a common literary technique in popular nineteenth-century literature, so what would have been passed over without notice as conventional by most readers Twain used for his own deliberate purposes, hiding his intentions in plain sight, as it were. Second, Silas Phelps, a part-time preacher, was preparing a sermon based on Acts 17 (57:316). Robert D. Arner points out that Acts 17 contains two lines that can be read as a condemnation of slavery (the MTP edition note on page 316 refers to his essay). Twain's allusion to the text can hardly be accidental; it is a sharp irony that Phelps, a slave owner as well as a preacher, would pick that particular chapter and then overlook its plain sense as he prepared his sermon. Here is a case of Twain's countertheological ridicule of the Moral Sense, which causes humans to plume themselves for observing small virtues while they commit large sins. And third, insofar as Silas Phelps may be seen as a typical citizen, and Pikesville as a typical town—just as St. Petersburg in *Tom Sawyer* has been previously shown to be—the whole

episode is another ill omen, one of many in the book, for Huck and Jim's hope for freedom.

14 Huck's distrust of Providence is also evident in "Huck Finn and Tom Sawyer among the Indians." There, he and Jim are opposed to Tom's plan to run off to Indian country because "we hadn't ever had such comfortable times before, & we reckoned we better let it alone as long as Providence warn't noticing" (6). Later in the story, the malign function of Providence is transferred to a "bad god, who was setting up nights to think up ways to bring them bad luck & bust up all their plans, & never fooled away a chance to do them all the harm he could" (132).

15 See Appendix D of the MTP edition of *Huckleberry Finn*, 804–806.

16 For a fuller discussion of the nature of conscience both in the "Carnival of Crime in Connecticut" and *Huckleberry Finn*, see Lawrence Berkove, "Poe, Twain, and the Nature of Conscience."

17 In his October 15, 1883, letter to Howells, Twain wrote "I never count my prospective chickens when I know that Providence knows where the nest is" (*Twain-Howells Letters* 1:445).

18 In addition to Lawrence Berkove's "The 'Poor Players' of *Huckleberry Finn*," which fundamentally influenced this chapter, essays by other scholars over the years participate in a minority but strongly supported defense of the novel's aesthetic and thematic unity. In *Writing "Huck Finn"* Doyno extensively connects Jim's debasement in the evasion chapters to the noxious practices that flourished under the convict-lease system and sees those last chapters as the socially critical culmination of a tragic novel. In "'Been Reading the Horrors in the Newspapers?': Octave Thanet's 'Trusty, No. 49' and the Arkansas Convict Lease System," Joseph Csicsila supports Doyno's argument with his analysis of "Trusty, No. 49," Octave Thanet's 1890 Arkansas story that attacks the notorious brutality of the convict-lease system. Berkove's essay "The Free Man of Color in *The Grandissimes* and Works by Harris and Mark Twain" demonstrates that first Cable, then Harris, and finally and most powerfully of all, Twain used the "free man of color" (f.m.c.) motif in their works as a bitter indictment of the reality of the false freedom offered by the grandiose but hollow term. Spencer Brown also glimpsed that the evasion chapters were functional in their attack on the sport Tom Sawyer and his real-life kind enjoyed in playing at freeing slaves. In short, the case for reading *Huckleberry Finn* as a successfully unified novel on more than one level has long been supported by overlapping arguments grounded in literary history and aesthetics.

19 Doyno believes an escape to the territories would make good sense from a legal point of view (*Writing "Huck Finn"* 230), but Twain made the West's realistic dangers and difficulties abundantly clear in *Roughing It* and especially in "Huck Finn and Tom Sawyer among the Indians," in which humans, nature, and the "bad god" collaborate in an uninterrupted series of disasters to Huck, Tom, and their friends.

20 Ironically, Jim's monetary value later drops precipitately to forty dollars, first when the King sells him on speculation in Pikesville (31:272), and next when he becomes a free man of color. Forty dollars is also what Tom gives him at the end of the novel for being such a "patient" and cooperative prisoner (360).

21 Helen Tunnicliff Catteral, ed., *Judicial Cases Concerning American Slavery and the Negro* (Washington, D.C.: Carnegie Institute of Washington, 1926–1937): 5:223–224.

22 An excellent firsthand account of how flimsy was the status of a free person of color is William R. Hogan and Edwin A. Davis's *William Johnson's Natchez: The Ante-bellum Diary of a Free Negro*. Hamilton Basso's *The Light Infantry Ball* deals fictionally with the same subject. That Twain was aware of the precariousness of the "freedom" of the free person of color is obvious in "Huck Finn and Tom Sawyer among the Indians." Jim leaves St. Petersburg to be with Huck and Tom because "there was white men around our little town that was plenty mean enough & ornery enough to steal Jim's papers from him & sell him down the river again; but they couldn't come that if he staid with us" (93).

23 "Tom Sawyer's Conspiracy," begun in 1897, one of the latest of several incomplete sequels to *Huckleberry Finn*, proves that this situation was not speculative. The first sentence of the fragment states "the Widow was hiring Jim for wages so he could buy his wife and children's freedom some time or other" (163). In the fragment, Jim chose to remain in St. Petersburg instead of moving to a free state. His freedom would be more restricted—"And they had tightened up the rules, and a nigger couldn't be out after dark at night, pass or no pass" (172)—but Jim would be near his family.

24 For a fuller discussion of the relationship of the three authors and their works, see Lawrence Berkove, "The Free Man of Color in *The Grandissimes* and Works by Harris and Mark Twain."

25 With similar insight, Justin Kaplan describes the early Mark Twain as a lecturer: "a daring manipulator of audience psychology and values, outrageous enough to hoax, surprise, and disorient, but careful not to offend" (30).

Chapter 5. *A Connecticut Yankee in King Arthur's Court*

1 See Henry Nash Smith, *Mark Twain's Fable of Progress: Political and Economic Ideas in* "A Connecticut Yankee"; and Alan Gribben, "Mark Twain, Business Man."

2 Overviews of the subject can be found in Philip Butcher, "'The Godfathership' of *A Connecticut Yankee*"; and James D. Williams, "The Use of History in Mark Twain's *A Connecticut Yankee.*" Examples of more specific studies are in Harold Aspiz, "Lecky's Influence on Mark Twain"; Howard G. Baetzhold, "The Course of Composition of *A Connecticut Yankee*"; and Fred W. Lorch, "Hawaiian Feudalism and Mark Twain's *A Connecticut Yankee in King Arthur's Court.*"

3 One of the sharpest criticisms of Hank is that of Chadwick Hansen. Also noting a consistent pattern in Hank's development toward becoming a dictator are Allen Guttman, "Mark Twain's *Connecticut Yankee*: Affirmation of the Vernacular Tradition?" and Judith Fetterley, "Yankee Showman and Reformer: The Character of Mark Twain's Hank Morgan." These critics, therefore, not only indicate Hank's unreliability as a narrator but also suggest authorial control and purpose in this development. Lorne Fienberg also recognizes Hank's unreliability. We part company with Fienberg, however, when he concludes that Hank epitomizes "the daimonic process of creative destruction," a necessary phase in a "dynamic view of progress."

4 All parenthetical page references are to the text of the 1979 MTP edition of *A Connecticut Yankee.* Where chapters are not identified in the text, they are cited in the parentheses as the number before the colon.

5 Bernard Bowron, Leo Marx, and Arnold Rose anticipate Smith's positing of a dichotomy in Twain with their demonstration in "Literature and Covert Culture" that cultural ambivalence is sometimes revealed in the same work when one position is overtly affirmed but a contradictory position is expressed covertly (382–383).

6 There are some interesting and ironic parallels between Hank's entrance into Abblasoure and the various sinister appearances of mysterious stranger figures in such Twain works as "The Notorious Jumping Frog of Calaveras County," "The Man That Corrupted Hadleyburg," "The Great Dark," and the "Mysterious Stranger" manuscripts. To the villagers, Hank was also a mysterious stranger who quickly proposed some deep changes in their community. He began by seeming friendly but ended by being perceived as evil. Similarly, it can be seen that from the perspective of sixth-century England, Hank is also a mysterious stranger. This point will be developed more fully in our last chapter.

7 "To me belongeth vengeance" (Deuteronomy 32:35) establishes revenge as an exclusive right of God. In seeking, therefore, to exact revenge, a trespass upon a divine prerogative, Hank admits to succumbing to a weakness of human nature. Additionally, although he repeatedly claims that he understands human nature, Hank is not as knowing as he thinks: he lacks depth. As he steadily grows in power, he increasingly misunderstands both himself and the way others see him. Despite his conviction that he is bringing democracy to England, his actions show him looking down condescendingly on his fellow humans and moving ever closer to becoming a tyrant.

8 Herman Melville's term for this is "Loose-Fish." In chapter 89 of *Moby-Dick*, Ishmael defines a Fast-Fish as a whale that is harpooned and physically secured by a party, and a Loose-Fish as one not yet so controlled. Then, extending metaphorically the terms beyond the whale fishery, he asks, rhetorically, "What are the Rights of Man and the Liberties of the World but Loose-Fish? . . . And what are you, reader, but a Loose-Fish and a Fast-Fish, too?" (310).

9 Melville, *Moby-Dick*, chapter 93.

10 For the background of Twain's knowledge of pre–Civil War free men of color and Reconstruction-era freedmen, see our chapter on *Huckleberry Finn*; Berkove, "The Free Man of Color in *The Grandissimes*"; Victor Doyno, *Writing* Huck Finn: *Mark Twain's Creative Process* (228–239); and Csicsila, "Been Reading."

11 A classical argument against utopia is that in order for it to exist, it is necessary to first create a utopian human nature.

12 Quoted in Chadwick Hansen, "The Once and Future Boss: Mark Twain's Yankee," 67.

13 The stock board made up of Round Table knights, for instance, precipitates the end of Arthur's reign, in chapter 42, by engaging in wildcat speculation. Greed gets the best of Launcelot when he discovers an opportunity to make a killing on the market. The tremendously inflated price of the stock as contrasted to its intrinsic worth is an ironic example of how slenderly Hank understands even his own notion of political economy.

14 Peter Messent regards this passage as introducing the subject of training into the book:

> Hank . . . judges her lack of compassion or remorse to be a result of training, rather than of moral culpability. (The implications of this judgment are crucial to the developing determinist strain in Twain's thought and his increasingly strong challenge to notions of individual moral agency and distinct and autono-

mous selfhood. In this respect, Twain's voice seems to merge with Hank. For if "training is all there is to a person," with all her or his thoughts and opinions "merely heredity and training," then "all that is original in us" disappears more or less completely from view, "can be covered up and hidden by the point of a cambric needle.") (92)

15   The exceptions to this desertion are Clarence, the fifty-two young boys, and, presumably, Hank's wife and child. Had their "training" been somehow more intensive than that of all the rest? This could be so in the case of Clarence, but the text is practically silent on the anonymous fifty-two, who are not even mentioned until the last chapters. It is doubtful, however, that their conditioning would have been more intensive than that of the West Pointers. We are left with the fact that they were young. Is Twain possibly saying that in order to be reliable, conditioning has to start at an early age? This would hardly be a profound insight, and it would not even apply to the case of Huckleberry Finn, who resisted being indoctrinated by St. Petersburg, his father, the Widow Douglas, and Tom Sawyer. The only other element common to all the exceptions was total devotion to Hank. But the reason for this element is nowhere even hinted at in the novel, and does not comport well with the idea of deterministic "training." As for the deserters, it is difficult to credit previous training as having remained so powerfully in their psyches as to motivate all of them—the armies, navies, factory workers, technicians, and graduates of all his academies and Sunday schools—to abandon Hank in the same instant, as it were, en masse. Determinism has nothing to contribute to the explanation of the interdict or the mass desertion. The best explanation for both is supernatural: the command of God—predestination, if you will—similar to the abrupt change that God caused to come over the Egyptians as the exodus began, so that they suddenly became willing to enrich the departing Israelites (Exodus 12:35-36).

16   Stanley Brodwin aptly applied to this situation in Twain's works the term "false consciousness," which he appropriated from Marxist thought. He cites Engels as having defined it as "an ideological process that does not allow the individual to understand 'the true motive forces impelling him'" ("Mark Twain's Theology" 243, n.8). In appropriating the term from Brodwin, we differ somewhat from him in applying the term to our purposes and redefining it as the mental tendency to eschew reflection and analysis and accept appearances at face value. Hank Morgan is an outstanding example of false consciousness in operation, but in Twain's fiction it is a general condition.

17   Several of these nightmares are recorded in Paine's *Biography* 2:1368-1369. Edgar J. Burde originally called attention to these and other important dreams of Twain by way of assessing Twain's ability as a pilot. Burde's interpretation of

the significance of the dreams was disputed by Edgar Branch ("The Pilot and the Writer"), but both critics agree on the fact that Twain's subconscious projected his concerns in dreams.

18 Hilton Obenzinger approaches this realization in his 2005 article, "Better Dreams: Political Satire and Twain's Final Exploding Novel," but the point was made earlier in Lawrence Berkove's 1984 article "The Reality of the Dream: Structural and Thematic Unity in *A Connecticut Yankee*."

19 Most commentators cite Hank's philosophical inconsistencies as proof that Twain is also inconsistent. This is neither a necessary nor a profitable inference. Some critics—for example, Allen Guttman, Judith Fetterley, and Chadwick Hansen—have presented evidence that there is a pattern to the steady drift of Hank toward "benevolent" despotism. In other words, the pattern indicates that Twain purposely depicted a self-contradictory Hank. Nor do the admitted similarities between some of Hank's views and some of Twain's oblige us to regard Hank as anything other than a fictititious character at all points in the novel. To read Hank otherwise is to deny Twain the right to create a character who seems at times to resemble his nonliterary self. This denial would break the novel by seeking to impose upon it the illogical assumption that because the protagonist at times resembles Clemens, it follows that Hank is autobiographical. The main obstacles to the recognition of *A Connecticut Yankee* as a fully integrated novel, therefore, have been the critical analyses of it, not the novel itself. If the fundamental difference between the author and his literary creature is respected, *A Connecticut Yankee* succeeds. Twain's conception of Hank as an unreliable narrator can be supported both by textual analysis and by his well-known description of Hank to Dan Beard as "a perfect ignoramus" (quoted in Paine's *Biography* 887–888) that distances the author from his literary creation.

20 For example, an almost unnoticed technique of Twain's to subtly undercut Hank's reliability as a narrator is the deferral of revealing that Morgan was Hank's last name to chapter 39 (out of forty-five chapters). It is significant that of all the surnames Twain could have given to Hank, he chose one with negative associations: with the character of Morgan le Fay; with the enormously wealthy and powerful contemporary financier J. P. Morgan, whom Foner reports Twain disliked (162, 301, 303); and with the notorious pirate Henry Morgan. The extreme delay enables Twain to both establish and obscure comparisons to individuals he regarded as disreputable.

21 Quoted in Cox, "Machinery," 99–100.

22 We are grateful to the late Frederick Anderson, who helped one of us locate this passage in an unpublished manuscript in the Mark Twain Papers.

23 See Howard G. Baetzhold's entry on *A Connecticut Yankee* in the *Mark Twain Encyclopedia*. He recapitulates an earlier essay, "The Course of Composition of *A Connecticut Yankee*: A Reinterpretation," on the course of the novel's composition and notes that as early as 1886, Twain had revealed to an audience his plan to have Hank, from behind electrified barbed wire fences, machine-gun Arthur's opponents. Baetzhold takes cognizance of the facts that Twain's views about the novel began shifting soon afterward and that Hank ultimately fought the chivalry of England instead of Arthur's enemies. Baetzhold, understandably, places interpretive emphasis on Twain's autobiographical remarks about the novel he was writing, whereas we place greater emphasis on the text itself and on the countertheology that constituted Twain's deepest convictions and that meshed with his creative impulses.

24 A brief but even earlier foreshadowing of the Battle of the Sand-Belt occurs as "A Word of Explanation," which precedes chapter 1. "M.T." and the "curious stranger," who turns out to be Hank, are in Warwick Castle with a group of tourists examining a bullet hole in a suit of chain mail. The docent attributes it to a Cromwellian soldier, but Hank offers his own explanation: "'Wit ye well, *I saw it done.*' Then, after a pause, added 'I did it myself.'" M.T.'s reaction is too apropos for Twain to have worded it coincidentally: "By the time I had recovered from the *electric* surprise of this remark, he was gone" (2, emphasis added). "Electric" thus works equally well as an appropriate contemporaneous metaphor and as allusion to Hank's surprise use of electricity in the battle.

25 Instead of "finger on the button," both the versions in the *Century* magazine (November 1889) and the subsequent first American edition read "hand on the cock." The editors of the 1983 MTP edition call attention in a note to the fact of sexual innendo in this reading and suggest that Twain changed the text once he became aware of it (636–637). It should be pointed out, however, that "cock" literally refers to both guns and valves. In both meanings, it shares with the rest of the passage an allusion to the Battle of the Sand-Belt.

26 The name of Hank's wife, Sandy, or Alisande ("all is sand"), is also linked, ironically, to the idea of the transience of time and to the final victory that time will have over Hank.

27 Some of the symbolic significance of the number thirteen is foreshadowed in chapter 7 when Hank completes installing a lightning rod in Merlin's tower and connecting it to embedded gunpowder on the thirteenth night of his preparing "miracle" (57). The next lightning storm allows Hank to effectuate his miracle. Also, in chapter 42 thirteen Gatling guns are emplaced to cover the twelve circles of deadly fences around the cave (421), a thirteenth circle.

28 Twain implies this very early in the novel when Hank questions "M.T.": "You know about transmigration of souls; do you know about transposition of epochs—and bodies?" ("A Word of Explanation" 2). The topic is not pursued, but even in its bare detail it supplies one of only two hints in the novel that offer an explanation as to how Hank found himself in sixth-century England. The other, related, hint occurs in Hank's recollection of his fight with one of his workmen: "At last I met my match, and I got my dose. It was during a misunderstanding conducted with crowbars with a fellow we used to call Hercules. He laid me out with a crusher alongside the head that made everything crack, and seemed to spring every joint in my skull and make it overlap its neighbor. Then the world went out in darkness" ("A Word of Explanation" 5). Most readers assume this passage to mean that not only was Hank knocked unconscious, but literally out of this world. But a blow to the skull from a crowbar wielded by a very powerful man ("Hercules") would almost certainly be fatal. Although this idea is also not pursued in the novel, Twain may be hinting that Hank was killed in his own time and place, and came to not in heaven but in another chronological circle of earthly hell, doomed—or damned—to another life-in-death dream existence even as he attempted to cope with recollections of the one he just left. Insofar as Twain affirms that this life is hell, all periods of time are also within hell, and that moving (being "transposed") from one epoch to another would be similar to someone in Dante's hell moving from one circle to another. In chapter 18, however, Twain might be distinguishing the immortal soul from the temporal person when Hank briefly and tragically glimpses his essential individuality as a "microscopic atom . . . in this plodding sad pilgrimage, this pathetic drift between the eternities" (162).

29 Despite drawing somewhat different conclusions about *A Connecticut Yankee* than Roger Salomon does, we find support for our position in his observations about the influence of Calvinism on Clemens (15–16) and about history following a pattern over which the individual has no influence (21–22). Salomon also quotes Clemens's bitter reaction to a work on optimistic evolution: "The world was made for man, and man was made to suffer and be damned" (50). That the idea of time's repeating itself was likely on Twain's mind as he wrote *A Connecticut Yankee* can be further adduced from a short work of the early 1900s, the "Passage from a Lecture" fragment. In it a character called the Mad Philosopher has formulated a "Law of Periodical Repetition," according to which "everything which has happened once must happen again and again and again—and not capriciously, but at regular periods, and each thing in its own period, not another's, and each obeying its own law. The eclipse of the sun . . . hint[s] to us that the same Nature which delights in periodical repetition in the

skies is the Nature which orders the affairs of the earth. Let us not underrate the value of that hint" (*Fables of Man* 401). The text of the novel also supports this idea in Hank's recording his story on a palimpsest. "Under the old dim writing of the Yankee historian appeared traces of a penmanship which was older and dimmer still" ("A Word of Explanation" 7).

30 Although we follow a different line of interpretation about the significance of the eclipse than David Ketterer does in his impressive essay, "Epoch-Eclipse and Apocalypse: Special 'Effects' in *A Connecticut Yankee*," we agree with an important part of his conclusion, that is, that *A Connecticut Yankee* expresses Twain's view that "all reality is a dream" (433–434).

31 In Twain's countertheology, following logically from God's omniscience and predestination, a visitor from another age might not even cause a temporary perturbation, for that visit would not be a miracle but also part of God's plan, and the time traveler would not be freer than anyone else to alter the course of the other age's history, which God had predestined before creation.

32 Brodwin notices this pattern of allusions and calls them a "parody" of Matthew 12:33–34 ("Wandering" 76). From this point on, our interpretations of the passage are different.

33 Hank consistently underestimates what he is up against. He discards his aspiration to being a magician, for example, without giving Merlin full credit for his achievements in that line. Although Hank regularly ridicules Merlin, Merlin performs real magic twice: once when he brings Arthur to the sword Excalibur, and once when he casts the spell that puts Hank to sleep for thirteen centuries. Merlin thus is a tangible example of the presence of the supernatural which elsewhere in the novel (and in *Huckleberry Finn*) operates quietly and invisibly behind the scenes.

34 This line is intriguingly similar to a famous sentence by Jonathan Swift which tells of "that Philosopher, who, while his Thoughts and Eyes were fixed upon the *Constellations*, found himself seduced by his *lower Parts* into a *Ditch*" ("A Discourse Concerning the Mechanical Operation of the Spirit &c.," 190). Both reflect ironically on individuals who lose touch with reality while indulging themselves in abstract speculation.

35 The illustrator Dan Beard was the first reader to intuit that Twain might have regarded Hank as a representative American. While the text, at the surface level, ingratiates Hank with readers by his seeming openness, good nature, good sense, benevolent intentions, and avowed opposition to the enemies of the common man (tyranny, ignorance, and superstition), Beard portrays him in his

heavily symbolic illustration "Hello-Central" (41:408) to resemble Uncle Sam, and Sandy to resemble Columbia. Note that Hank's leggings are striped like the flag and that he has a beard. Sandy's gown is star-spangled. Behind Hank, on the table, are items that resemble a powder horn and a tomahawk. The cradle has a repeated fleur-de-lis motif suggestive of the French Revolution. And over Hank's head is a sign with a conventional American sentiment: "God Bless Our Home."

36 Covici, in his *Mark Twain Encyclopedia* entry on "Humor," packs a lot of insight into his observation that "the humor of Mark Twain often turns out to be no laughing matter" (380). The countertheological approach of this book bears out the validity of that comment.

37 According to D. Justin Schove's *Chronology of Eclipses and Comets AD 1–1000*, there were in fact no solar eclipses in western Europe in 528.

38 We gratefully acknowledge the insights of students who, in our Mark Twain classes, selected the poker and euchre option for their class papers: Elizabeth Ryan, Kevin Peshkopia, Jacqueline Licalzi, Dennis Gerathy, and Julie Richter.

39 Explosions and gunplay punctuate Hank's rise to power and his transformation into an unfeeling tyrant. In chapter 27, for instance, when Hank dispatches a couple of hostile knights with a dynamite bomb, he says, "Yes, it was a neat thing, very neat and pretty to see. It resembled a steamboat explosion on the Mississippi; and during the next fifteen minutes we stood under a steady drizzle of microscopic fragments of knights and hardware and horse-flesh" (272). Considering that Mississippi River steamboat explosions were normally regarded as horrible disasters, that Clemens's brother Henry was mortally injured in one, and that Twain never forgot the anguish of watching his brother and others die, Hank's jocular description is loaded by Twain to be bitterly ironic.

40 It is no accident that the first of the schools Hank establishes is an equivalent of a West Point ("one of my deepest secrets" [10:83]), where selected students are taught to wage nineteenth-century war. (Philip Leon's *Mark Twain and West Point* establishes Twain's familiarity and close associations with West Point and also casts light on Twain's "Man-Factories.") But against whom? At this early stage of his influence, there appear to be no enemies, domestic or foreign, against whom he needs defense. At some level of his mind, therefore, he is planning offense. In chapter 25 Hank listens with great pleasure to a cadet from his military academy lay out the "science of war" and "wallow in details of battle and siege, of supply, transportation, mining and countermining . . . infantry, cavalry, artillery, and all about siege guns, field guns, gatling guns, rifled guns, smooth bores, musket practice, revolver practice" (243). This passage closely

resembles the scene in Book II of *Gulliver's Travels* in which Gulliver enthusiastically tells the king of Brobdingnag of the wonderful effects of gunpowder and is surprised when the king responds with horror at the "inhuman" invention (7:134–135). Like Gulliver, Hank is unable to see himself as others see him or to understand what terrible things he has taught. This episode is therefore another reason to regard Hank as an unreliable narrator, and not to confuse him with the biographical Clemens.

The bulk of chapter 10 ("Beginnings of Civilization") might look progressive on a first reading, but Hank's development of a Sunday school system and his encouragement of a wide variety of Protestant congregations have nothing to do with a desire that the people worship God sincerely but everything to do with his wish to weaken and break the monopoly of the church, his greatest competitor after Merlin. One of his larger delusions, however, is his institution of "Man-Factories." From a modern perspective, but one Twain was certain to hold, manhood is a quality which cannot be mass-produced in a factory.

41 The small number of Hank's party may also be an allusion to Calvinism insofar as they are the "elect" Hank intends to "save." If so, this is another manifestation of Hank's hubristic drift toward godhood.

Chapter 6. *No. 44, The Mysterious Stranger*

1 A few notable exceptions to such pessimistic readings of Twain's late period include Sholom Kahn's *Mark Twain's* Mysterious Stranger: *A Study of the Manuscript Texts*, William Macnaughton's *Mark Twain's Last Years as a Writer*, and Michael Kiskis's "Coming Back to Humor: The Comic Voice in Mark Twain's *Autobiography*."

2 Susan Gillman, *Dark Twins: Imposture and Identity in Mark Twain's America*.

3 These titles are as established by the authoritative Mark Twain Papers edition of *Mysterious Stranger Manuscripts* (1969).

4 John Tuckey's "Mark Twain's Later Dialogue," Gillman's *Dark Twins*, and Susan Harris's *Mark Twain's Escape from Time: A Study of Patterns and Images* are notable exceptions.

5 For a more detailed discussion of distinctions between the various Mysterious Stranger manuscripts, see Joseph Csicsila, "Religious Satire to Tragedy of Consciousness: The Evolution of Theme in Mark Twain's 'Mysterious Stranger' Manuscripts."

6 See, for example, Jason Gary Horn, *Mark Twain and William James: Crafting a Free Self*, 123–124.

7 At a metaphorical level, August's flight from Eseldorf and Father Adolf's culture of religious cruelty to Castle Rosenfeld, which Sholom Kahn has pointed out Twain likened in his descriptions to that of the human mind, echoes the totality of the project of *No. 44, the Mysterious Stranger* for Twain: freedom from oppressive religious ideology via the exploration of psychology as a means for understanding the human mind.

8 Noteworthy is the observation that Twain's use of the name Forty-Four antedates *No. 44, The Mysterious Stranger* by at least three years. In the unfinished "Mysterious Stranger" fragment composed between November and December 1898 and published as "Schoolhouse Hill" in Gibson's edition of Twain's *Mysterious Stranger Manuscripts*, Twain presents the story of Satan's angelic son, who also introduces himself as Forty-Four to the inhabitants of a small village. Twain's working notes for "Schoolhouse Hill" indicate that this peculiar name (first conceived as "404," which Twain later changed to "94," "45," and lastly "44") probably derives from the notion that the Forty-Four of this particular tale, as one of Satan's multitudinous offspring, is the member of an enormously large family: "I am No. 45 in New Series 986,000,000. I have seen all my brothers and sisters at one time or another, and I know them by Number and features. There are some billions of them" (*Mysterious Stranger Manuscripts*, 444). Several scholars have, in addition, offered interpretations attempting to account for an even more profound (perhaps autobiographical) explanation and origin of the name Forty-Four, a summary of which is provided in Gibson's textual notes to the *Mysterious Stranger Manuscripts*. But because Twain clearly developed the name Forty-Four for the earlier "Schoolhouse Hill," our analysis is not so much concerned with the source of the name Forty-Four as it is with how Twain is able to utilize it in *No. 44, The Mysterious Stranger*—two very separate yet equally important issues. In short, it is our argument that Twain created the name August effectually in response to the name Forty-Four and embedded within it a significance to amplify and deepen not only the intimate correlation between the two protagonists of *No. 44, The Mysterious Stranger* but also the original relevance of the name "Forty-Four."

9 Twain's short story "The Facts Concerning the Recent Carnival of Crime in Connecticut" (1876) is also indebted to Poe's use of metaphorical alter egos. See Berkove, "Poe, Twain, and the Nature of Conscience."

10 See Gribben, *Mark Twain's Library*, 130.

11 For a detailed analysis, see Joop Berding's "John Dewey's Participatory Philosophy of Education, Experience and Curriculum."

12 See Berding, "John Dewey's Participatory Philosophy."

13 See Gregg Camfield, "Transcendental Hedonism?: Sex, Song, Food and Drink in *No. 44, The Mysterious Stranger* and 'My Platonic Sweetheart,'" for further discussion of sexuality in *No. 44, The Mysterious Stranger.*

14 Martin von Giesbach is, according to our analysis, the third version of August's Dream-Self mentioned in the story. The first and most central, we argue, is Forty-Four. The second is Emil, who is variously identified in the text as August's Duplicate and August's Dream-Self with flesh (see, for example, August's discussion of Emil on 124–125). Forty-Four, we contend, is August's authentic Dream-Self throughout the novel. Emil and Martin, on the other hand, merely perform the role of August's Dream-Self in certain situations—temporary props created by Forty-Four, if you will—mainly for the purpose of illustrating Forty-Four's "lessons" regarding the dual nature of the individual, which also aids, of course, in disguising Forty-Four's true identity until the very end of the narrative.

15 James articulates his theory of "the Soul" in a lengthy discussion in *Principles of Psychology* in the context of describing the unification of the selves. James offers numerous historical descriptions of the "pure ego," including "the Soul" (342) in the chapter titled "The Consciousness of the Self," but in all of these descriptions, James sees the "pure ego" as the "pure principle of personal identity" or, put another way, as the "transcendental principle of unity" (330).

16 For two excellent analyses of the minstrel episode in *No. 44, The Mysterious Stranger*, see Sharon McCoy, "'I Ain' No Dread Being': The Minstrel Mask as Alter Ego"; and Henry Wonham, "Mark Twain's Last Cakewalk: Racialized Performance in *No. 44, The Mysterious Stranger.*"

17 See Lawrence Berkove, "'A Difficult Case': W. D. Howells's Impression of Mark Twain."

18 Interestingly, Forty-Four's argument here that we are all merely thoughts "wandering forlorn among the empty eternities" echoes an assertion Hank Morgan makes about his own existence in *A Connecticut Yankee* during the well-known "training is everything" passage at the beginning of chapter 18: "And as for me, all that I think about in this plodding sad pilgrimage, this pathetic drift between the eternities, is to look out and humbly live a pure and high and blameless life, and save that one microscopic atom in me that is truly *me*: the rest may land in Sheol and welcome, for all I care" (162).

19 In "Imagination and Redemption: 44 in the Third Version of *The Mysteri-*

ous Stranger," Robert Lowery argues that the final chapter is "neither nihilistic nor pessimistic" (110). His argument is that because August is able to transcend the misery of the human condition through self-education, *No. 44, The Mysterious Stranger* should be read as an optimistic work of fiction.

20 Another point on which Forty-Four's reliability might be questioned is his final advice to August to "Dream other dreams, and better" (186). According to Twain's countertheological vision, human nature is such that we are by definition so prone to error that any choices August makes will be flawed. This would mean that in addition to the other problems we identify about the ending, Forty-Four's advice is also impractical because of what Twain would have believed to be August's built-in shortcomings as a human being.

21 For fuller discussion, see chapter 5.

Chapter 7. The Last Letters from Earth

1 "Letters from the Earth" first appeared in the collection of the same name edited by Bernard DeVoto in 1962. The piece was reedited and republished in Baetzhold and McCullough, *The Bible According to Mark Twain*. The latter is currently the most reliable version of "Letters from the Earth." The composition of "Letters from the Earth" is thought to have taken place in November and December 1909. See Macnaughton, *Mark Twain's Last Years as a Writer*, 237.

2 See, for instance, DeVoto, *Mark Twain at Work*; Justin Kaplan, *Mr. Clemens and Mark Twain*; and Hamlin Hill, *Mark Twain: God's Fool*.

3 See Laura Skandera Trombley, *Mark Twain in the Company of Women*, "'She Wanted to Kill': Jean Clemens and Postictal Psychosis," "Mark Twain's Last Work of Realism: The Ashcroft-Lyon Manuscript," and "Mark Twain's *Annus Horribilis* of 1908–09." In the second piece, Trombley affirms Hill's contention that wherever Twain was in those last ten years amounted to a hell for him.

4 See Michael Kiskis, "Coming Back to Humor: The Comic Voice in Mark Twain's *Autobiography*."

5 See Susan K. Harris, "Hadleyburg: Mark Twain's Dual Attack on Banal Theology and Banal Literature."

6 Even if it were ordered that the Richardses and the others fall to temptation, according to the tenets of Calvinism, they would still be considered guilty.

7 See Edgar Branch, *The Literary Apprenticeship of Mark Twain*, 150–151.

8 Although there really is a place called Black Jack in Arkansas, a fact of which Twain conceivably could have been aware, he obviously saw ironic possibilities

for a village of this appellation being associated with a holy miracle due to its definition as a card game used in gambling.

9 See chapter 4, n.7, for our interpretation of the Grangerford-Shepherdson episode, and chapter 5 for our discussion of this idea in *A Connecticut Yankee*.

10 Here Twain appears to confuse the Catholic church's dogma of the Immaculate Conception with the notion of the virgin birth, a fairly common error. According to the *Catechism of the Catholic Church* (2002), the Immaculate Conception, as Pope Pius IX proclaimed in 1854, refers to the fact that Mary, from the instant of *her* conception as a human being, "was preserved immune from the stain of original sin" (124). The "virgin birth," by contrast, refers to the fact that Jesus Christ "was conceived by the Holy Spirit without human seed" (903).

11 Quoted in Caroline Thomas Harnsberger, *Mark Twain's Views of Religion*, 26.

12 Gribben, in *Mark Twain's Library*, notes that Twain inscribed the year 1907 in his copy of Noyes's *Views of Religion*, an indication that Twain likely read and commented in the margins of the book in 1907.

13 Quoted in Caroline Thomas Harnsberger, *Mark Twain's Views of Religion*, 26.

14 See Paine, *Mark Twain: A Biography*, 776, 1354.

15 For an extended discussion of this idea, see Joseph Csicsila, "From Religious Satire to Tragedy of Consciousness: The Evolution of Theme in Mark Twain's 'Mysterious Stranger' Manuscripts."

16 The most authoritative edition of these writings appears in Baetzhold and McCullough's *The Bible According to Mark Twain*, whose texts we follow.

17 See the introduction to Baetzhold and McCullough's *The Bible According to Mark Twain*.

18 Twain also had this same statement inscribed on his wife's headstone.

19 To be specific, Edward Tudor is restored to his true identity as Prince of Wales; Tom Canty is restored as both a commoner and a compassionate human being; Valet de Chambers is returned to his status as a slave; Tom Driscoll is returned to his proper identity as the son of Percy Driscoll; and the Richardses, like the other leading citizens of Hadleyburg, resume their identities as deceptive, self-interested individuals, despite their "training" to be honest people.

20 See, for example, Baetzhold and McCullough, *The Bible According to Mark Twain*, 213-217.

Adams, Percy G. *Travel Literature and the Evolution of the Novel.* Lexington: UP of Kentucky, 1981.

Allen, Charles A. "Mark Twain and Conscience." *Literature and Psychology* 7 (May 1957): 17–21.

Arner, Robert D. "Acts Seventeen and Huckleberry Finn: A Note on Silas Phelps' Sermon." *Mark Twain Journal* 16 (Summer 1972): 12.

Aspiz, Harold. "Lecky's Influence on Mark Twain." *Science and Society* 26 (Winter 1962): 15–25.

Baetzhold, Howard G. "Carlyle, Thomas." In *The Mark Twain Encyclopedia*, ed. J. R. Le Master and James D. Wilson, 126–128. New York: Garland, 1993.

———. *"A Connecticut Yankee in King Arthur's Court."* In *The Mark Twain Encyclopedia*, ed. J. R. Le Master and James D. Wilson, 174–179. New York: Garland, 1993.

———. "The Course of Composition of *A Connecticut Yankee*: A Reinterpretation." *American Literature* 33 (1961): 195–214.

———. *Mark Twain and John Bull: The British Connection.* Bloomington: Indiana UP, 1970.

Baetzhold, Howard G., and Joseph B. McCullough, eds. *The Bible According to Mark Twain.* Athens: U of Georgia P, 1995.

Baldanza, Frank. *Mark Twain: An Introduction and Interpretation.* New York: Barnes and Noble, 1961.

———. "The Structure of *Huckleberry Finn*." *American Literature* 27 (November 1955): 347–355.

Basso, Hamilton. *The Light Infantry Ball.* Garden City, N.Y.: Doubleday, 1959.

Bellamy, Gladys. *Mark Twain as a Literary Artist.* Norman: U of Oklahoma P, 1950.

Berding, Joop W. A. "John Dewey's Participatory Philosophy of Education, Experience and Curriculum." Ph.D. diss., Free University, Amsterdam, 1999.

Berkove, Lawrence I. "*A Connecticut Yankee*: A Serious Hoax." *Essays in Arts and Sciences* 19 (May 1990): 28–44.

———. "*Connecticut Yankee*: Twain's Other Masterpiece." In *Making Mark Twain Work in the Classroom*, ed. James S. Leonard, 88–109. Durham, N.C.: Duke UP, 1999.

———. "Dan De Quille's 'Jim Gillis: The Thoreau of the Sierras.'" *Mark Twain Circular* 2, nos. 3–4 (1988): 1–2.

———. "'A Difficult Case': W. D. Howells's Impression of Mark Twain." *Studies in Short Fiction* 31, no. 4 (Fall 1994): 607–615.

———, ed. "Editor's Preface." In *The Best Short Stories of Mark Twain*, xix–xxv. New York: Modern Library, 2004.

———. *Ethical Records of Twain and His Circle of Sagebrush Journalists.* Quarry Farm Papers No. 5. Elmira, N.Y.: Elmira College Center for Mark Twain Studies, 1994.

———. "The Free Man of Color in *The Grandissimes* and Works by Harris and Mark Twain." *Southern Quarterly* 18, no. 4 (Summer 1980): 60–73.

———. "The Gospel According to Hank Morgan's Newspaper." *Essays in Arts and Sciences* 20 (October 1991): 32–42.

———, ed. *Insider Stories of the Comstock Lode and Nevada's Mining Frontier 1859–1909: Primary Sources in American Social History.* 2 vols. Lewiston, N.Y.: Edwin Mellen Press, 2007.

———. "Mark Twain's Hostility to Joseph." *CEA Critic* 62, no. 3 (Summer 2000): 39–47.

———. "Nevada Influences on Mark Twain." In *A Companion to Mark Twain*, ed. Peter Messent and Louis J. Budd, 157–171. Oxford: Blackwell, 2005.

———. "'No Mere Accidental Incidents': *Roughing It* as a Novel." *Mark Twain Annual* 1 (2003): 7–17.

———. "Poe, Twain, and the Nature of Conscience." *ESQ* 46, no. 4 (2000): 239–252.

———. "The 'Poor Players' of *Huckleberry Finn*." *Papers of the Michigan Academy* 53 (1968): 291–310.

———. "The Reality of the Dream: Structural and Thematic Unity in *A Connecticut Yankee*." *Mark Twain Journal* 22, no. 1 (Spring 1984): 8–14.

———. "The Trickster God in *Roughing It*." *Thalia* 18, nos. 1–2 (1998): 21–30.

Bierce, Ambrose. *The Collected Works of Ambrose Bierce.* 12 vols. New York: Neale, 1909–1912.

———. "Town Crier." *San Francisco News-Letter and California Advertiser,* September 11, 1869.

Blair, Walter. *Mark Twain and Huck Finn.* Berkeley: U of California P, 1960.

Boettner, Loraine. *The Reformed Doctrine of Predestination.* Philadelphia: Presbyterian and Reformed Publishing, 1973.

Booth, Wayne C. *The Rhetoric of Fiction.* Chicago: U of Chicago P, 1961.

Boswell's Life of Johnson. Ed. George Birkbeck Hill and Rev. L. F. Powell. Vol. 2. Oxford: Clarendon Press, 1934.

Bowron, Bernard, Leo Marx, and Arnold Rose. "Literature and Covert Culture." *American Quarterly* 9, no. 4 (Winter 1957): 382–383.

Branch, Edgar M. *The Literary Apprenticeship of Mark Twain.* 1950. Repr., New York: Russell and Russell, 1966.

———. "Mark Twain: The Pilot and the Writer." *Mark Twain Journal* 23, no. 2 (Fall 1985): 28–43.

Briden, Earl F. "Conscience." In *The Mark Twain Encyclopedia,* ed. J. R. Le Master and James D. Wilson, 179–181. New York: Garland, 1993.

Brodwin, Stanley. "Blackness and the Adamic Myth in Mark Twain's *Pudd'nhead Wilson.*" *Texas Studies in Language and Literature* 15, no. 1 (Spring 1973): 167–176.

———. "Mark Twain and the Myth of the Daring Jest." In *The Mythologizing of Mark Twain,* ed. Sara deSaussure Davis and Philip D. Beidler, 136–157, 173–177. Tuscaloosa: U of Alabama P, 1984.

———. "Mark Twain in the Pulpit." In *One Hundred Years of Huckleberry Finn: The Boy, His Book, and American Culture,* ed. Robert Sattelmeyer and J. Donald Crowley, 371–385. Columbia: U of Missouri P, 1985.

———. "Mark Twain's Masks of Satan: The Final Phase." *American Literature* 45, no. 2 (May 1973): 206–227.

———. "Mark Twain's Theology: The Gods of a Brevet Presbyterian." In *Cambridge Companion to Mark Twain,* ed. Forrest G. Robinson, 220–248. New York: Cambridge UP, 1995.

———. "The Theology of Mark Twain: Banished Adam and the Bible." In *Critical Essays on Mark Twain, 1910–1980,* ed. Louis J. Budd, 176–193. Boston: G. K. Hall, 1982.

———. "*The Tragedy of Pudd'nhead Wilson.*" In *The Mark Twain Encyclopedia,* ed. J. R. Le Master and James D. Wilson, 595–599. New York: Garland, 1993.

———. "Wandering between Two Gods: Theological Realism in *Connecticut Yankee*." *Studies in the Literary Imagination* 16, no. 2 (1983): 57–82.

Brown, Spencer. "*Huckleberry Finn* for Our Time." *Michigan Quarterly Review* 6, no. 1 (Winter 1967): 41–46.

Budd, Lou, ed. *Mark Twain: Collected Tales, Sketches, Speeches, and Essays, 1852–1890, 1891–1910.* 2 vols. New York: Library of America, 1992.

———. "Mark Twain's Fingerprints in *Pudd'nhead Wilson*." In *New Directions in American Humor*, ed. David E. E. Sloane, 171–185. Tuscaloosa: U of Alabama P, 1998.

———. *Our Mark Twain: The Making of His Public Personality.* Philadelphia: U of Pennsylvania P, 1983.

Burde, Edgar J. "Mark Twain: The Writer as Pilot." *PMLA* 93 (1978): 878–892.

Bush, Harold K., Jr. "Demythologizing Adam: Mark Twain and the Nature of Man." In *Critical Essays on the Myth of the American Adam*, ed. Viorica Patea and Maria Euginia Diaz, 147–162. Salamanca, Spain: U of Salamanca P, 2001.

———. *Mark Twain and the Spiritual Crisis of the Gilded Age.* Birmingham: U of Alabama P, 2006.

———. "Mark Twain's American Adam: Humor as Site for Hope and Apocalypse." *Christianity and Literature* 53, no. 3 (Spring 2004): 291–314.

———. "'A Moralist in Disguise': Mark Twain and American Religion." In *A Historical Guide to Mark Twain*, ed. Shelly Fisher Fishkin, 55–94. Oxford: Oxford UP, 2002.

Butcher, Philip. "'The Godfathership' of *A Connecticut Yankee*." *CLA Journal* 12, no. 3 (March 1969): 189–198.

Cable, George Washington. *The Grandissimes: A Story of Creole Life (1879–80).* Ed. Newton Arvin. New York: Hill and Wang, 1957.

———. "My Politics" [1889]. In *The Negro Question*, ed. Arlin Turner, 2–25. New York: Norton, 1958.

Camfield, Gregg. *Sentimental Twain: Samuel Clemens in the Maze of Moral Philosophy.* Philadelphia: U of Pennsylvania P, 1994.

———. "Transcendental Hedonism? Sex, Song, Food, and Drink in *No. 44, The Mysterious Stranger* and 'My Platonic Sweetheart.'" In *Centenary Reflections on Mark Twain's "No. 44, The Mysterious Stranger,"* ed. Joseph Csicsila and Chad Rohman, 127–143. Columbia: U of Missouri P, 2009.

Campbell, Jack K. *Colonel Francis W. Parker: The Children's Crusader.* New York: Columbia Teachers' College P, 1967.

Carlyle, Thomas. *Sartor Resartus: The Life and Opinions of Herr Teufels-dröckh*. New York: Scribners, 1897.

Caron, James. *Mark Twain: Unsanctified Newspaper Reporter*. Columbia: U of Missouri P, 2008.

Carter, Everett. "The Meaning of *A Connecticut Yankee*." *American Literature* 50, no. 3 (November 1978): 418–440.

Catteral, Helen Tunnicliff, ed. *Judicial Cases Concerning American Slavery and the Negro, III*. Washington, D.C.: GPO, 1932.

Coulombe, Joseph L. *Mark Twain and the American West*. Columbia: U of Missouri P, 2003.

Covici, Pascal, Jr. "Hoax." In *The Mark Twain Encyclopedia*, ed. J. R. Le Master and James D. Wilson, 362. New York: Garland, 1993.

———. "Humor." In *The Mark Twain Encyclopedia*, ed. J. R. Le Master and James D. Wilson, 377–380. New York: Garland, 1993.

———. *Mark Twain's Humor: The Image of a World*. Dallas: Southern Methodist UP, 1962.

Cox, James M. "*A Connecticut Yankee in King Arthur's Court*: The Machinery of Self-Preservation." *Yale Review* 50 (Autumn 1960): 89–102.

———. "Remarks on the Sad Initiation of Huckleberry Finn." *Sewanee Review* 62 (Summer 1954): 389–405.

Csicsila, Joseph. "'Been Reading the Horrors in the Newspapers?': Octave Thanet's 'Trusty, No. 49' and the Arkansas Convict Lease System." *Essays in Arts and Sciences* 34, no. 2 (2005): 65–68.

———. *Canons by Consensus: Critical Trends and American Literature Anthologies*. Tuscaloosa: U of Alabama P, 2004.

———. "'The Child Learns by Doing': Mark Twain and the Turn-of-the-Century Education Reform." *Mark Twain Annual* 6 (2008): 91–100.

———. "Life's Rich Pageant: The Education of August Feldner in Mark Twain's *No. 44, The Mysterious Stranger*." *Studies in American Humor* ser. 3, no. 4 (1997): 54–67.

———. "Religious Satire to Tragedy of Consciousness: The Evolution of Theme in Mark Twain's 'Mysterious Stranger' Manuscripts." *Essays in Arts and Sciences* 27 (October 1998): 53–70.

Csicsila, Joseph, and Chad Rohman, eds. *Centenary Reflections on Mark Twain's "No. 44, The Mysterious Stranger."* Columbia: U of Missouri P, 2009.

Cummings, Sherwood. *Mark Twain and Science: Adventures of a Mind*. Baton Rouge: Louisiana State UP, 1988.

Daiches, David. "Mark Twain as Hamlet." In *More Literary Essays*, 238–247. Chicago: U of Chicago P, 1968.

Davis, Chester L. "Mark Twain's Religious Beliefs as Indicated by Notations in His Books: *History of European Morals* by William Edward Hartpole Lecky." *Twainian* 14, no. 3 (May–June 1955): 1–4; 14, no. 4 (July–August 1955): 1–4; 14, no. 5 (September–October 1955): 1–4; 14, no. 6 (November–December 1955): 3–4.

Dempsey, Terrell. *Searching for Jim: Slavery in Sam Clemens's World*. Columbia: U of Missouri P, 2001.

De Quille, Dan. *The Big Bonanza* [1876]. Introduction by Oscar Lewis. New York: Knopf, 1947.

———. "Natural or Supernatural . . . The 'Thoreau of the Sierras.'" *Salt Lake City Daily Tribune*, July 19, 1891.

———. *Washoe Rambles*. Los Angeles: Westernlore Press, 1963.

DeVoto, Bernard. *Mark Twain at Work*. Cambridge, Mass.: Harvard UP, 1942.

———, ed. *Mark Twain in Eruption: Hitherto Unpublished Pages about Men and Events*. New York: Harper and Bros., 1940.

Doane, T. W. *Bible Myths and Their Parallels in Other Religions*. New York: Truth Seeker, 1882.

Donnelly, Mabel C. "Henry Ward Beecher and Infant Damnation." *The Harriet Beecher Stowe House and Library* (January/February 1992): 3.

Doyno, Victor. "Foreword" and "Textual Addendum." In *Adventures of Huckleberry Finn: The Only Comprehensive Edition*, xiii–xvii, 365–418. New York: Random House, 1996.

———, ed. Huck Finn: *The Complete Buffalo and Erie County Public Library Manuscript—Teaching and Research Digital Edition*. 2002.

———. "Introduction." In *Extract from Captain Stormfield's Visit to Heaven*. Amherst, N.Y.: Prometheus Books, 2002.

———. *Writing "Huck Finn": Mark Twain's Creative Process*. Philadelphia: U of Pennsylvania P, 1991.

Driscoll, Kerry. "The Fluid Identity of 'Petrified Man.'" *American Literary Realism* 41, no. 3 (Winter 2009): 214–231.

———. "'Man Factories' and the 'White Indians' of Camelot: Re-reading the Native Subtext of *A Connecticut Yankee in King Arthur's Court*." *Mark Twain Annual* 2 (2004): 6–25.

———. "'Only Heedlessly a Savage': Mark Twain's 'Indian' Identity." *Mark Twain Journal* 6 (Winter 2001): 5–17.

Dunne, Michael. *Calvinist Humor in American Literature*. Baton Rouge: Louisiana State UP, 2007.

Ensor, Allison R. "Mark Twain's Yankee and the Prophet [*sic*] of Baal." *American Literary Realism* 14, no. 1 (Spring 1981): 38–42.

Fanning, Philip Ashley. *Mark Twain and Orion Clemens: Brothers, Partners, Strangers*. Tuscaloosa: U of Alabama P, 2003.

Farnam, Henry W. *Chapters in the History of Social Legislation in the United States to 1860*. Ed. Clive Day. Washington, D.C.: GPO, 1938.

Fetterley, Judith. "The Sanctioned Rebel." *Studies in the Novel* 3 (Fall 1971): 293–304.

———. "Yankee Showman and Reformer: The Character of Mark Twain's Hank Morgan." *Texas Studies in Language and Literature* 14 (1973): 667–679.

Fienberg, Lorne. "Twain's Connecticut Yankee: The Entrepreneur as a Daimonic Hero." *Modern Fiction Studies* 28, no. 2 (Summer 1982): 155–167.

Foner, Philip S. *Mark Twain: Social Critic*. New York: International Publishers, 1958.

Fulton, Joe. *Mark Twain in the Margins: The Quarry Farm Marginalia and the Composition of "A Connecticut Yankee in King Arthur's Court."* Tuscaloosa: U of Alabama P, 2000.

———. "Mark Twain's Theological Travels." *Mark Twain Annual* 5 (2007): 43–56.

———. *The Reverend Mark Twain: Theological Burlesque, Form, and Content*. Columbus: Ohio State UP, 2006.

Galton, Francis. *Finger Prints*. [1892]. Introduction by Harold Cummins. New York: Da Capo Press, 1965.

Gillman, Susan. *Dark Twins: Imposture and Identity in Mark Twain's America*. Chicago: U of Chicago P, 1989.

Gribben, Alan. "Mark Twain, Business Man: The Margins of Profit." *Studies in American Humor* 1 (new series) (June 1982): 24–43.

———. *Mark Twain's Library: A Reconstruction*. 2 vols. Boston: G. K. Hall, 1980.

———. "'That Pair of Spiritual Derelicts': The Poe-Twain Relationship." *Poe Studies* 18 (1985): 17–21.

———. "Those Other Thematic Patterns in Mark Twain's Writings." *Studies in American Fiction* 13 (Autumn 1985): 185–200.

Gross, Seymour L. "Mark Twain and Catholicism." *Critic* 17 (April–May 1959): 9, 12, 88–91.

Guttman, Allen. "Mark Twain's *Connecticut Yankee*: Affirmation of the Vernacular Tradition?" *New England Quarterly* 33 (1960): 232–237.

Hansen, Chadwick. "The Once and Future Boss: Mark Twain's Yankee." *Nineteenth-Century Fiction* 28 (1973): 62–73.

Harnsberger, Caroline Thomas. *Mark Twain's Views of Religion*. Evanston, Ill.: Schori Press, 1961.

Harris, Joel Chandler. "Free Joe and the Rest of the World." In *Free Joe and Other Georgian Sketches*, 3–39. New York: Collier, 1887.

Harris, Susan K. "Hadleyburg: Mark Twain's Dual Attack on Banal Theology and Banal Literature." *American Literary Realism* 16 (Autumn 1983): 240–252.

———. *Mark Twain's Escape from Time: A Study of Patterns and Images*. Columbia: U of Missouri P, 1982.

Herts, Alice. *The Children's Educational Theatre*. New York: Harper and Bros., 1901.

Hill, Hamlin. "The Composition and Structure of *The Adventures of Tom Sawyer*." *American Literature* 32 (January 1961): 379–392.

———. *Mark Twain: God's Fool*. New York: Harper and Row, 1973.

Hill, Hamlin, and Walter Blair. *The Art of "Huckleberry Finn."* San Francisco: Chandler, 1962.

Hirrel, Leo P. *Children of Wrath: New School Calvinism and Antebellum Reform*. Lexington: UP of Kentucky, 1998.

Hodge, Charles. *Systematic Theology*. 3 vols. Grand Rapids, Mich.: Wm. B. Eerdmans, 1946.

Hoffman, Daniel. "Black Magic—and White." In *Mark Twain's Wound: A Casebook*, ed. Lewis Leary, 311–334. New York: Crowell, 1962.

———. *Form and Fable in American Fiction*. New York: Oxford UP, 1961.

Hogan, William R., and Edwin A. Davis, eds. *William Johnson's Natchez: The Ante-bellum Diary of a Free Negro*. Baton Rouge: Louisiana State UP, 1979.

The Holy Bible (King James Version). Iowa City, Iowa: World Bible, 1992.

Horn, Jason Gary. *Mark Twain and William James: Crafting a Free Self*. Columbia: U of Missouri P, 1996.

Howells, William Dean. "A Difficult Case." In *A Pair of Patient Lovers*, 145–220. New York: Harper, 1901.

———. *My Mark Twain*. New York: Harper and Bros., 1910.

James, William. *A Pluralistic Universe*. Ed. and introduction by Richard J. Bernstein. Cambridge, Mass.: Harvard UP, 1977.

——. *The Principles of Psychology.* New York: Holt, 1890.

——. *The Varieties of Religious Experience: A Study in Human Nature.* New York: Longmans, 1902.

Jones, Alexander E. "Heterodox Thought in Mark Twain's Hannibal." *Arkansas Historical Quarterly* 10, no. 4 (Autumn 1951): 244–257.

——. "Mark Twain and the Determinism of *What Is Man?*" *American Literature* 29 (March 1957): 1–17.

Kahn, Sholom. *Mark Twain's Mysterious Stranger: A Study of the Manuscript Texts.* Columbia: U of Missouri P, 1978.

Kaplan, Justin. *Mr. Clemens and Mark Twain.* New York: Simon and Schuster, 1966.

Kazin, Alfred. *An American Procession.* New York: Knopf, 1984.

——. *God and the American Writer.* New York: Knopf, 1997.

Ketterer, David. "Epoch-Eclipse and Apocalypse: Special 'Effects' in *A Connecticut Yankee*," rev. of *A Connecticut Yankee in King Arthur's Court*, ed. Allison R. Ensor, 417–434. New York: Norton, 1982.

Kiskis, Michael. "Coming Back to Humor: The Comic Voice in Mark Twain's *Autobiography.*" In *Mark Twain's Humor: Critical Essays*, ed. David E. E. Sloane, 539–568. New York: Garland, 1993.

——. *Mark Twain's Own Autobiography.* Madison: U of Wisconsin P, 1990.

LeMaster, J. R., and James D. Wilson, eds. *The Mark Twain Encyclopedia.* New York: Garland, 1993.

Leon, Philip W. *Mark Twain and West Point.* Toronto: ECW Press, 1996.

Le Sage, Alain René. *The Adventures of Gil Blas de Santillana* [1735]. 2 vols. Trans. Tobias Smollett. London: Oxford UP, 1928.

Longstreet, Augustus Baldwin. *Georgia Scenes* [1835]. New York: Sagamore Press, 1957.

Lorch, Fred W. "Hawaiian Feudalism and Mark Twain's *A Connecticut Yankee in King Arthur's Court.*" *American Literature* 30 (1958): 50–66.

Lowery, Robert. "Imagination and Redemption: 44 in the Third Version of *The Mysterious Stranger.*" *Southern Review* 18 (1982): 100–110.

Macnaughton, William. *Mark Twain's Last Years as a Writer.* Columbia: U of Missouri P, 1979.

Mailloux, Steven. *Rhetorical Power.* Ithaca, N.Y.: Cornell UP, 1989.

Marx, Leo. "Mr. Eliot, Mr. Trilling, and *Huckleberry Finn.*" *American Scholar* 22, no. 4 (Autumn 1953): 423–440.

Matthiessen, F. O. *The James Family.* New York: Knopf, 1947.

McCoy, Sharon. "'I Ain' No Dread Being': The Minstrel Mask as Alter

Ego." In *Centenary Reflections on Mark Twain's "No. 44, The Mysterious Stranger,"* ed. Joseph Csicsila and Chad Rohman, 13–40. Columbia: U of Missouri P, 2009.

McNutt, James C. "Mark Twain and the American Indian: Earthly Realism and Heavenly Idealism." *American Indian Quarterly* 4 (August 1978): 223–242.

Melton, Jeffrey. *Mark Twain, Travel Books, and Tourism.* Tuscaloosa: U of Alabama P, 2002.

Melville, Herman. *Moby-Dick* [1851, 2nd ed.]. Ed. Hershel Parker and Harrison Hayford. New York: W. W. Norton, 2002.

Messent, Peter. *The Cambridge Introduction to Mark Twain.* New York: Cambridge UP, 2007.

Noll, Mark A. *A History of Christianity in the United States and Canada.* Grand Rapids, Mich.: Wm. B. Eerdmans, 1992.

Obenzinger, Hilton. "Better Dreams: Political Satire and Twain's Final Exploding Novel." *Arizona Quarterly* 61, no. 1 (2005): 165–184.

Paine, Albert Bigelow. *Mark Twain: A Biography.* 4 vols. New York: Harper and Bros., 1912.

Paine, Thomas. *The Age of Reason.* In *The Life and Major Writings of Thomas Paine,* ed. Philip S. Foner. Secaucus, N.J.: Citadel, 1974.

Parker, Francis. *Talks on Pedagogies: An Outline of the Theory of Concentration.* New York: Kellogg, 1894.

Parker, Hershel. "*Pudd'nhead Wilson*: Jack-Leg Author, Unreadable Text, and Sense-Making Critics." In *Flawed Texts and Verbal Icons: Literary Authority in American Fiction,* 115–145. Evanston, Ill.: Northwestern UP, 1984.

Parrington, Vernon. *Main Currents in American Thought.* 2 vols. 1927. Repr., New York: Harcourt, Brace, 1954.

Perry, Ralph Barton. *The Thought and Character of William James.* Boston: Little, Brown, 1935.

Phipps, William E. *Mark Twain's Religion.* Macon, Ga.: Mercer UP, 2003.

Quirk, Tom. "Determinism." In *The Mark Twain Encyclopedia,* ed. J. R. Le Master and James D. Wilson, 216–218. New York: Garland, 1993.

———. *Mark Twain and Human Nature.* Columbia: U of Missouri P, 2007.

Rasmussen, Kent. *Mark Twain A to Z.* New York: Facts on File, 1995.

Reade, Charles. *Bible Characters.* London: Chatto and Windus, 1888.

Riasanovsky, Nicholas Valentine. *Nicholas I and Official Nationality in Russia, 1825–1855.* Berkeley: U of California P, 1959.

Robinson, Forrest G. "Dreaming Better Dreams: The Late Writing of Mark Twain." In *A Companion to Mark Twain*, ed. Peter Messent and Louis J. Budd, 449–465. Oxford: Blackwell, 2005.

———. *In Bad Faith: The Dynamics of Deception in Mark Twain's America*. Cambridge, Mass.: Harvard UP, 1986.

———. "'Seeing the Elephant': Some Perspectives on Mark Twain's *Roughing It*." *American Studies* 21, no. 2 (Fall 1980): 43–64.

———. "Social Play and Bad Faith in *The Adventures of Tom Sawyer*." *Nineteenth Century Fiction* 39 (June 1984): 1–24.

———. "An 'Unconscious and Profitable Cerebration': Mark Twain and Literary Intentionality." *Nineteenth-Century Literature* 50, no. 3 (December 1995): 357–380.

Salomon, Roger. *Twain and the Image of History*. New Haven, Conn.: Yale UP, 1961.

Scharnhorst, Gary, ed. *Critical Essays on "The Adventures of Tom Sawyer."* New York: G. K. Hall, 1993.

———. "Human Nature." In *The Mark Twain Encyclopedia*, ed. J. R. Le Master and James D. Wilson, 375–377. New York: Garland, 1993.

Schove, D. Justin. *Chronology of Eclipses and Comets AD 1–1000*. Bury St. Edmunds, Suffolk: Boydell Press, 1984.

Smith, Henry Nash. "Introduction." In *Adventures of Huckleberry Finn*, v–xxix. Boston: Houghton Mifflin, 1958.

———. *Mark Twain: The Development of a Writer*. Cambridge, Mass.: Harvard UP, 1962.

———. *Mark Twain's Fable of Progress: Political and Economic Ideas in "A Connecticut Yankee."* New Brunswick, N.J.: Rutgers UP, 1964.

———. "Mark Twain's Hannibal: From St. Petersburg to Eseldorf." *Texas Studies in English* 37 (1958): 3–23.

Smith, Morton. "The Southern Tradition." In *Reformed Theology in America: A History of Its Modern Development*, ed. David F. Wells, 189–207. Grand Rapids, Mich.: Baker Books, 1997.

Solomon, Eric. "*Huckleberry Finn* Once More." *College English* 22 (December 1960): 172–178.

Stahl, John Daniel. "*The Prince and the Pauper*." In *The Mark Twain Encyclopedia*, ed. J. R. Le Master and James D. Wilson, 591–592. New York: Garland, 1993.

Steinbrink, Jeffrey. *Getting to Be Mark Twain*. Berkeley: U of California P.

Swift, Jonathan. "A Discourse Concerning the Mechanical Operation of the

Spirit, &c." In *A Tale of a Tub with Other Early Works: The Prose Works of Jonathan Swift*, vol. 1. Ed. Herbert Davis. Oxford: Blackwell, 1957.

———. *Gulliver's Travels* [1726]. In *The Prose Works of Jonathan Swift*, vol. 2. Ed. Herbert Davis. Oxford: Blackwell, 1959.

Tomlinson, David O. "Calvinism." In *The Mark Twain Encyclopedia*, ed. J. R. Le Master and James D. Wilson, 118–122. New York: Garland, 1993.

Towers, Tom H. "'I Never Thought We Might Want to Come Back': Strategies of Transcendence in *Tom Sawyer*." *Modern Fiction Studies* 21 (Winter 1975–1976): 509–520.

Tracy, Robert. "Myth and Reality in *The Adventures of Tom Sawyer*." *Southern Review* 4 (Spring 1968): 530–541.

Trombley, Laura Skandera. *Mark Twain in the Company of Women*. Philadelphia: U of Pennsylvania P, 1994.

———. "Mark Twain's *Annus Horribilis* of 1908–09." *American Literary Realism* 40, no. 2 (Winter 2008): 114–136.

———. "Mark Twain's Last Work of Realism: The Ashcroft-Lyon Manuscript." *Essays in Arts and Sciences* 23 (October 1994): 39–48.

———. "'She Wanted to Kill': Jean Clemens and Postictal Psychosis." *American Literary Realism* 37 (April 2005): 225–237.

Tuckey, John. *Mark Twain and Little Satan: The Writing of "The Mysterious Stranger."* West Lafayette, Ind.: Purdue UP, 1963.

———. "Mark Twain's Later Dialogue: The 'Me' and the Machine." *American Literature* 41 (January 1970): 532–542.

Twain, Mark. *Adventures of Huckleberry Finn* [1885]. Ed. Victor Fischer and Lin Salamo. Berkeley: U of California P, 2003.

———. *The Adventures of Tom Sawyer* [1876]. Ed. Paul Baender and John C. Gerber. Berkeley: U of California P, 1982.

———. *A Connecticut Yankee in King Arthur's Court* [1889]. Ed. Bernard L. Stein. Berkeley: U of California P, 1983.

———. *Eve's Diary: Translated from the Original MS*. New York: Harper and Bros., 1906.

———. *Fables of Man*. Ed. John S. Tuckey. Berkeley: U of California P, 1972.

———. "Huck Finn and Tom Sawyer among the Indians." In *Mark Twain's Hannibal, Huck and Tom*. Ed. Walter Blair, 81–140. Berkeley: U of California P, 1969.

———. "Letters from the Earth" [1909]. In *Letters from the Earth*. Ed. Bernard DeVoto, 1–55. New York: Harper and Row, 1962.

———. *Life on the Mississippi* [1883]. New York: Viking Penguin, 1984.

——. *Mark Twain–Howells Letters: The Correspondence of Samuel L. Clemens and William D. Howells, 1872–1910*. Vol. 2. Ed. Henry Nash Smith and William M. Gibson. Cambridge, Mass.: Harvard UP, 1968.

——. *Mark Twain's Autobiography*. Ed. Albert Bigelow Paine. New York: Harper and Brothers, 1924.

——. *Mark Twain's Letters*. Vol. 2. Ed. Albert Bigelow Paine. New York: Harper and Bros., 1912.

——. *Mark Twain's Letters*. Vol. 4, 1870–1871. Ed. Victor Fischer and Michael B. Frank. Berkeley: U of California P, 1995.

——. *Mark Twain's Notebook* [1935]. Ed. Albert Bigelow Paine. New York: Cooper Square, 1972.

——. *Mysterious Stranger Manuscripts*. Ed. and introduction by William M. Gibson. Berkeley: U of California P, 1969.

——. *Notebooks and Journals*. Vol. 3. Ed. Robert Pack Browning, Michael B. Frank, and Lin Salamo. Berkeley: U of California P, 1979.

——. *Roughing It* [1872]. Ed. Franklin R. Rogers and Paul Baender. Berkeley: U of California P, 1972.

——. *Roughing It*. Ed. Harriet Elinor Smith and Edgar Marquess Branch. Berkeley: U of California P, 1993.

——. "Tom Sawyer's Conspiracy." In *Mark Twain's Hannibal, Huck and Tom*. Ed. Walter Blair, 152–242. Berkeley: U of California P, 1969.

——. "Villagers 1840–3." In *Mark Twain's Hannibal, Huck and Tom*. Ed. Walter Blair, 23–40. Berkeley: U of California P, 1969.

——. *What Is Man? and Other Philosophical Writings*. Ed. Paul Baender. Berkeley: U of California P, 1973.

——. *Which Was the Dream? and Other Symbolic Writings*. Ed. John S. Tuckey. Berkeley: U of California P, 1968.

Wagenknecht, Edward. *Mark Twain: The Man and His Work*. Rev. ed. Norman: U of Oklahoma P, 1961.

Warburton, Ben A. *Calvinism: Its History and Basic Principles, Its Fruits and Its Future, and Its Practical Application to Life*. Grand Rapids, Mich.: Wm. B. Eerdmans, 1955.

Warfield, Benjamin B. *Selected Shorter Writings of Benjamin B. Warfield*. 3 vols. Ed. John E. Meeter. Nutley, N.J.: Presbyterian and Reformed Publishing, 1970.

Wecter, Dixon. *Sam Clemens of Hannibal: The Formative Years of America's Great Indigenous Writer*. Boston: Houghton Mifflin, 1952.

The Westminster Confession of Faith (American Version) [1789]. Suwanee, Ga.: Great Commission Publications, 2007.

Wigger, Anne P. "The Source of Fingerprint Material in Mark Twain's *Pudd'nhead Wilson and Those Extraordinary Twins.*" *American Literature* 28 (1957): 517–520.

Williams, James D. "The Use of History in Mark Twain's *A Connecticut Yankee.*" *PMLA* 80 (1965): 102–110.

Wilson, James D. "History as Palimpsest: The Layers of Time in *Life on the Mississippi.*" *Journal of the American Studies Association of Texas* 25 (October 1994): 32–39.

———. "Religious and Esthetic Vision in Mark Twain's Early Career." *Canadian Review of American Studies* 17, no. 2 (Summer 1986): 155–172.

Wolff, Cynthia Griffin. "*The Adventures of Tom Sawyer*: A Nightmare Vision of American Boyhood." *Massachusetts Review* 21 (Winter 1980): 637–652.

Wonham, Henry B. "Mark Twain's Last Cakewalk: Racialized Performance in *No. 44, The Mysterious Stranger.*" In *Centenary Reflections on Mark Twain's "No. 44, The Mysterious Stranger,"* ed. Joseph Csicsila and Chad Rohman, 41–50. Columbia: U of Missouri P, 2009.

Yates, Norris W. "The 'Counter-Conversion' of *Huckleberry Finn.*" *American Literature* 32, no. 1 (March 1960): 1–10.